Ready Reproducibles
Year-Round Instructional and Decorative Resources

Carson-Dellosa Publishing Company, Inc.
Greensboro, North Carolina

CREDITS:

Editor: Erin Seltzer
Layout Design: Jon Nawrocik
Cover Design: Annette Hollister-Papp
Cover Illustrations: Wayne Miller
Inside Illustrations: Wayne Miller, Julie Kinlaw, Mike Duggins

ISBN 0-88724-917-5

TABLE OF CONTENTS

TABLE OF CONTENTS CONTINUED

TABLE OF CONTENTS CONTINUED

HOW TO USE THIS BOOK

Ready Reproducibles: Year-Round Instructional and Decorative Resources includes patterns, stationery and calendar templates, and literature lists for every season and 11 topics commonly taught in kindergarten and first-grade classrooms.

Students can use patterns in this book:

- as manipulatives in math centers.
- as pictures to color and glue into alphabet books.
- as game cards to identify words that rhyme.
- as visuals for showing what they know on graphic organizers.
- as stationery.
- for drawing and writing about monthly topics or holidays.
- for front covers for books they publish.
- for making cards for special days.
- for framing pieces of seasonal or holiday art.

Teachers can:

- use the literature lists for each month and each topic to help choose books or recommend books to parents.
- use the calendar and newsletter templates as communication tools.
- use patterns for bulletin board displays, holiday decorations, and birthday and weather graphs.
- use patterns to label cubbies, desks, and supplies.
- use patterns when writing about field trips or other class events. The appropriate pictures provide visual clues for early emergent readers in the classroom.
- use the patterns to help novice English language learners acquire new vocabulary. First, begin with picture to picture matching games. Point to each item, say the name of it in English, and show students how to find matches. Then, say, "Point to a ______." or "Show me ______." (Students who are learning a new language often feel more comfortable with visual responses.) After students can non-verbally identify people and things, teach them what the pictures' corresponding words look like. (Remember to introduce a few words at a time.) Next, have students match pictures to the appropriate words. Once students master picture to word matches, have them work on matching words to words. Students will retain more vocabulary if the words they are learning are related to school or home life. The best pictures and vocabulary words to begin with for these games are names of classmates and places at school.
- use awards to recognize students' strengths and good work.
- use the high frequency words as a classroom word wall or for student practice at home. Simply copy the words on sturdy, colorful construction paper. Then, add two words at a time to a word wall or have caregivers display them on refrigerators at home.
- use the notes home to say thank you, share what students miss during absences, let a caregiver know that his child lost a tooth, etc.

The possibilities for using these patterns and templates are endless, so enjoy! Let the resources in *Ready Reproducibles* brighten the classroom and students' minds!

January

January

JANUARY LITERATURE SELECTIONS

All the Colors of the Earth by Sheila Hamanka (HarperTrophy, 1999)

All the Colors We Are: The Story of How We Get Our Skin Color by Katie Kissinger (Redleaf Press, 1994)

Chicken Soup with Rice: A Book of Months by Maurice Sendak (HarperCollins Juvenile Books, 1962)

The Dancing Dragon by Marcia K. Vaughan (Mondo Pub, 1996)

Happy Birthday, Martin Luther King by Jean Marzollo (Scholastic, 1995)

Martin's Big Words: The Life of Martin Luther King, Jr. by Doreen Rappaport (Hyperion Books, 2001)

Miss Bindergarten Celebrates the 100th Day of Kindergarten by Joseph Slate (Dutton Books, 1998)

My Dream of Martin Luther King by Faith Ringgold (Dragonfly, 1998)

The 100th Day of School by Angela Shelf Medearis (Cartwheel Books, 1996)

Peace Begins With You by Katherine Scholes (Little Brown & Company, 1994)

Sam and the Lucky Money by Karen Chinn (Lee & Low Books, 1995)

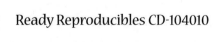

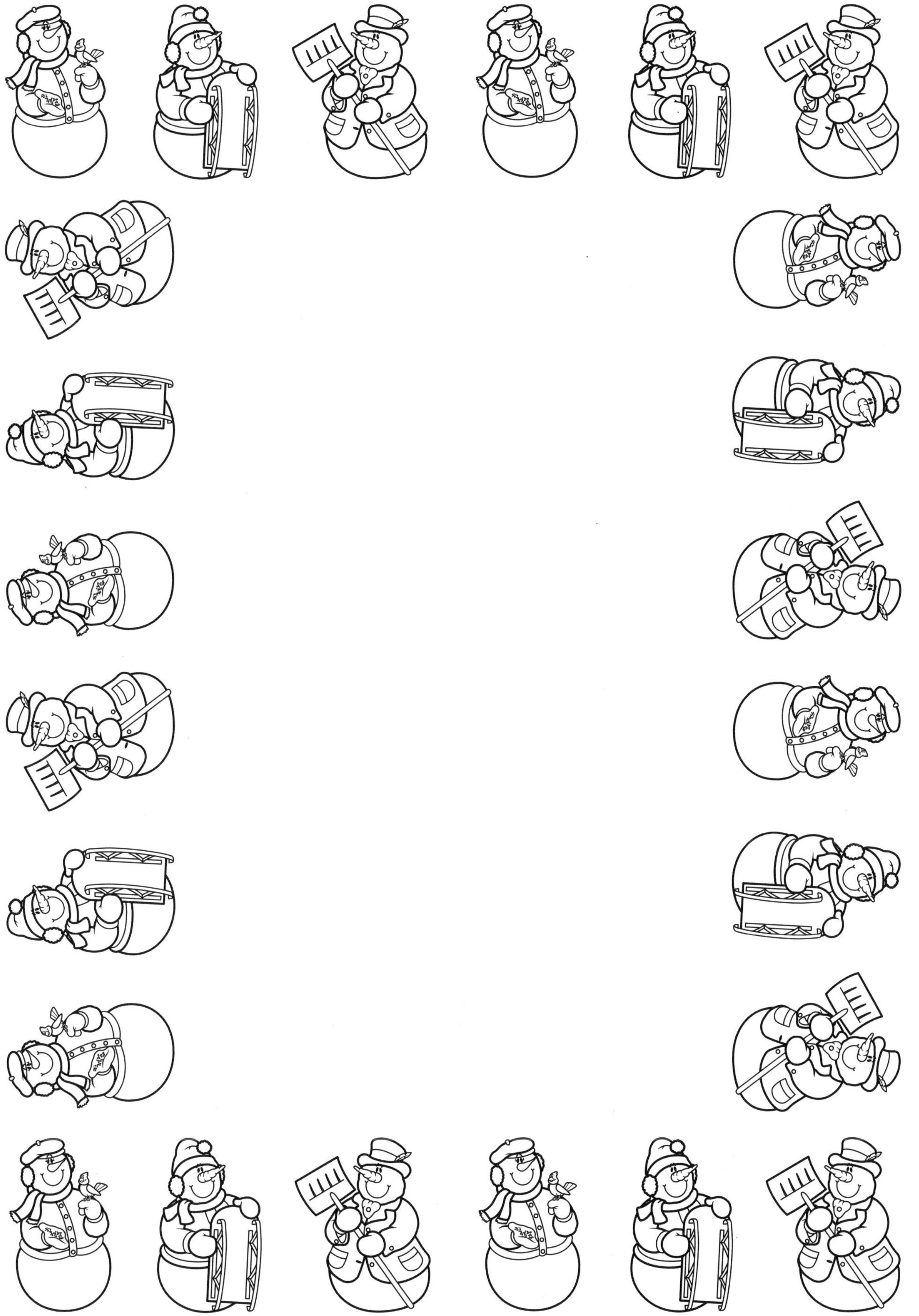

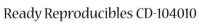

JANUARY

SCHOOL

January

Sunday	Monday	Tuesday	Wednesday	Thursday	Friday	Saturday

January Gazette

Teacher ______________________ Date ______________

IN THE NEWS

TAKE NOTE

WHAT'S COMING UP

HAPPY
NEW YEAR
12
1
2
3
4
5
6
7
8
9
10
11

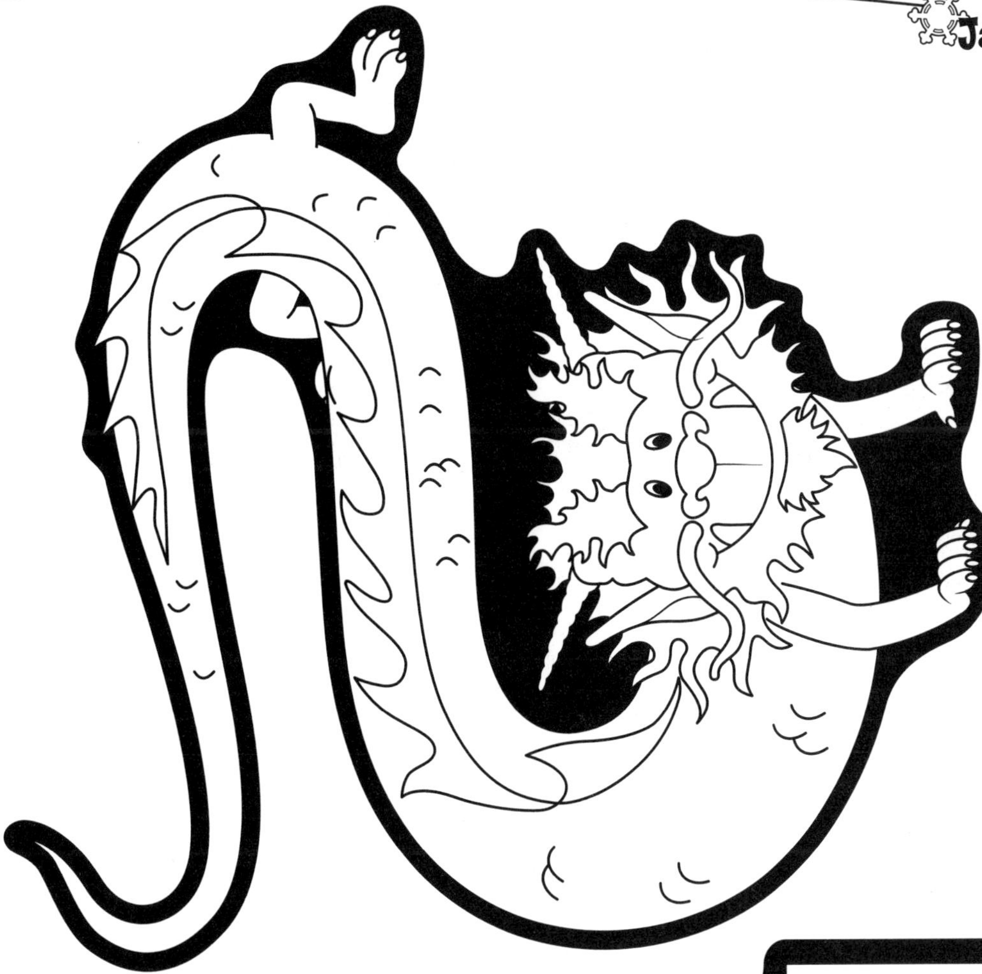

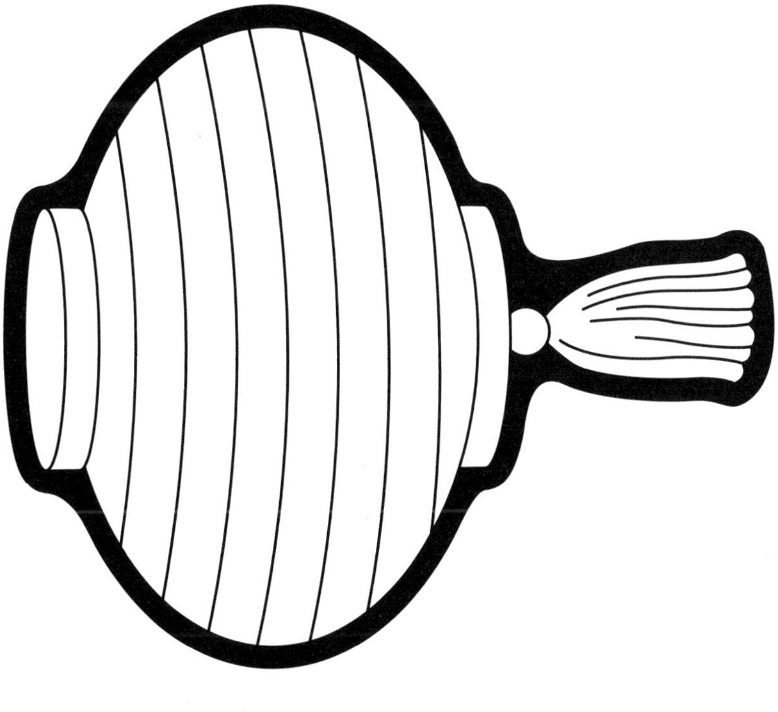

friend

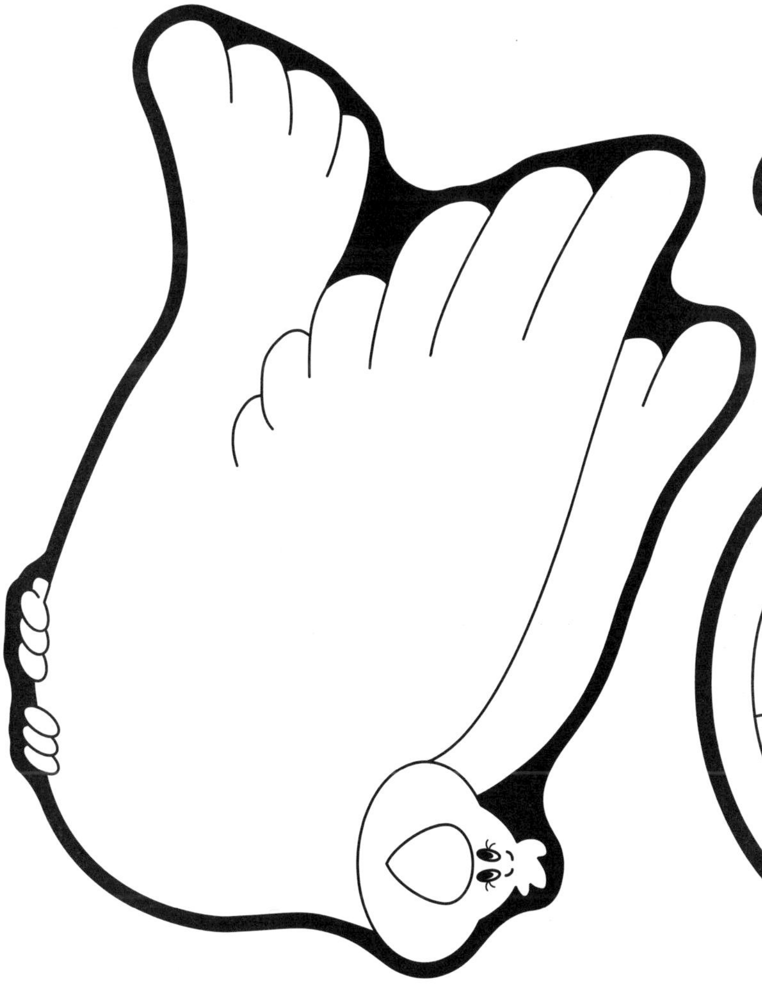

February

February

FEBRUARY LITERATURE SELECTIONS

Abe Lincoln's Hat by Martha Brenner (Random House Books for Young Readers, 1994)

Abiyoyo by Pete Seeger (Aladdin Library, 1994)

Abraham Lincoln by Edgar Parin D'Aulaire (Yearling Books, 1987)

Aunt Harriet's Underground Railroad in the Sky by Faith Ringgold (Dragonfly, 1995)

Follow the Drinking Gourd by Jeanette Winter (Dragonfly, 1992)

Gifts of Our People by Portia George (Judson Press, 1995)

Honest Abe by Edith Kunhardt (HarperTrophy, 1998)

I See the Rhythm by Toyomi Igus (Children's Press, 1998)

It's Groundhog Day! by Steven Kroll (Scholastic, 1991)

Junie B. Jones and the Mushy Gushy Valentine by Barbara Park (Random House Books for Young Readers, 1999)

A Picture Book of George Washington by David A. Adler (Holiday House, 1990)

Sister Anne's Hands by Marybeth Lorbiecki (Puffin, 2000)

The Valentine Bears by Eve Bunting (Clarion Books, 1985)

FEBRUARY

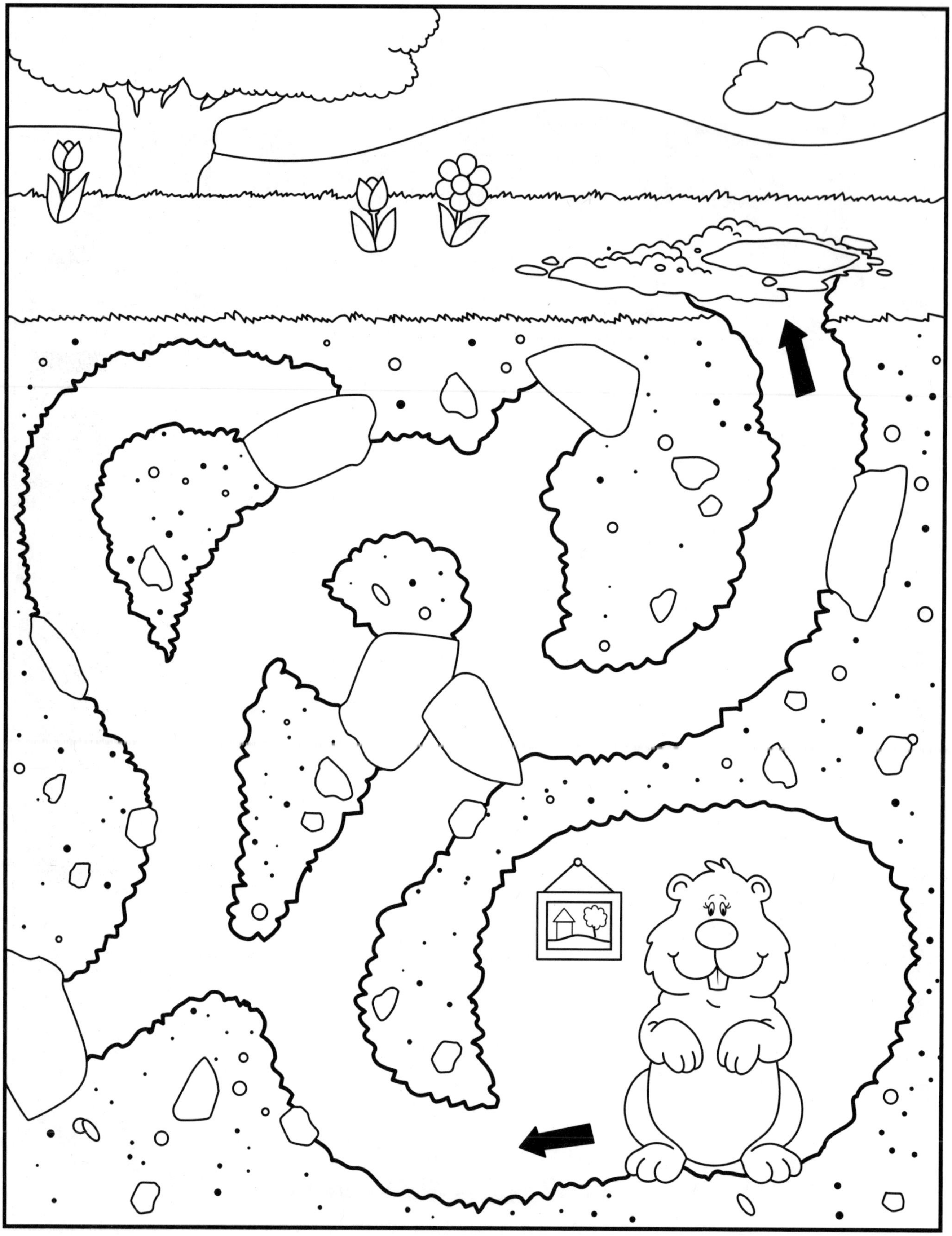

FRIENDS FOREVER LOVE

February

FOR YOU PAL

Sunday	Monday	Tuesday	Wednesday	Thursday	Friday	Saturday

February Gazette

Teacher ______________________ Date ______________

IN THE NEWS

WHAT'S COMING UP

TAKE NOTE

KID'S CORNER

Draw a picture of someone you love.

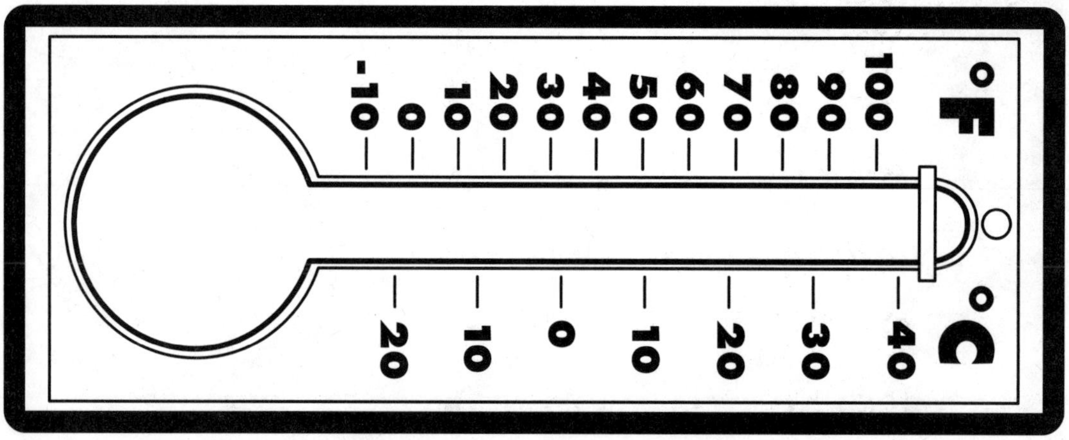

°F

100
90
80
70
60
50
40
30
20
10
0
-10

°C

40
30
20
10
0
10
20

LIBERTY
IN GOD WE
TRUST
2004

IN GOD WE TRUST
LIBERTY
2002

IN GOD WE TRUST
LIBERTY
2003

LIBERTY
IN GOD
WE TRUST
2004

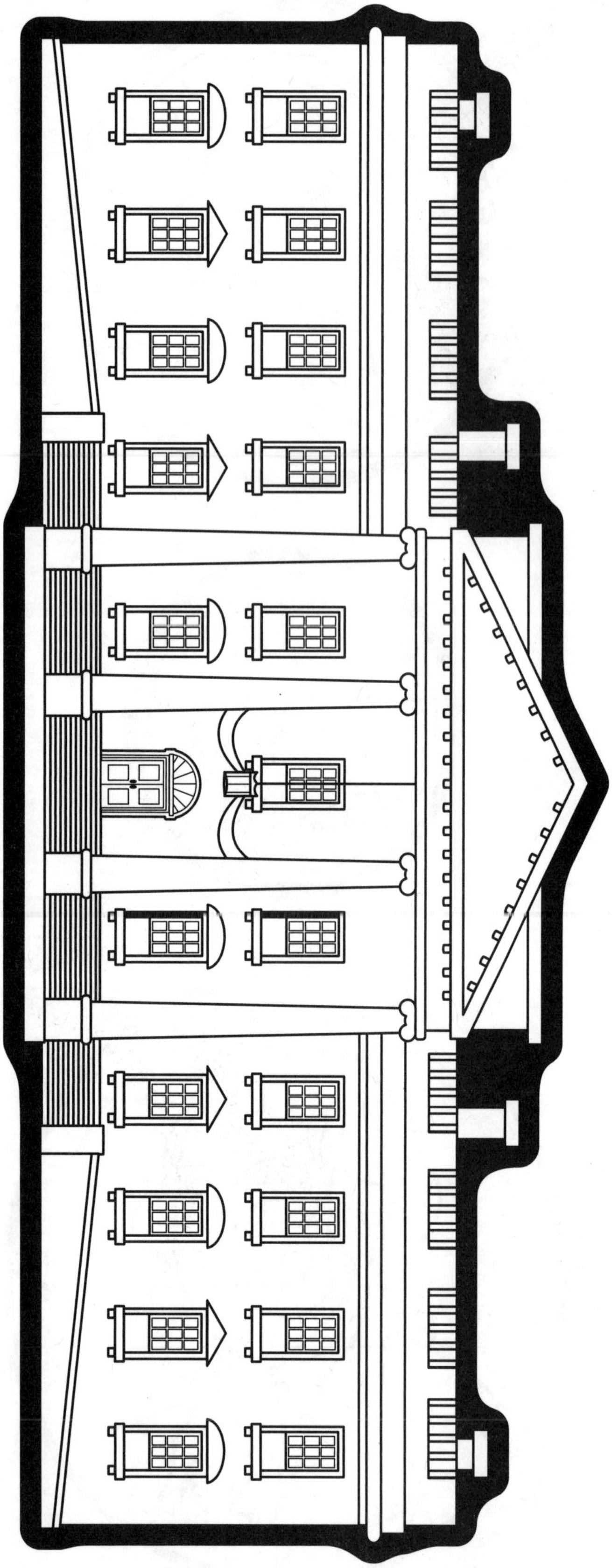

THE UNITED STATES OF AMERICA

GREAT
YOU'RE SWEET
BE MINE
FRIENDS
SWEET

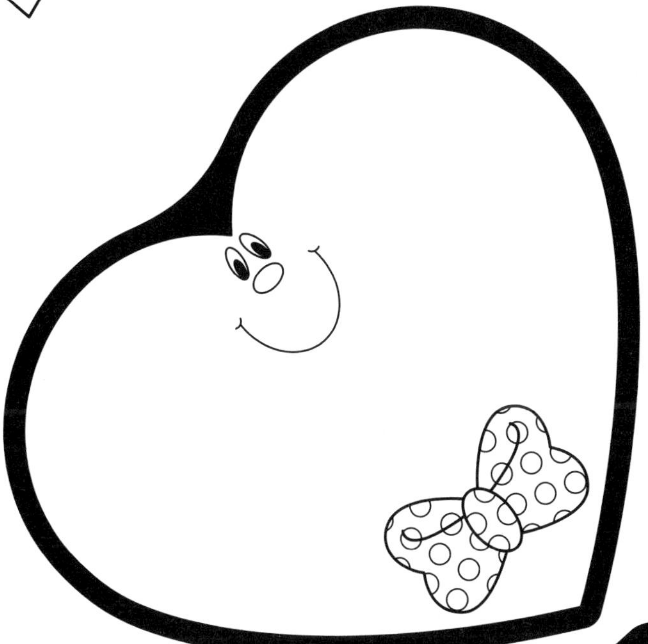

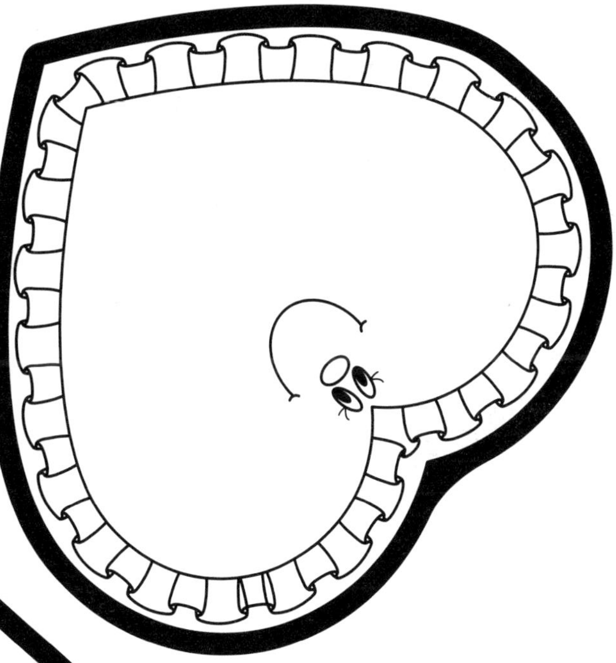

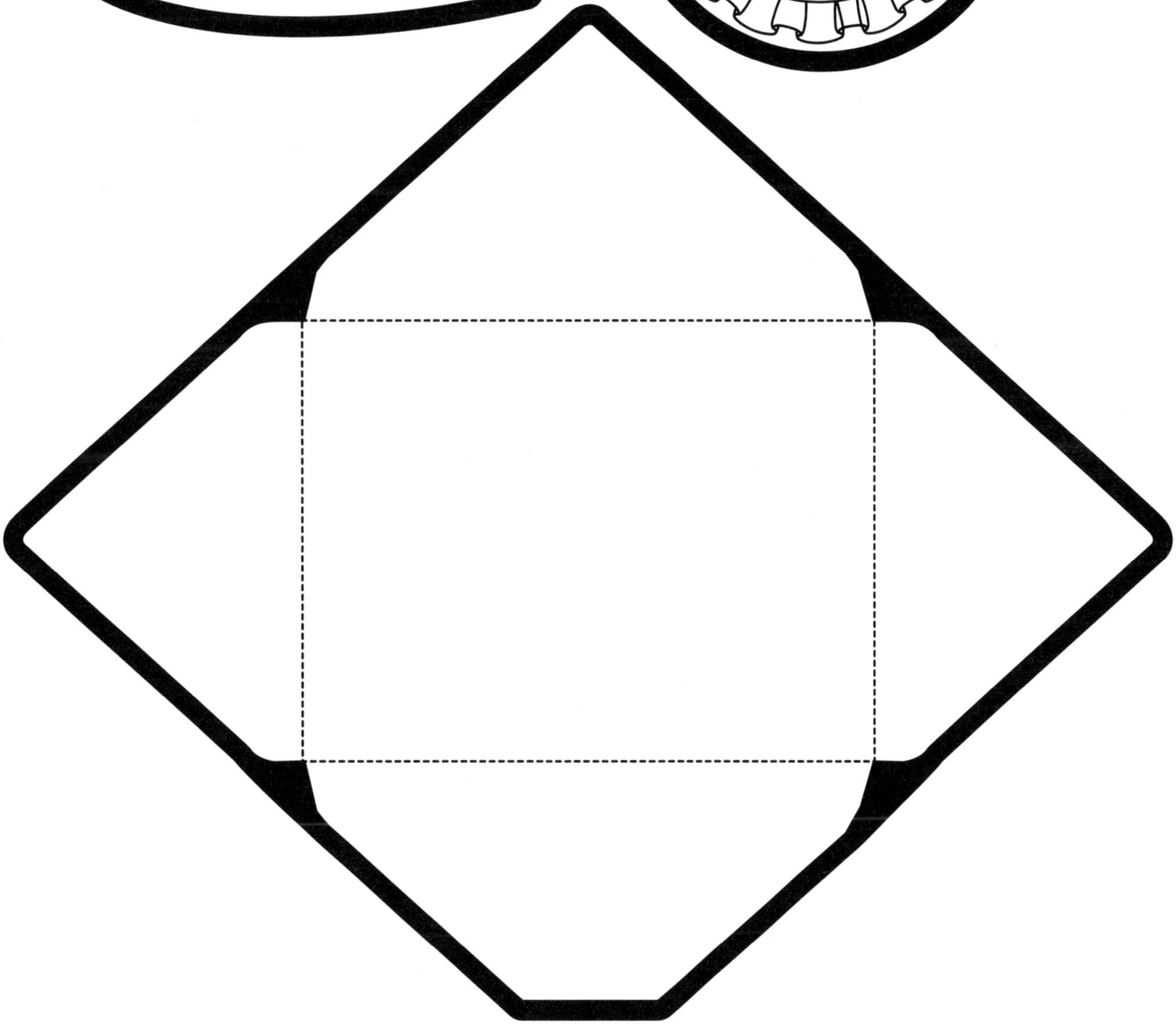

I love

March

March

MARCH LITERATURE SELECTIONS

Amazing Grace by Mary Hoffman (Dramatic Pub Co., 1998)

Amelia's Road by Linda Jacobs Altman (Lee & Low Books, 1995)

Andy and the Lion by James Daugherty (Puffin, 1989)

Chester's Way by Kevin Henkes (Harcourt, 1993)

Feel the Wind by Arthur Dorros (HarperTrophy, 1990)

Gilberto and the Wind by Marie Hall Ets (Puffin, 1978)

Handsigns: A Sign Language Alphabet by Kathleen Fain (Chronicle Books, 1995)

I Look Like a Girl by Sheila Hamanaka (Morrow Junior, 1999)

Just Us Women by Jeannette Caines (HarperTrophy, 1984)

Leo the Late Bloomer by Robert Kraus (HarperCollins Juvenile Books, 1971)

Moses Goes to a Concert by Isaac Macmillan (Sunburst, 2002)

My Spring Robin by Anne Rockwell (Aladdin Library, 1996)

A Rainbow of My Own by Don Freeman (Bt Bound, 1999)

Simple Signs by Cindy Wheeler (Puffin, 1997)

St. Patrick's Day in the Morning by Eve Bunting (Clarion Books, 1983)

MARCH

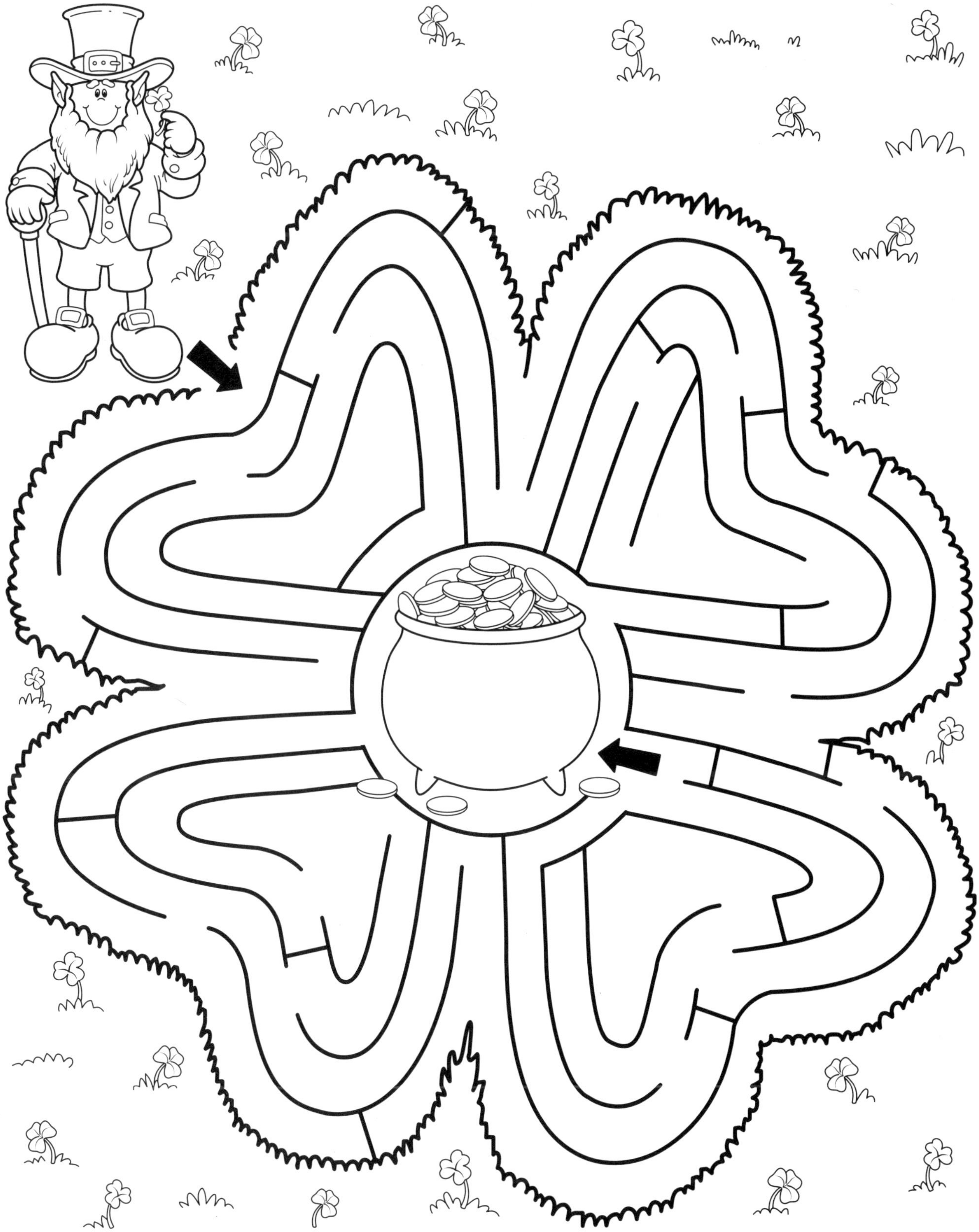

March

Sunday	Monday	Tuesday	Wednesday	Thursday	Friday	Saturday

March Gazette

Teacher ______________________________ Date ________________

IN THE NEWS

TAKE NOTE

WHAT'S COMING UP

KID'S CORNER

Color the kite.

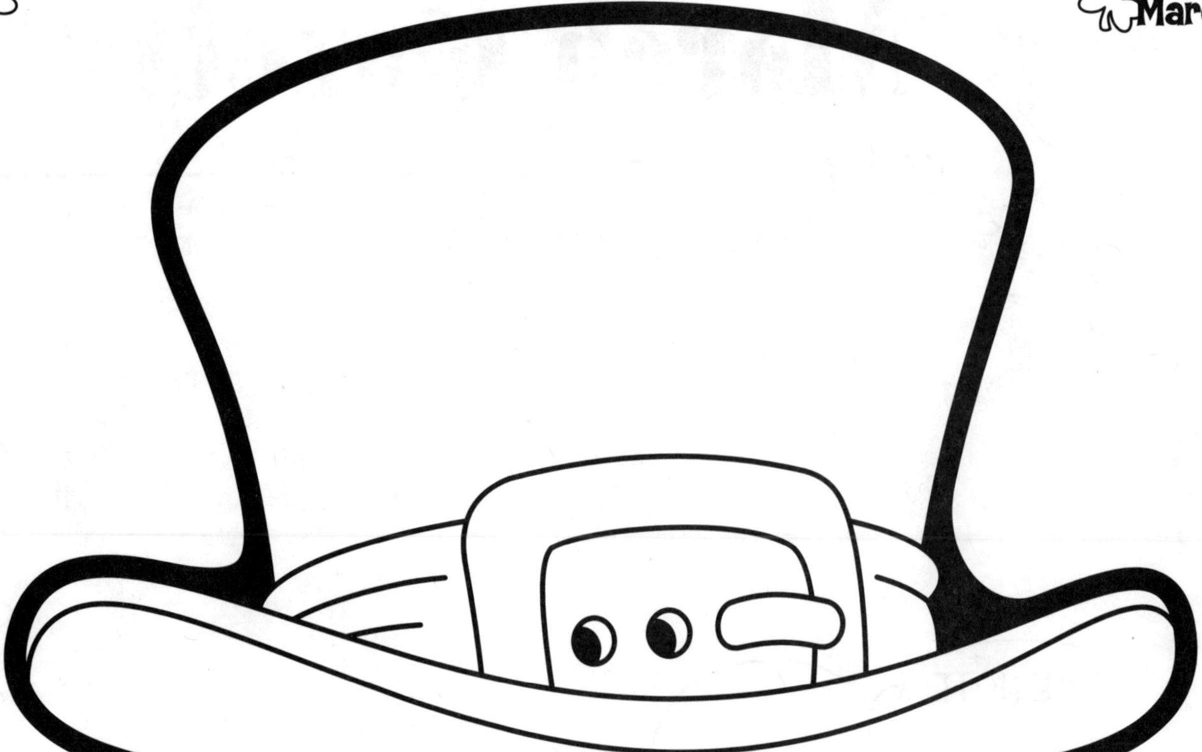

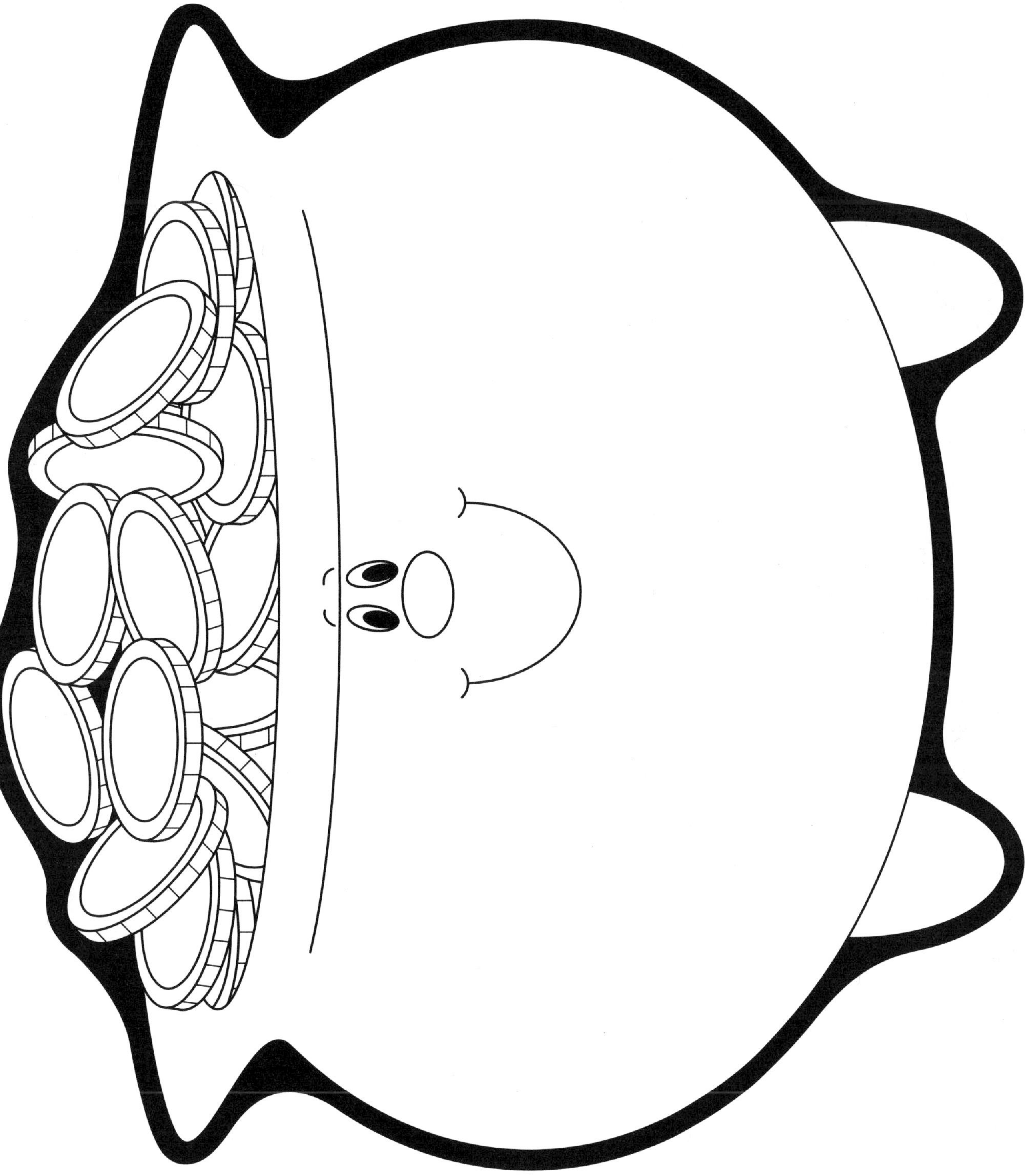

April

April

APRIL LITERATURE SELECTIONS

Brother Eagle, Sister Sky: A Message from Chief Seattle illustrated by Susan Jeffers (Dial Books for Young Readers, 1991)

Chicken Sunday by Patricia Polacco (Philomel Books, 1992)

Day of Delight: A Jewish Sabbath in Ethiopia by Maxine Rose Schur (Dial Books for Young Readers, 1994)

The Earth is Painted Green: A Garden of Poems edited by Barbara Brenner (Byron Preiss Publications, 2000)

The Egg Tree by Katherine Milhous (Atheneum, 1971)

Honey, I Love and Other Love Poems by Eloise Greenfield (HarperTrophy, 1986)

Just a Dream by Chris Van Allsburg (Houghton Mifflin Co., 1990)

Listen to the Rain by Bill Martin Jr. and John Archambault (Henry Holt & Company, Inc., 1988)

The Lorax by Dr. Seuss (Random House Books for Young Readers, 1971)

Make Way for Ducklings by Robert McCloskey (Puffin, 1999)

Old Elm Speaks: Tree Poems by Kristine O'Connell George (Houghton Mifflin, Co., 1998)

Puddles by Jonathan London (Puffin, 1999)

Rabbit's Good News by Ruth Lercher Bornstein (Houghton Mifflin, Co., 1997)

APRIL

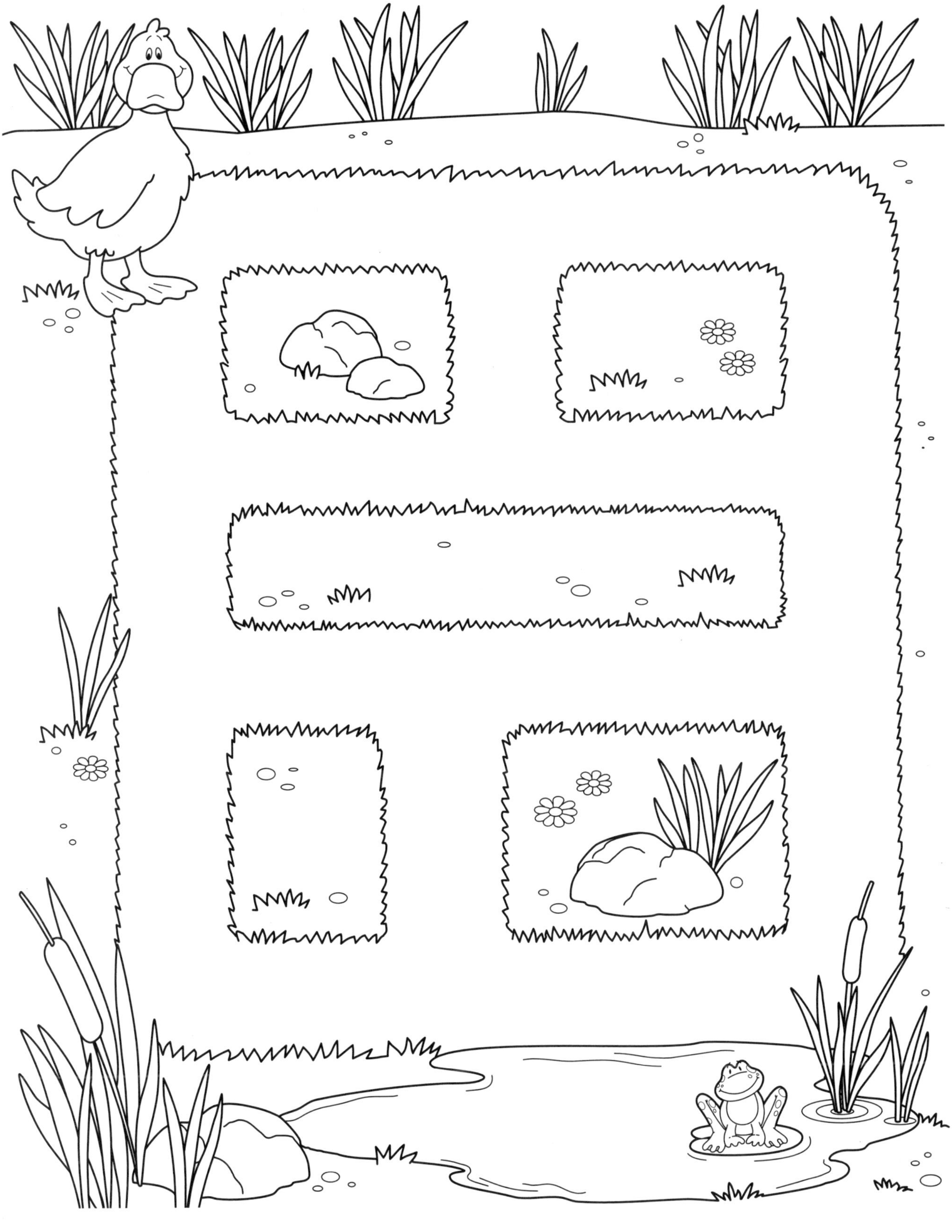

April

Sunday	Monday	Tuesday	Wednesday	Thursday	Friday	Saturday

April Gazette

Teacher ______________________ Date ______________

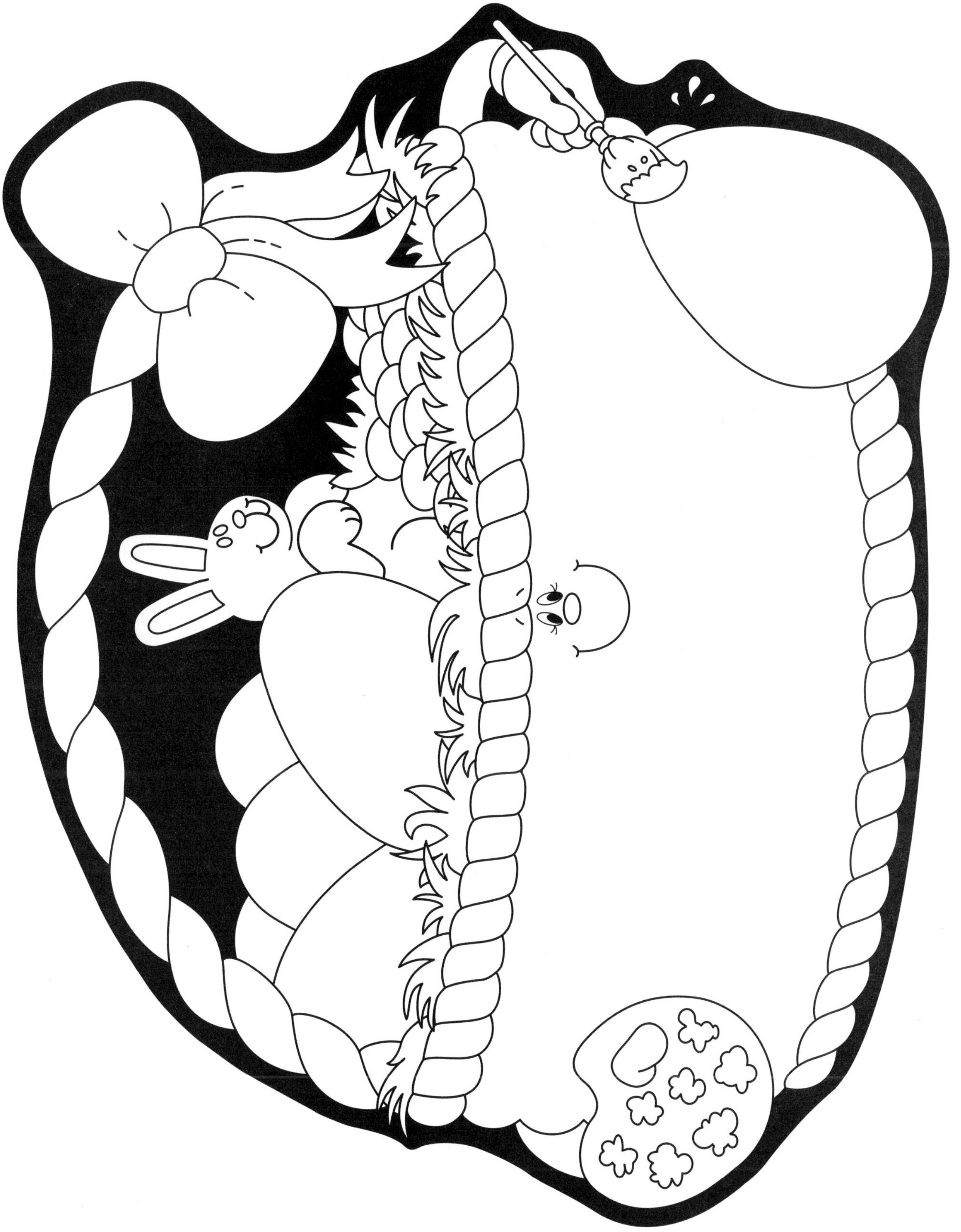

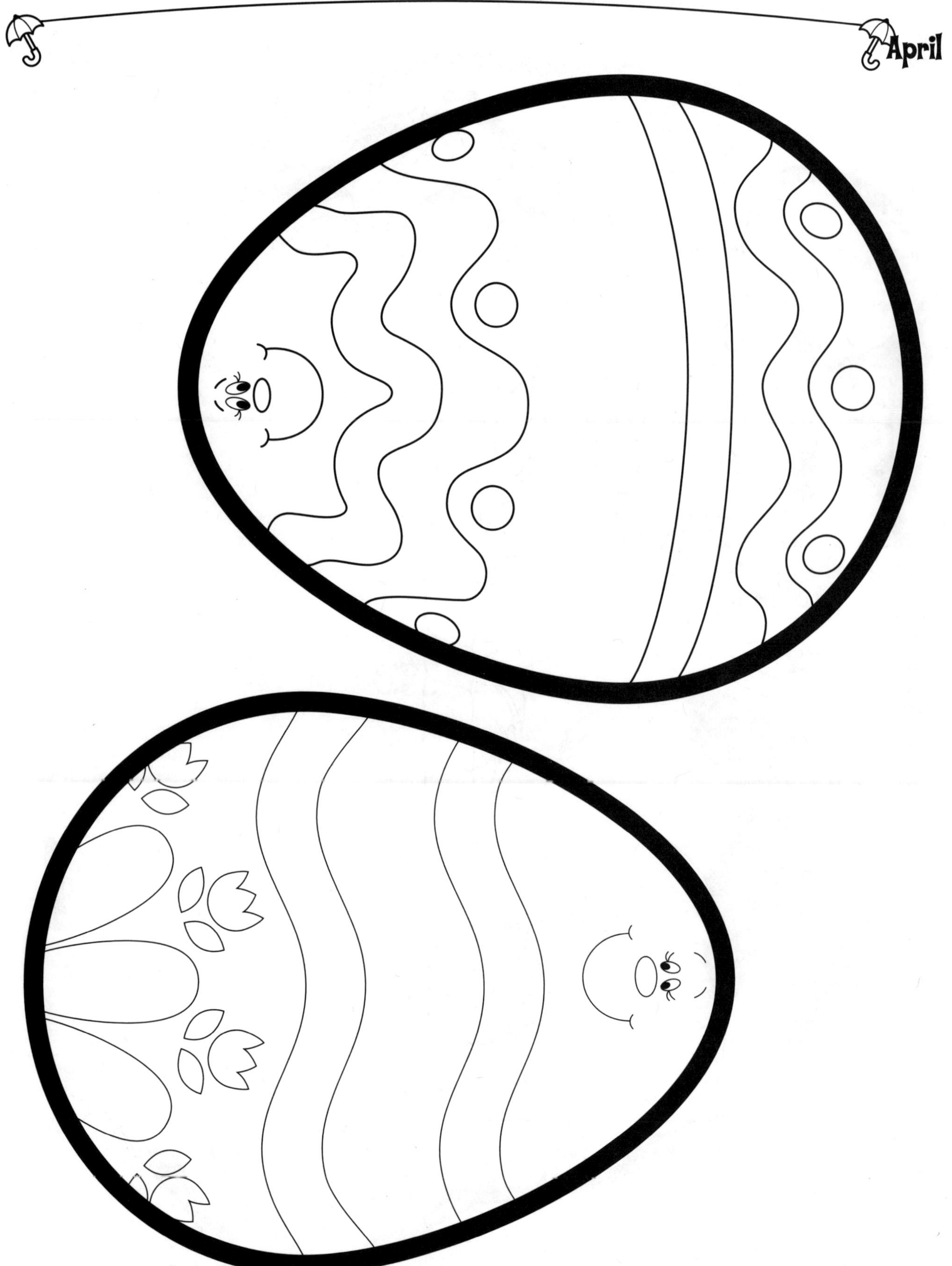

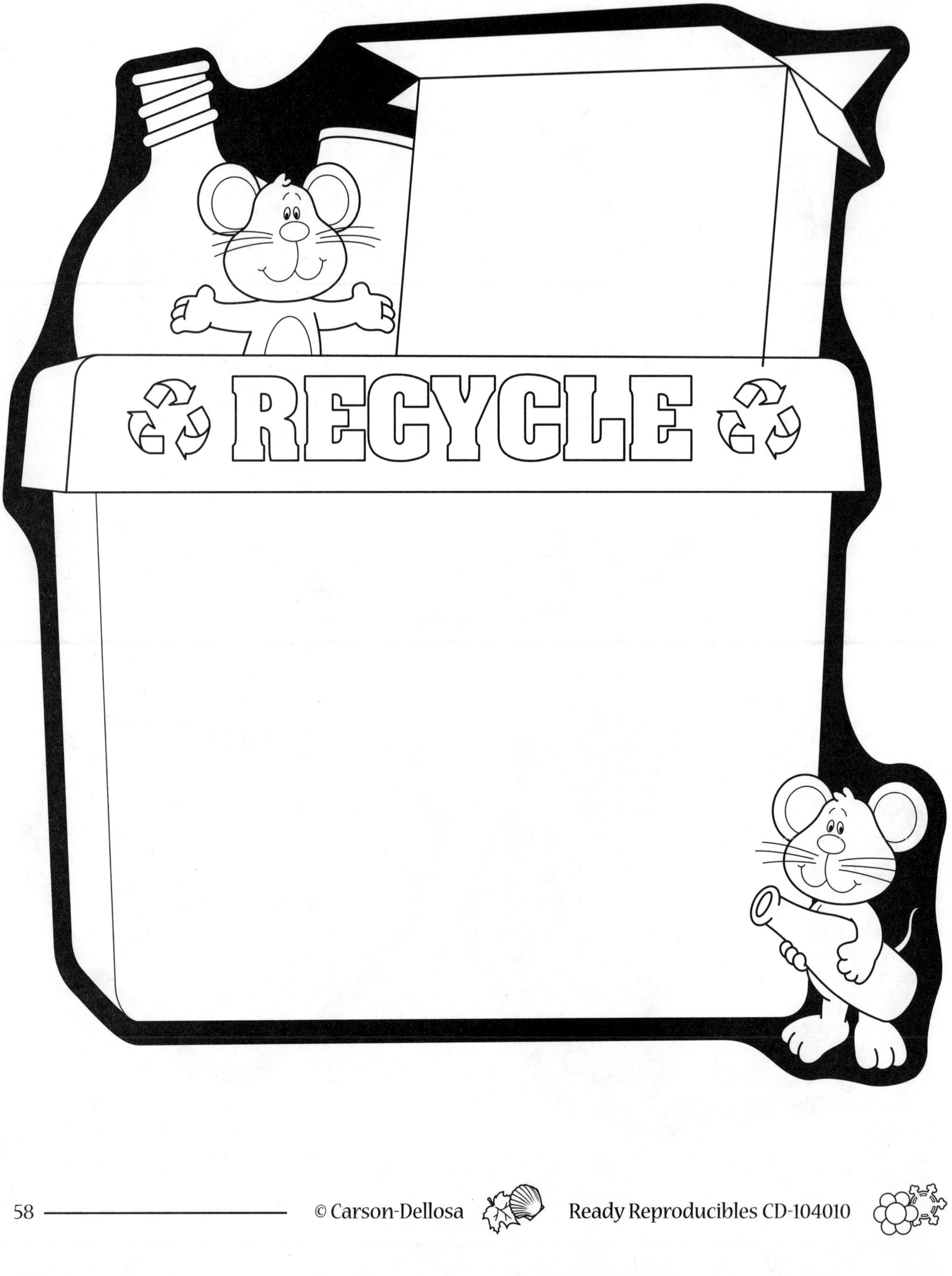

RECYCLE

May

May

MAY LITERATURE SELECTIONS

Alison's Zinnia by Anita Lobel (HarperTrophy, 1996)

The Carrot Seed by Ruth Krauss (HarperTrophy, 1989)

A Chair for My Mother by Vera B. Williams (William Morrow & Company, 1983)

Families Are Different by Nina Pellegrini (Holiday House, 1991)

Fathers, Mothers, Sisters, Brothers: A Collection of Family Poems by Mary Ann Hoberman (Turtleback Books, 2001)

Farmer Duck by Martin Waddell (Candlewick Press, 1996)

Flower Garden by Eve Bunting (Voyager Books, 2000)

From Seed to Plant by Gail Gibbons (Holiday House, 1993)

Hooray for Mother's Day! by Catherine Lukas (Simon & Schuster, 2003)

Jack's Garden by Henry Cole (HarperTrophy, 1997)

My Momma Had a Dancing Heart by Libba Moore Gray (Orchard Books, 1999)

Planting a Rainbow by Lois Ehlert (Harcourt, 1992)

Sunflower House by Eve Bunting (Voyager Books, 1999)

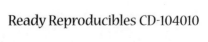

MAY

May

Sunday	Monday	Tuesday	Wednesday	Thursday	Friday	Saturday

May Gazette

Teacher ______________________ Date __________

IN THE NEWS

TAKE NOTE

WHAT'S COMING UP

KID'S CORNER

Connect the dots.

June

June

JUNE LITERATURE SELECTIONS

A House for Hermit Crab by Eric Carle (Aladdin Library, 2002)

How to Hide an Octopus and Other Sea Creatures by Ruth Heller (Grosset & Dunlap, 1992)

Inch by Inch by Leo Lionni (Astor Honor, 1962)

In Daddy's Arms I Am Tall: African-Americans Celebrating Fathers by Javaka Steptoe (Lee & Low Books, 2001)

in the swim by Douglas Florian (Voyager Books, 2001)

Like Jake and Me by Mavis Jukes (Knopf Books for Young Readers, 1984)

One Hot Summer Day by Nina Crews (Greenwillow, 1995)

My Father's Hands by Joanne Ryder (William Morrow, 1994)

Night Shift Daddy by Eileen Spinelli (Hyperion Press, 2000)

Papa, Please Get the Moon for Me by Eric Carle (Simon & Schuster Children's Publishing, 1991)

A Perfect Father's Day by Eve Bunting (Clarion Books, 1993)

Tar Beach by Faith Ringgold (Dragonfly, 1996)

Ten Flashing Fireflies by Philemon Sturges (North-South Books, 1997)

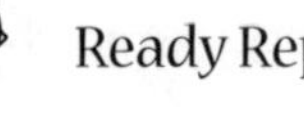

JUNE

MAP

June

Sunday	Monday	Tuesday	Wednesday	Thursday	Friday	Saturday

June Gazette

Teacher ______________________________ Date ______________

IN THE NEWS

TAKE NOTE

WHAT'S COMING UP

KID'S CORNER

Color the picture below.

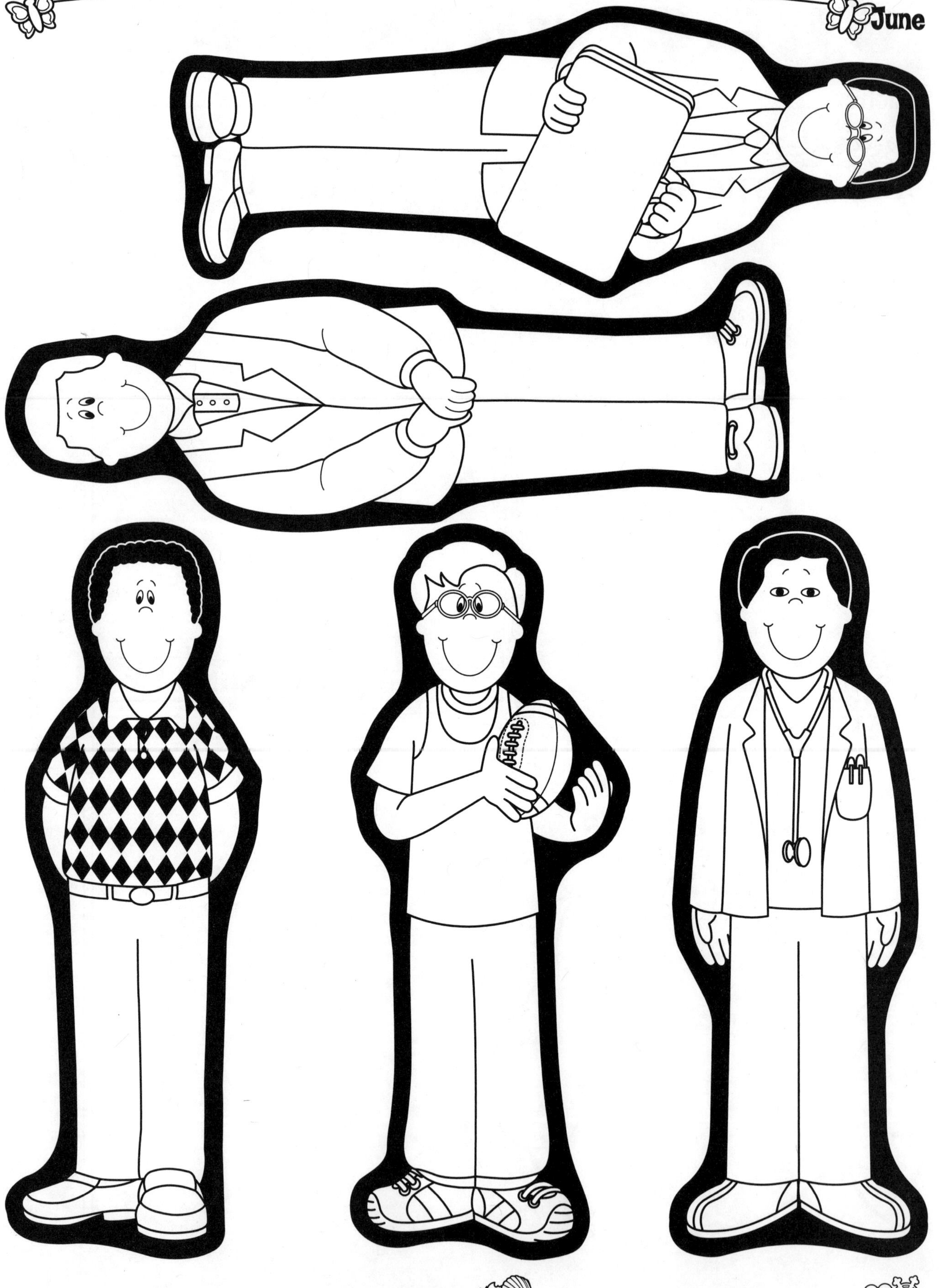

July

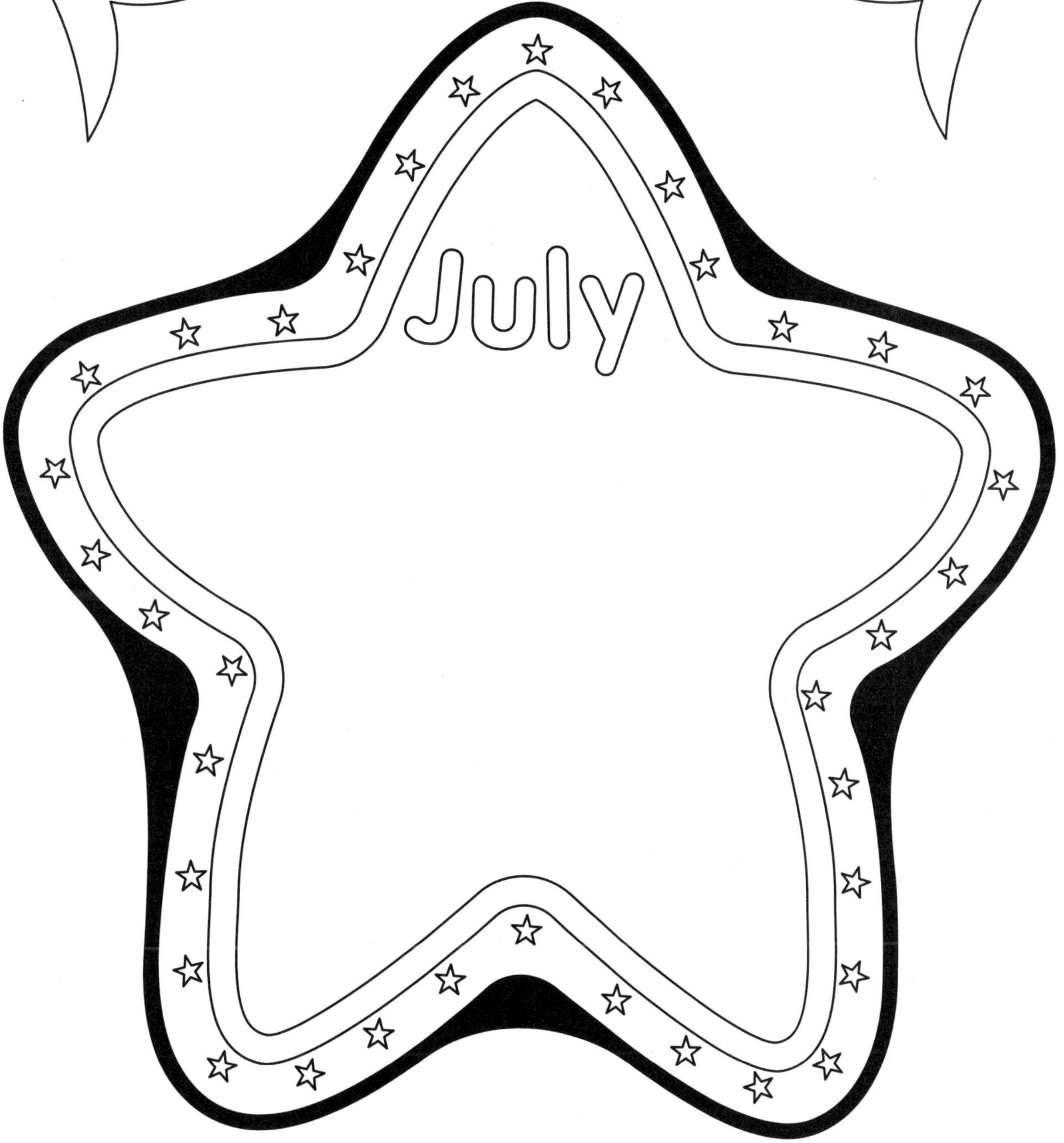

July

JULY LITERATURE SELECTIONS

Arthur Goes to Camp by Marc Brown (Little Brown & Company, 1984)

Beat the Drum, Independence Day Has Come: Poems for the Fourth of July edited by Lee B. Hopkins (Boyds Mill Press, 1993)

Blueberries for Sal by Robert McCloskey (Puffin, 1976)

Canada Day by Patricia J. Murphy (Children's Press, 2002)

The Fourth of July Story by Alice Dalgliesh (Aladdin Paperbacks, 1987)

Hats Off for the Fourth of July by Harriet Ziefert (Viking Childrens Books, 2000)

Henry and Mudge in the Green Time by Cynthia Rylant (Aladdin Library, 1996)

Ira Sleeps Over by Bernard Waber (Houghton Mifflin/ Walter Lorraine Books, 1975)

One Hundred Hungry Ants by Bonnie MacKain (Scholastic Paperbacks, 1996)

Picnic with Piggins by Jane Yolen (Voyager Books, 1993)

The Teddy Bears' Picnic by Jimmy Kennedy (Aladdin Library, 2000)

There's an Ant in Anthony by Bernard Most (HarperTrophy, 1992)

JULY

Ketchup

July

Sunday	Monday	Tuesday	Wednesday	Thursday	Friday	Saturday

July Gazette

Teacher______________________________ Date________________

IN THE NEWS

TAKE NOTE

WHAT'S COMING UP

KID'S CORNER

boat
pool
swim
sun
basket
picnic

p	b	o	a	t	t
s	i	i	e	e	s
w	l	c	k	b	u
i	d	s	n	d	n
m	a	h	i	i	i
b	p	o	o	l	c

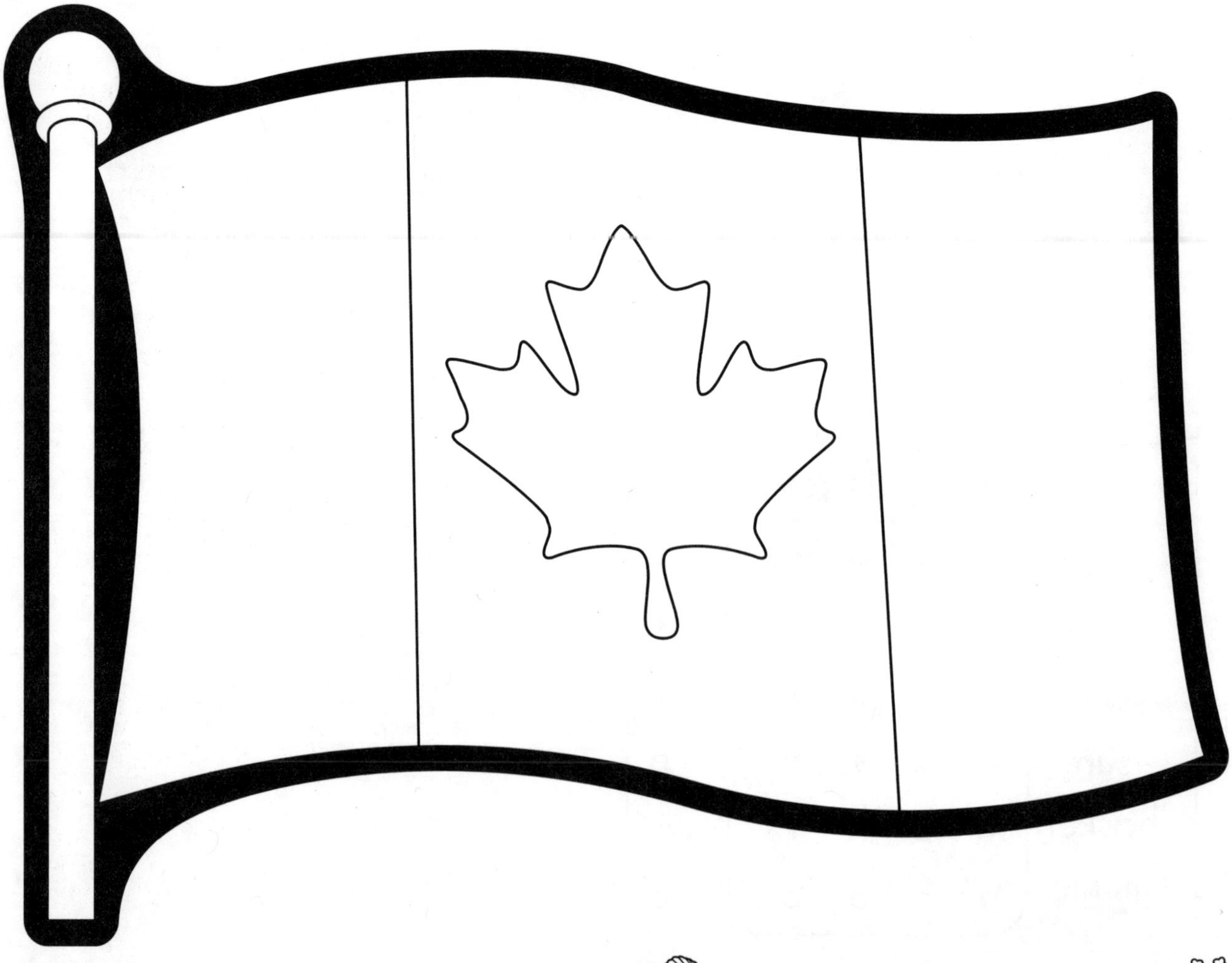

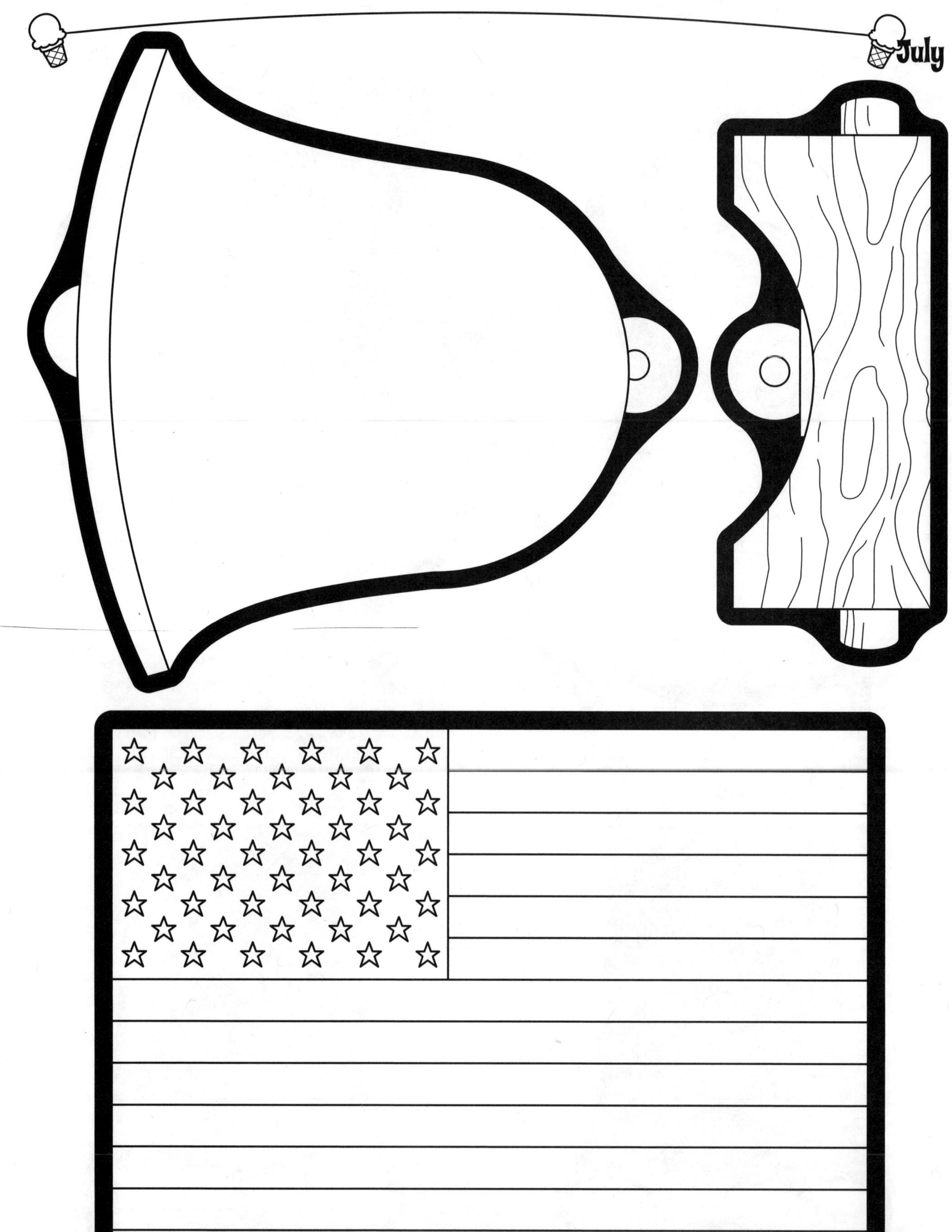

August
August

AUGUST LITERATURE SELECTIONS

The Brand New Kid by Katherine Couric (Doubleday, 2000)

Bread and Jam for Frances by Russell Hoban (HarperCollins, 1993)

Chicka Chicka Boom Boom by Bill Martin Jr. and John Archambault (Aladdin Library, 2000)

The First Strawberries: A Cherokee Story by Joseph Bruchac (Puffin, 1998)

Hooway for Wodney Wat by Helen Lester (Houghton Mifflin/ Walter Lorraine Books, 2002)

How Do You Know It's Summer? by Allan Fowler (Children's Press, 1992)

It's Summer! by Linda Glaser (Millbrook Press, 2003)

Jamberry by Bruce Degen (HarperTrophy, 1985)

Little Mouse, the Red Ripe Strawberry, and the Big Hungry Bear by Audrey Wood (Child's Play International, Ltd., 1984)

Norma Jean, Jumping Bean by Joanna Cole (Random House Books for Young Readers, 1987)

The Rainbow Fish by Marcus Pfister (North South Books, 1995)

When Sophie Gets Angry—Really, Really Angry... by Molly Bang (Scholastic, 1999)

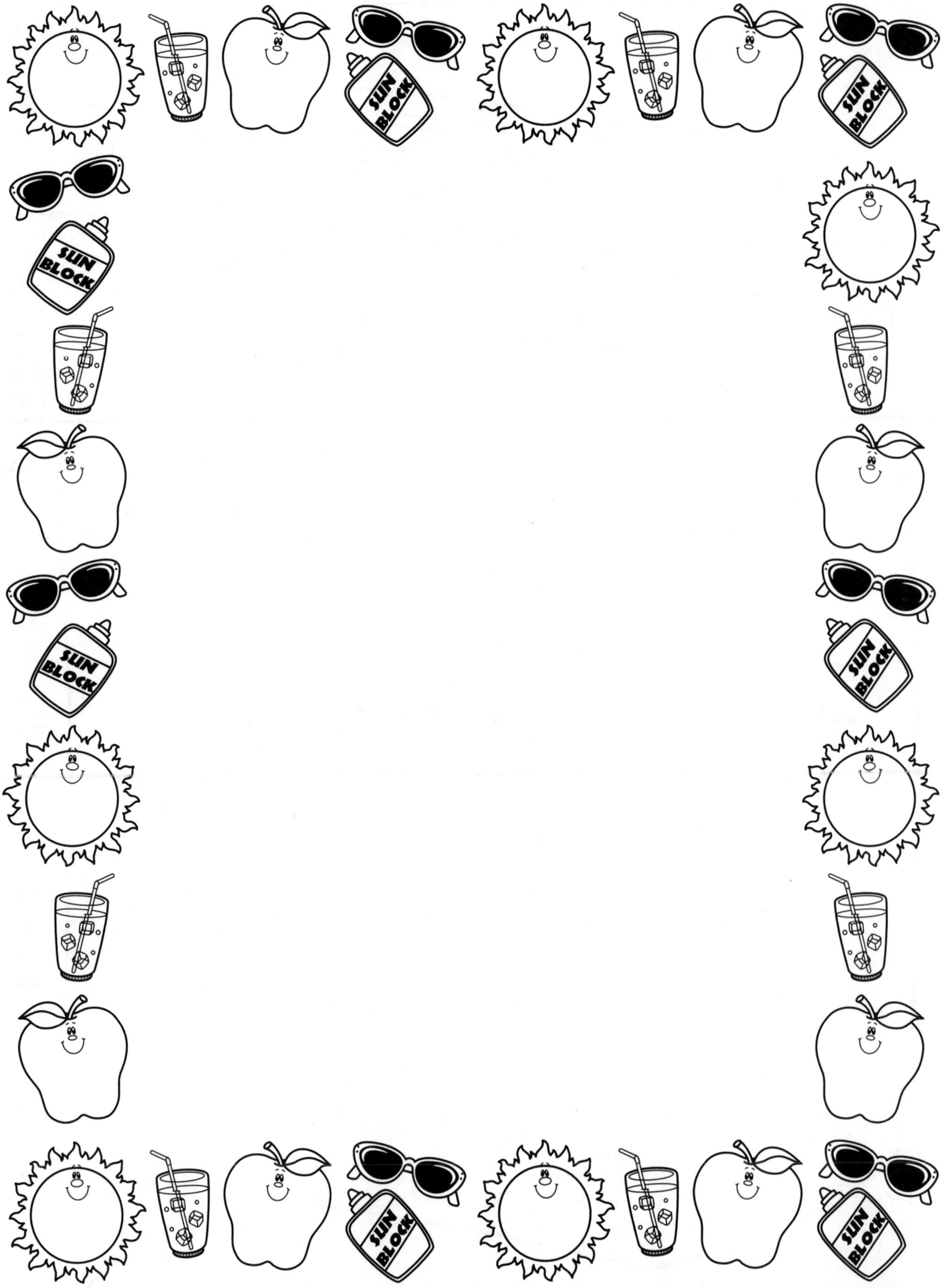

AUGUST

SCHOOL

AUGUST

Sunday	Monday	Tuesday	Wednesday	Thursday	Friday	Saturday

AUGUST GAZETTE

Teacher ______________________ Date ____________

IN THE NEWS

WHAT'S COMING UP

TAKE NOTE

KID'S CORNER
Color the sand castle.

September

September

SEPTEMBER LITERATURE SELECTIONS

Abuela by Arthur Dorros (Puffin, 1997)

Apple Picking Time by Michele B. Slawson (Dragonfly, 1998)

The Berenstain Bears and the Week at Grandma's by Jan Berenstain (Random House Books for Young Readers, 1986)

Cherry Pies and Lullabies by Lynn Reiser (Greenwillow, 1998)

How Do Apples Grow? by Betsy Maestro (HarperTrophy, 1993)

Grandfather's Journey by Allen Say (Houghton Mifflin/Walter Lorraine Books, 1993)

Lots of Grandparents by Shelley Rotner (Millbrook Press, 2003)

Lupita's Papalote/ El Papalote de Lupita by Lupe-Ruiz Flores (Piñata Books, 2002)

Nana Upstairs and Nana Downstairs by Tomie de Paola (Putnam Publishing Group, 2000)

Pablo's Tree by Pat Mora (Simon & Schuster Children's Publishing, 1994)

The Relatives Came by Cynthia Rylant (Aladdin Paperbacks, 1993)

A Sip of Aesop by Jane Yolen (Scholastic, 2000)

SEPTEMBER

September

Sunday	Monday	Tuesday	Wednesday	Thursday	Friday	Saturday

September Gazette

Teacher ______________________________ Date ____________________

IN THE NEWS

TAKE NOTE

WHAT'S COMING UP

KID'S CORNER

Fred

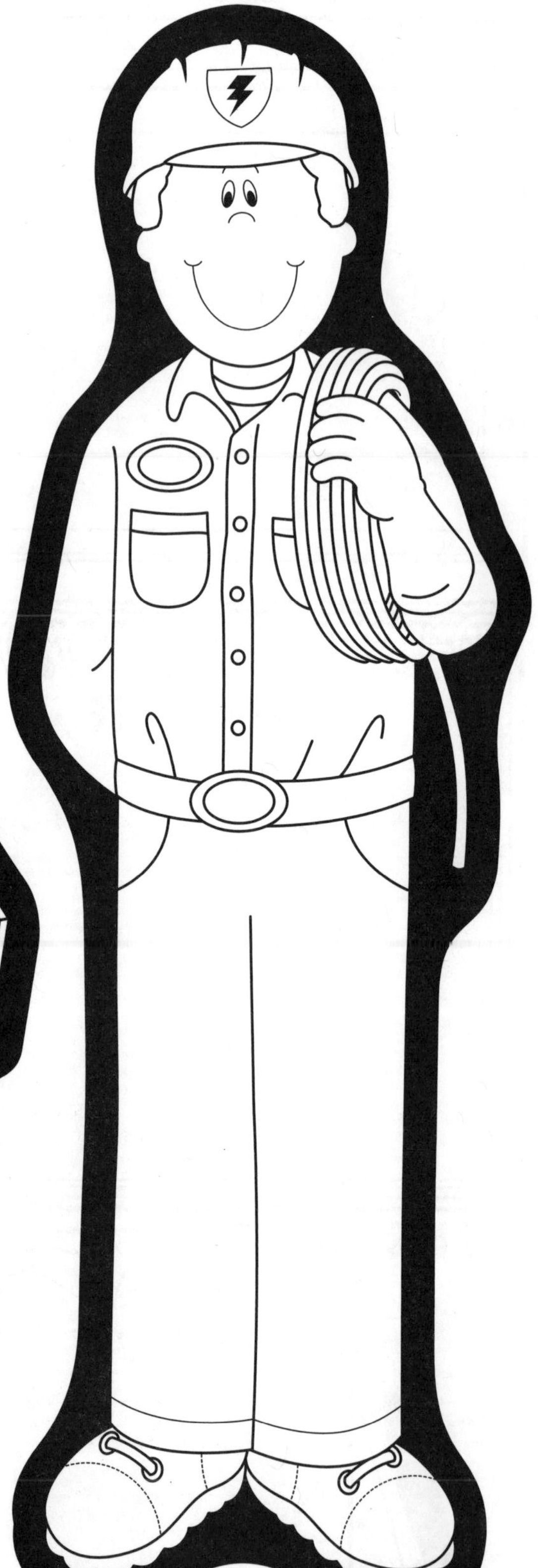

October
October

OCTOBER LITERATURE SELECTIONS

The Biggest Pumpkin Ever by Steven Kroll (Scholastic, 1985)

Dem Bones by Bob Barner (Chronicle Books, 1996)

Go Away, Big Green Monster by Ed Emberly (Little Brown & Company, 1993)

The Little Old Lady Who Was Not Afraid of Anything by Linda Williams (HarperTrophy, 1988)

Look What I Did With a Leaf by Morteza E. Sohi (Walker and Co., 1995)

A Picture Book of Christopher Columbus by David A. Adler (Holiday House, 1992)

Pumpkin Pumpkin by Jeanne Titherington (HarperTrophy, 1990)

Red Leaf, Yellow Leaf by Lois Ehlert (Harcourt, 1991)

Scarecrow by Cynthia Rylant (Voyager Books, 2001)

Stellaluna by Janell Cannon (Harcourt, 1993)

Where the Wild Things Are by Maurice Sendak (HarperTrophy, 1988)

Why Do Leaves Change Color? by Betsy Maestro (HarperTrophy, 1994)

OCTOBER

October

Sunday	Monday	Tuesday	Wednesday	Thursday	Friday	Saturday

October Gazette

Teacher ____________________ Date ____________

IN THE NEWS

WHAT'S COMING UP

TAKE NOTE

KID'S CORNER

Find the hidden words.

acorn leaf
autumn fun
fall tree

l	f	a	l	l	n
e	a	o	f	m	n
a	t	c	u	u	f
f	e	t	o	r	u
f	u	v	e	r	n
a	t	r	e	e	n

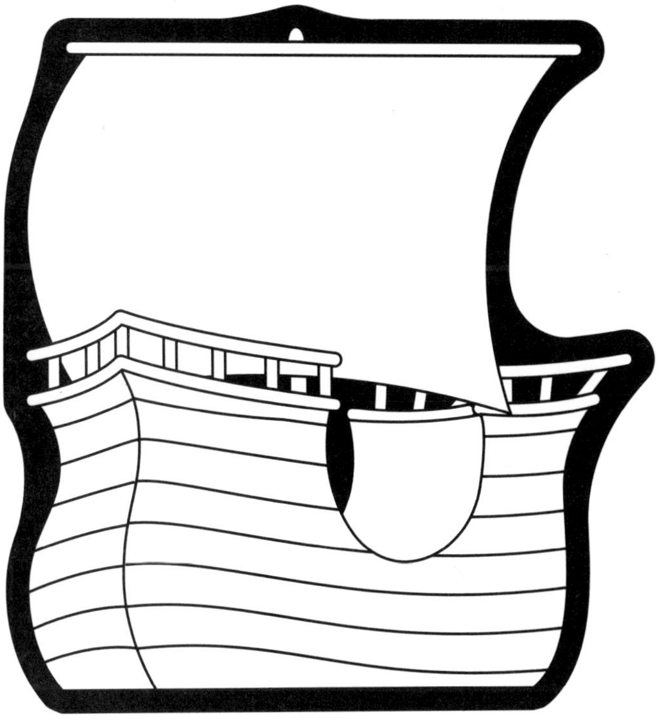

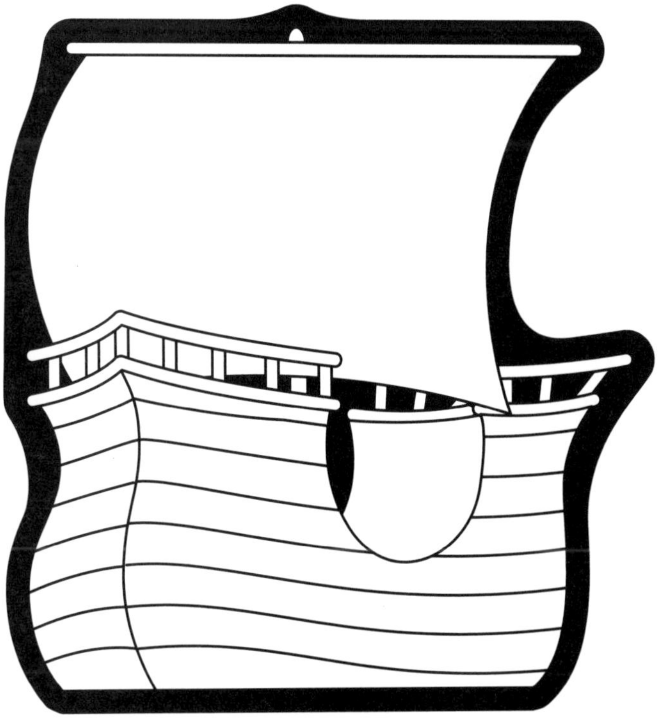

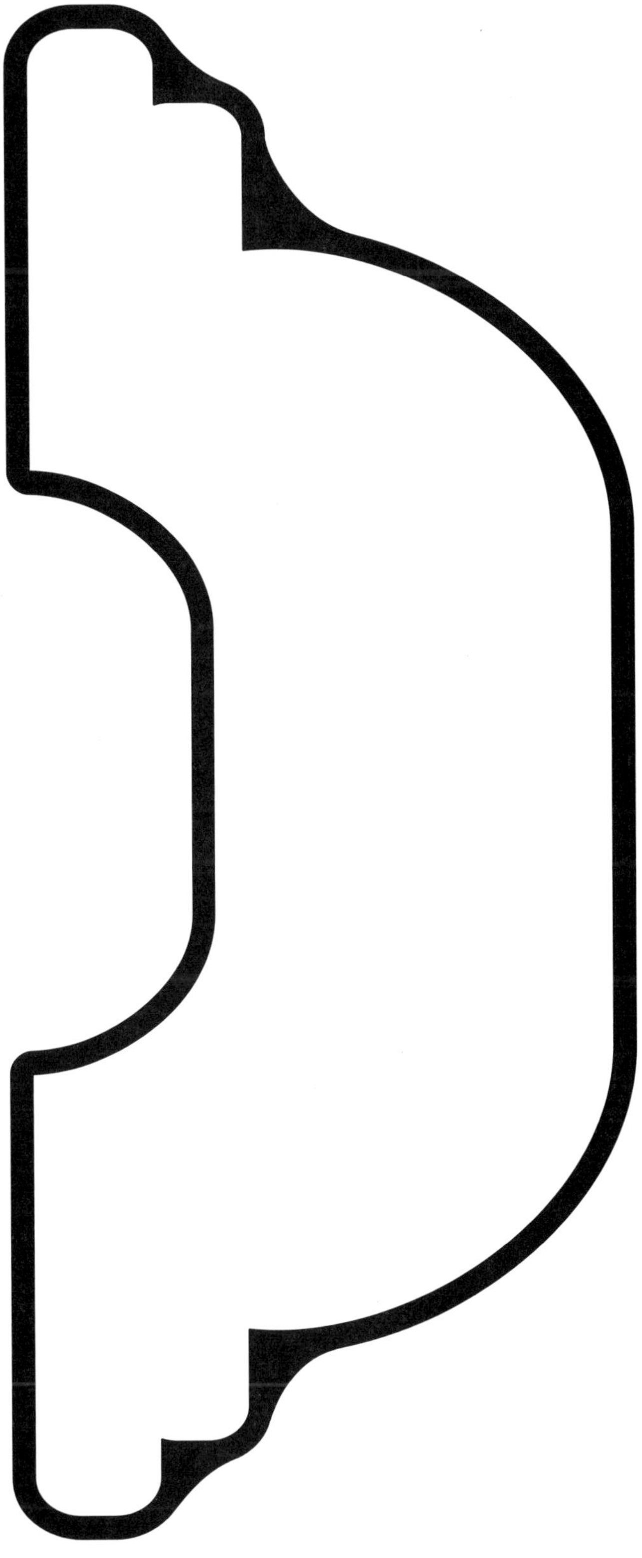

Christopher Columbus

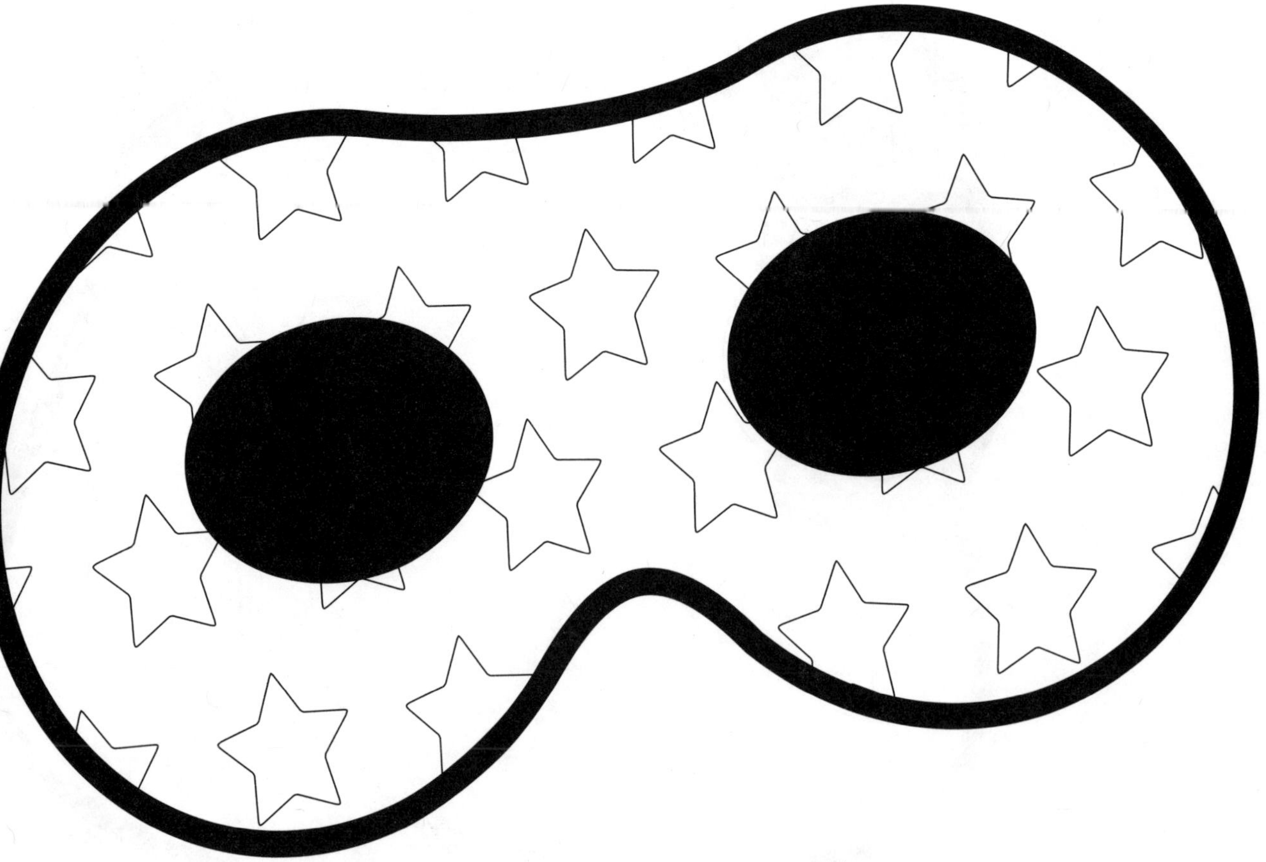

November

November

NOVEMBER LITERATURE SELECTIONS

All About Turkeys by Jim Arnosky (Scholastic, 1998)

The Day Gogo Went to Vote by Elinor Sisulu (Megan Tingley, 1999)

Growing Vegetable Soup by Lois Ehlert (Voyager Books, 1990)

Harvest Year by Chris Peterson (Boyds Mill Press, 1996)

How Many Days to America? A Thanksgiving Story by Eve Bunting (Clarion Books, 1990)

Itse Selu: Cherokee Harvest Festival by Daniel Pennington (Charlesbridge Publishing, 1994)

The Moon Lady by Amy Tan (Aladdin Library, 1995)

Night Lights: A Sukkot Story by Barbara Diamond Goldin (Harcourt, 1995)

Thanksgiving Day by Gail Gibbons (Holiday House, 1983)

The Thanksgiving Story by Alice Dalgliesh (Holiday House, 1978)

I Know an Old Lady Who Swallowed a Pie by Alison Jackson (Puffin, 2002)

A Turkey for Thanksgiving by Eve Bunting (Clarion Books, 1995)

The Wind and the Sukkah by Aydel Lebovics (Merkos Linyonei Chinuch, 1990)

Veterans Day by Mir Tamim Ansary (Heinemann Library, 2001)

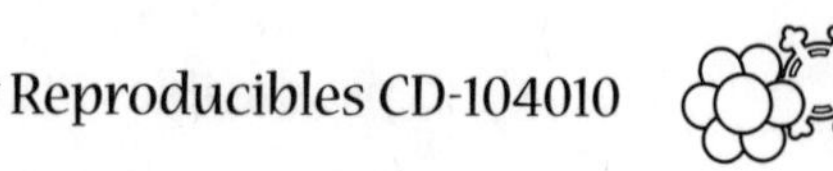

NOVEMBER

November

Sunday	Monday	Tuesday	Wednesday	Thursday	Friday	Saturday

November Gazette

Teacher ______________________ Date ______________

IN THE NEWS

TAKE NOTE

WHAT'S COMING UP

KID'S CORNER

Draw what's inside a pumpkin.

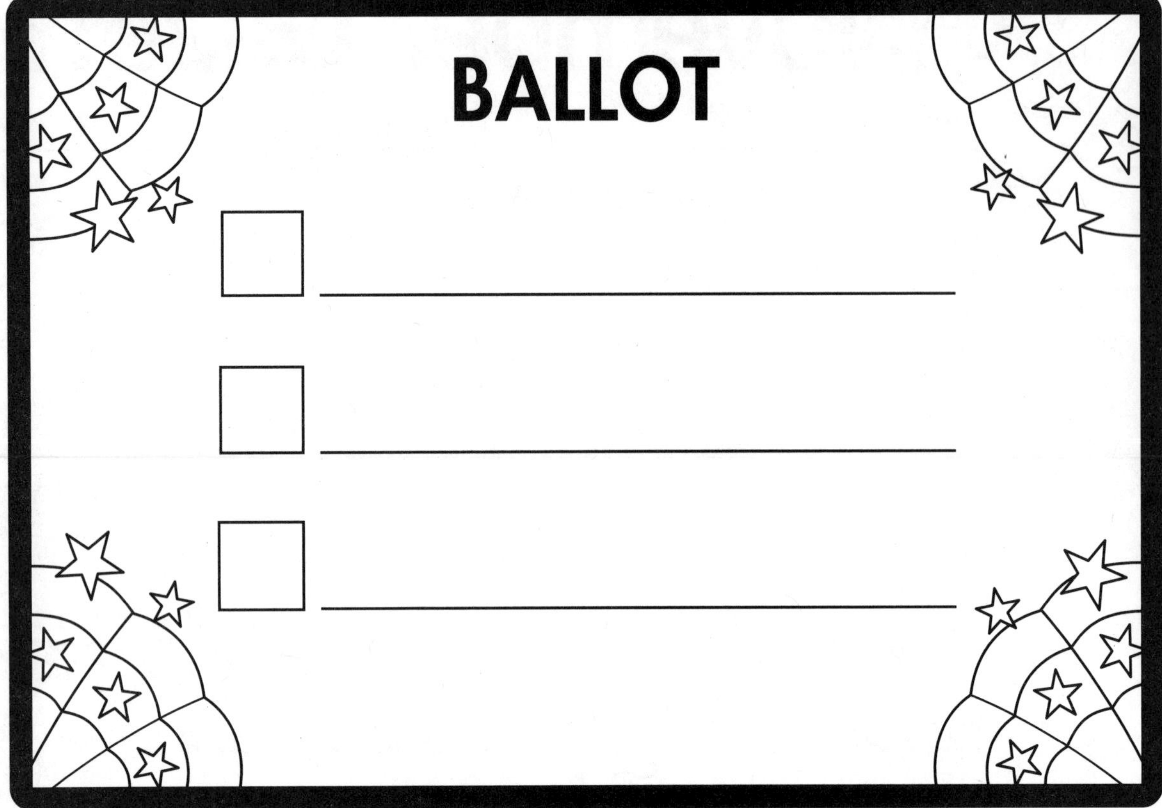
BALLOT

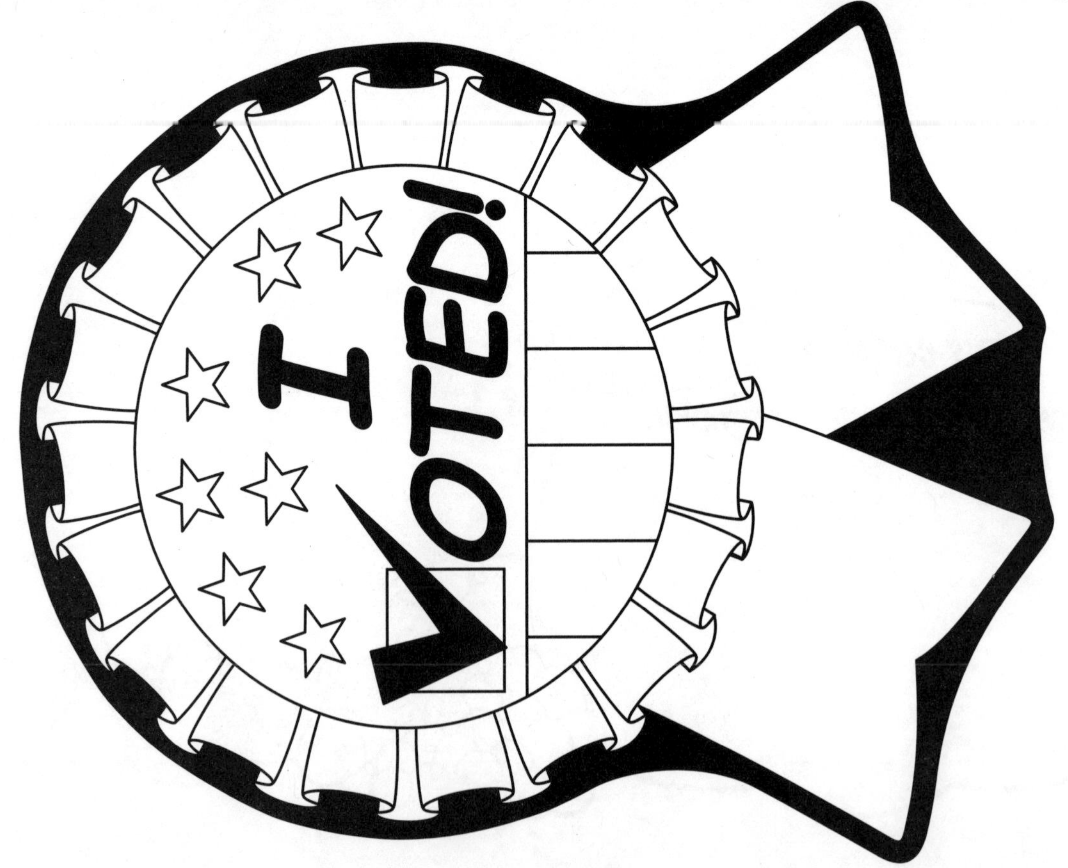
I
VOTED!

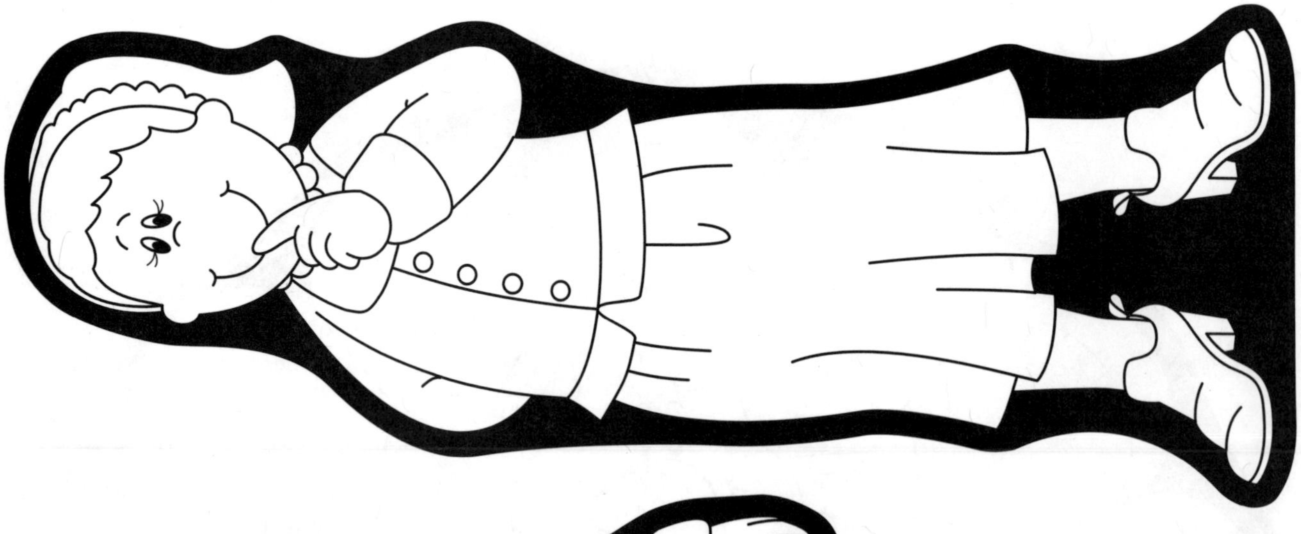

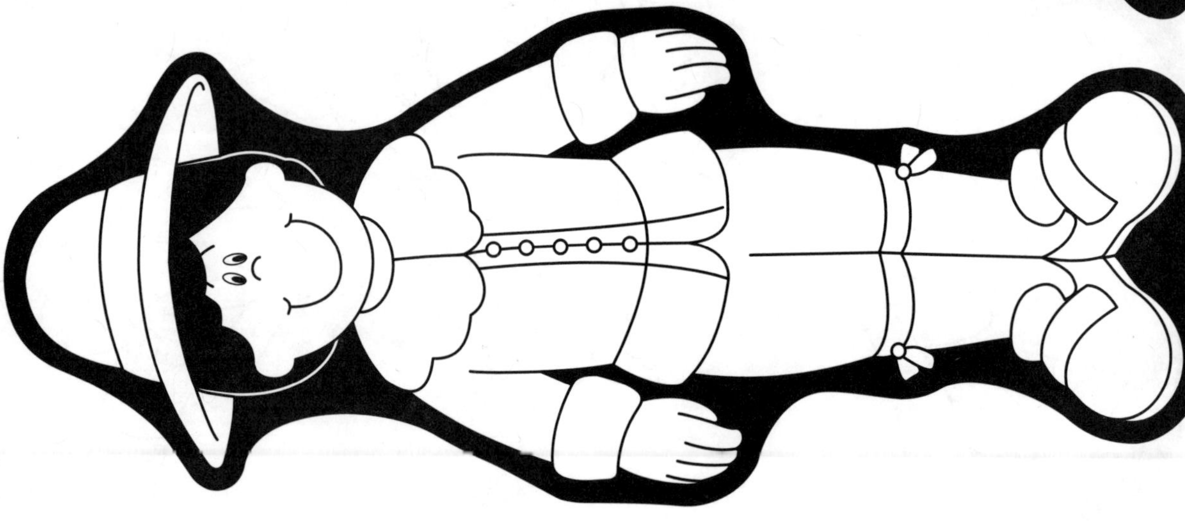

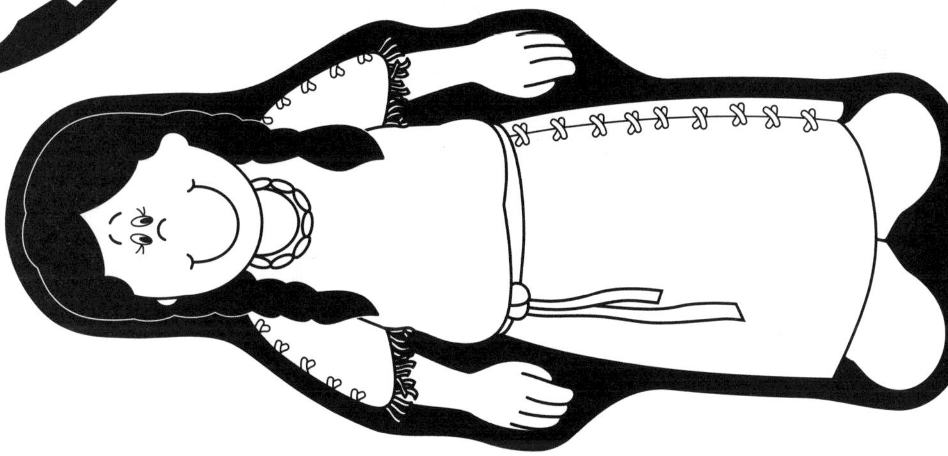

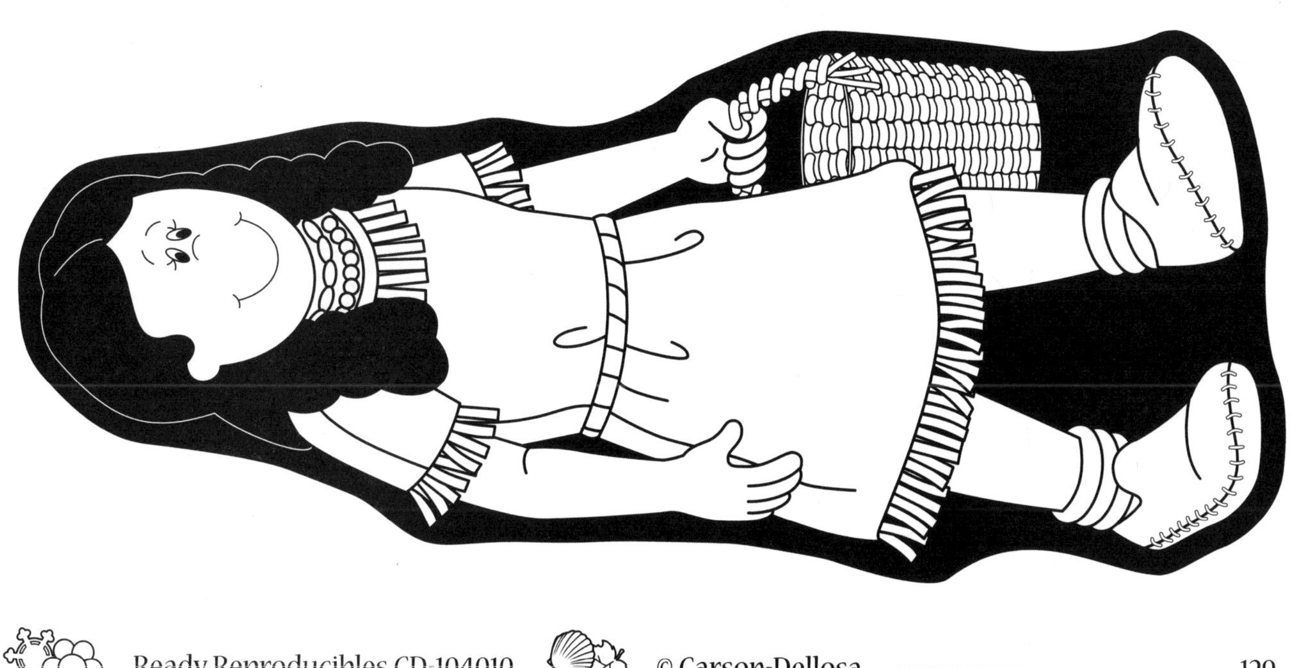

December

DECEMBER LITERATURE SELECTIONS

The Gift of the Magi illustrated by Lisbeth Zwerger (Aladdin Library, 1997)

The Gingerbread Baby by Jan Brett (Putnam Publishing Group, 1999)

Hanukkah Lights, Hanukkah Nights by Leslie Kimmelman (HarperTrophy, 1994)

In the Snow: Who's Been Here? by Lindsay Barret George (HarperTrophy, 1999)

The Legend of the Christmas Tree by Rick Osborne (Zonderkidz, 2001)

The Legend of the Poinsettia by Tomie de Paola (Putnam Publishing Group, 1997)

The Magic Dreidels: A Hanukkah Story by Eric A. Kimmel (Holiday House, 1997)

The Mitten: A Ukrainian Folktale by Jan Brett (Scholastic, 1990)

My First Kwanzaa Book by Deborah M. Newton Chocolate (Scholastic, 1999)

The Night of Las Posadas by Tomie de Paola (Putnam Publishing Group, 2001)

Seven Candles for Kwanzaa by Andrea Davis Pinkney (Puffin, 1998)

DECEMBER

December

Sunday	Monday	Tuesday	Wednesday	Thursday	Friday	Saturday

December Gazette

Teacher ____________________ Date__________

IN THE NEWS

TAKE NOTE

WHAT'S COMING UP

KID'S CORNER

1★ 2 3 4 5 6 7 8 9 10 11 12 13 14 15 16 17 18 19

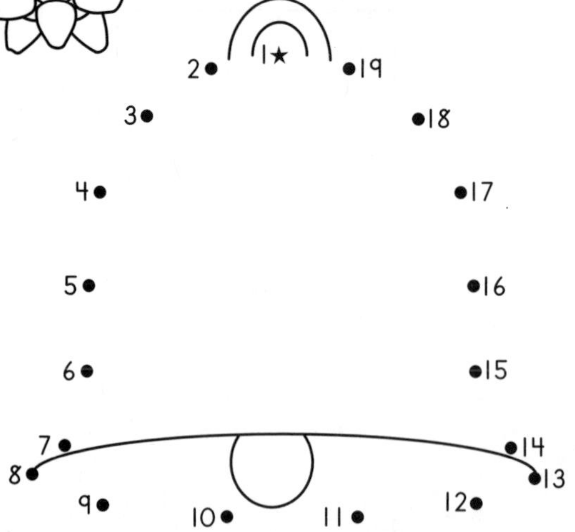

ש
Shin

ה
Hey

נ
Nun

ג
Gimmel

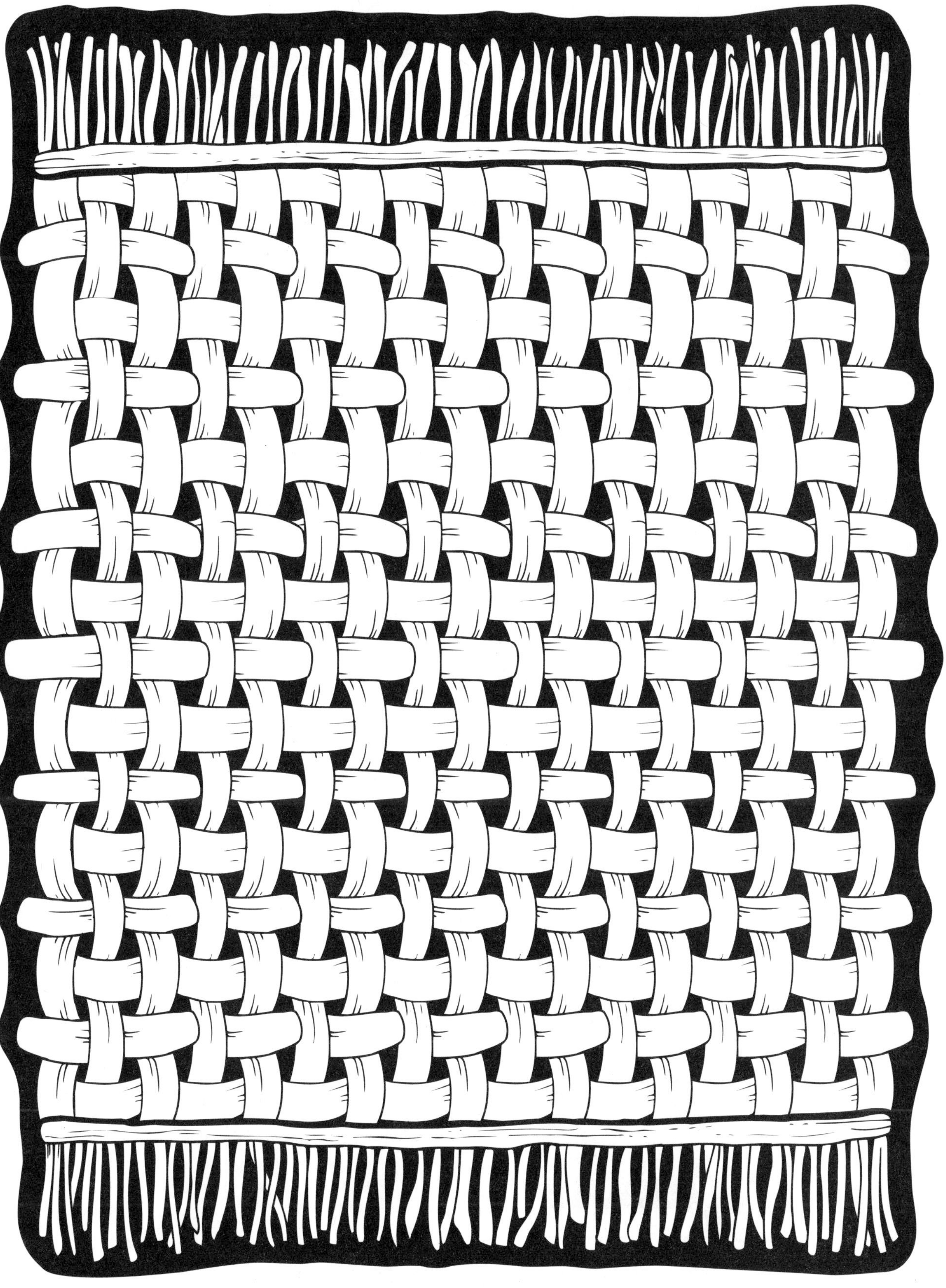

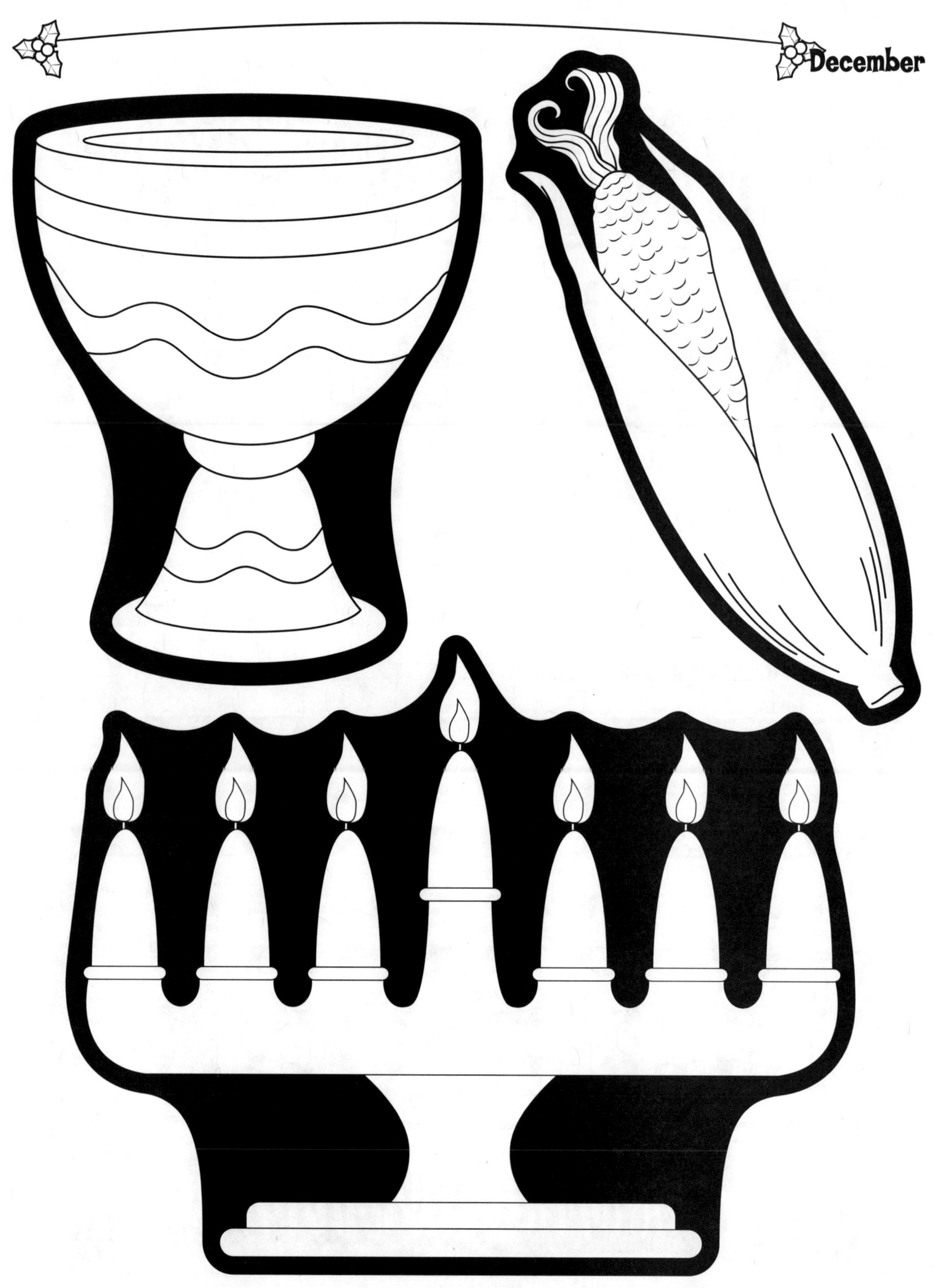

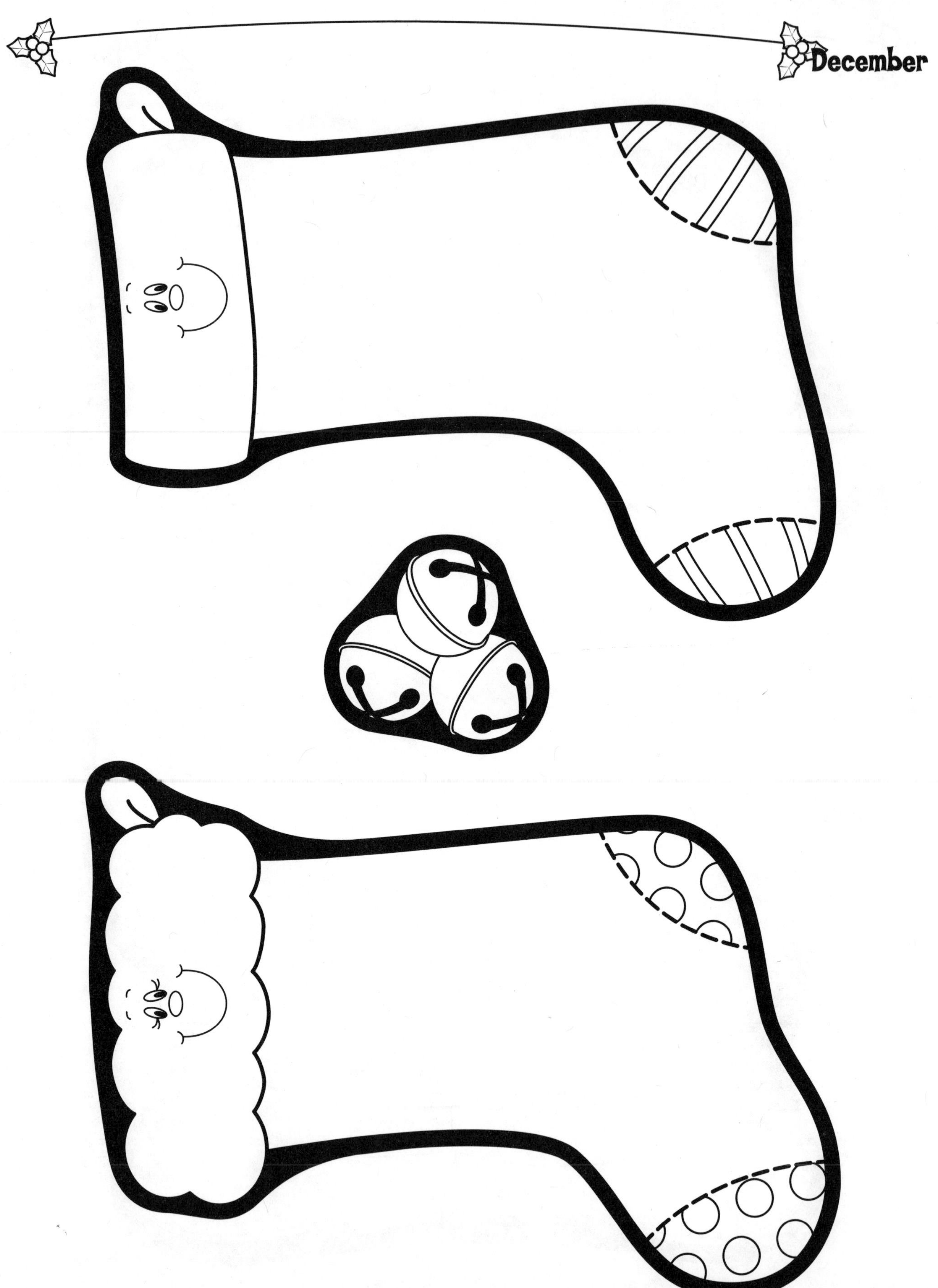

Winter

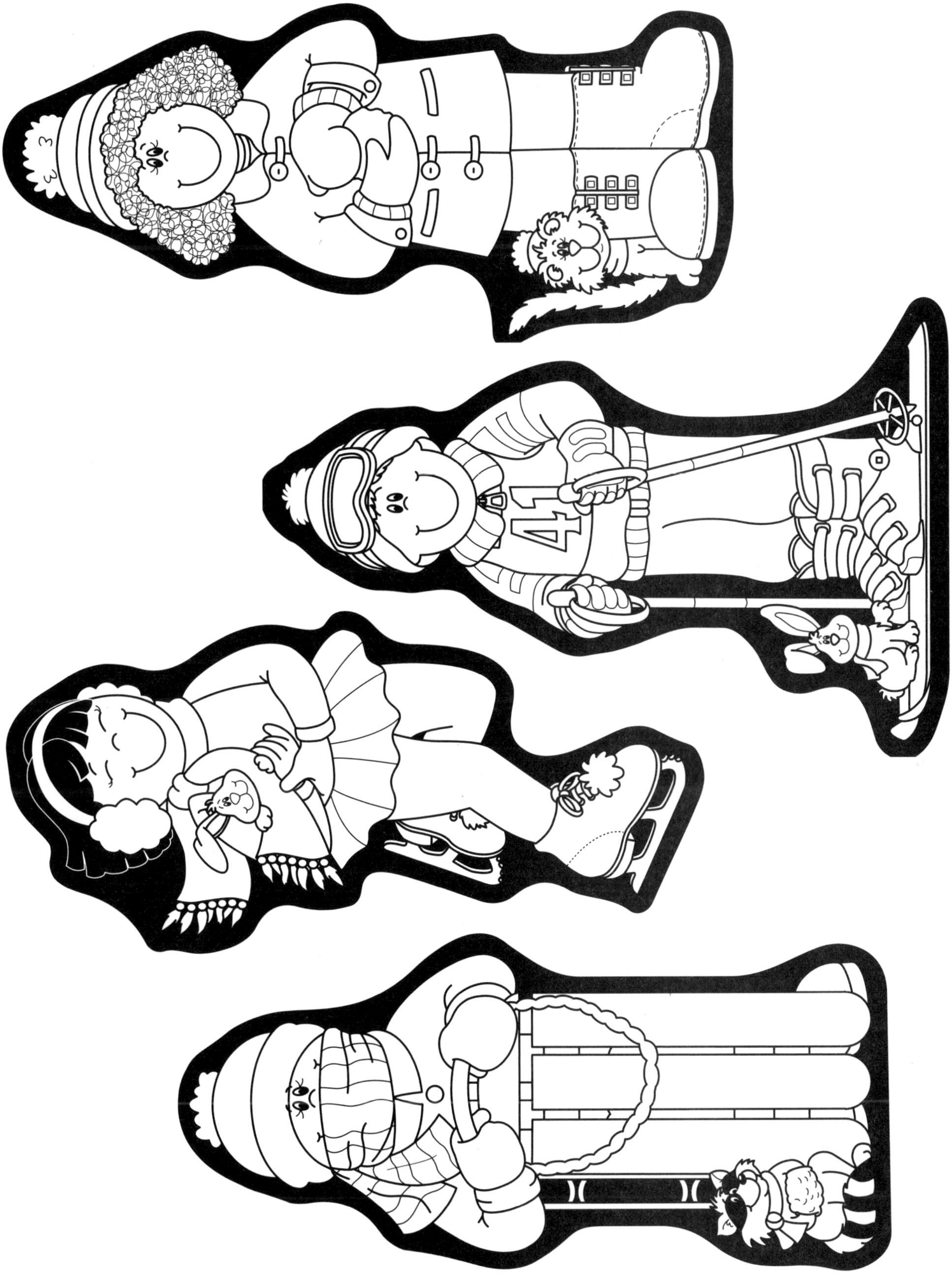

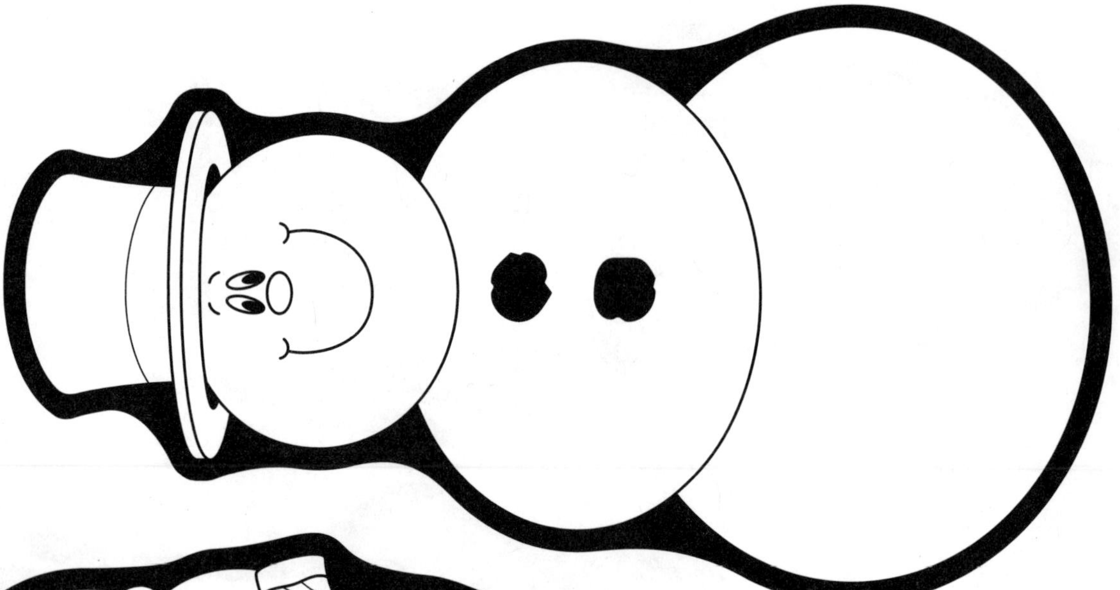

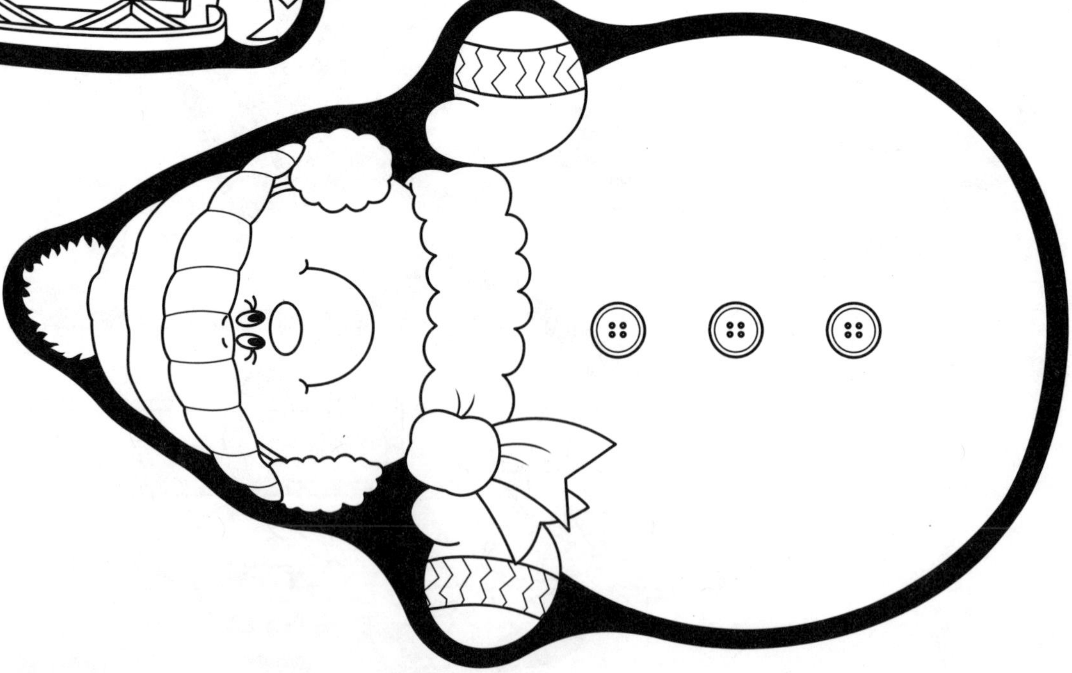

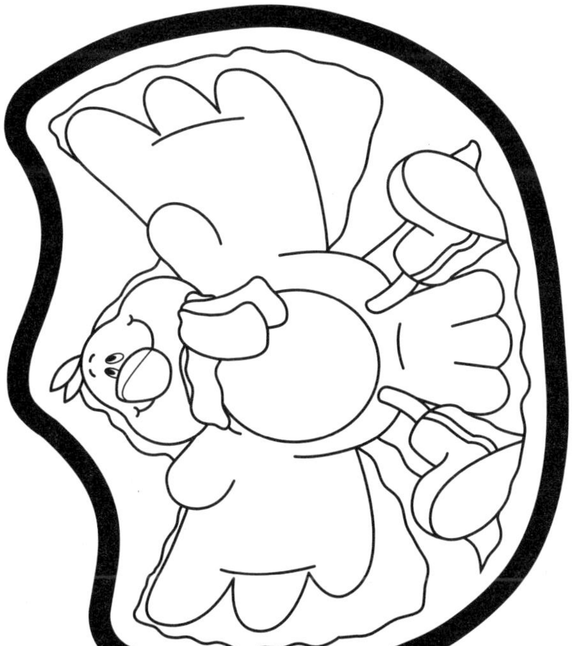

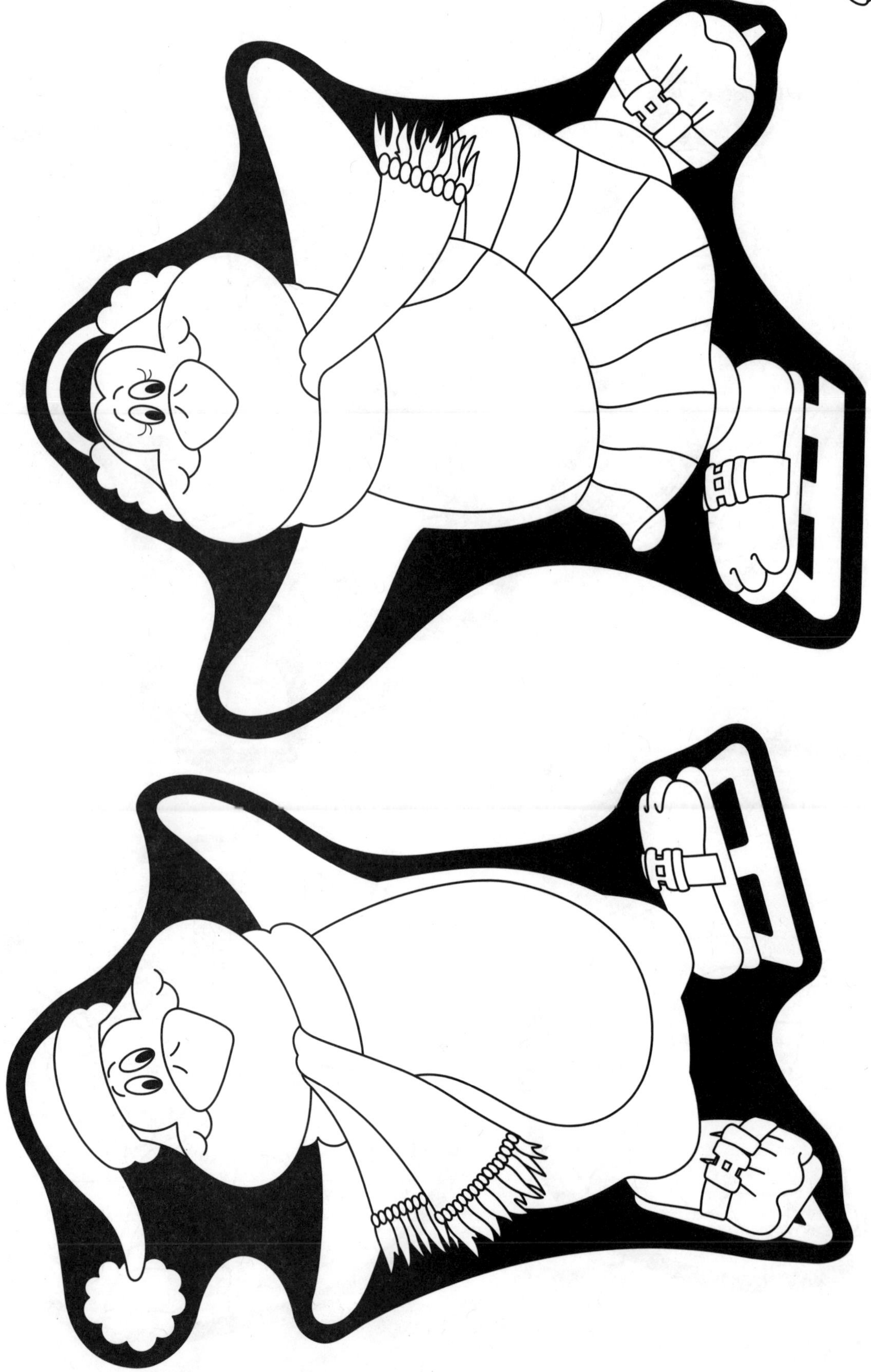

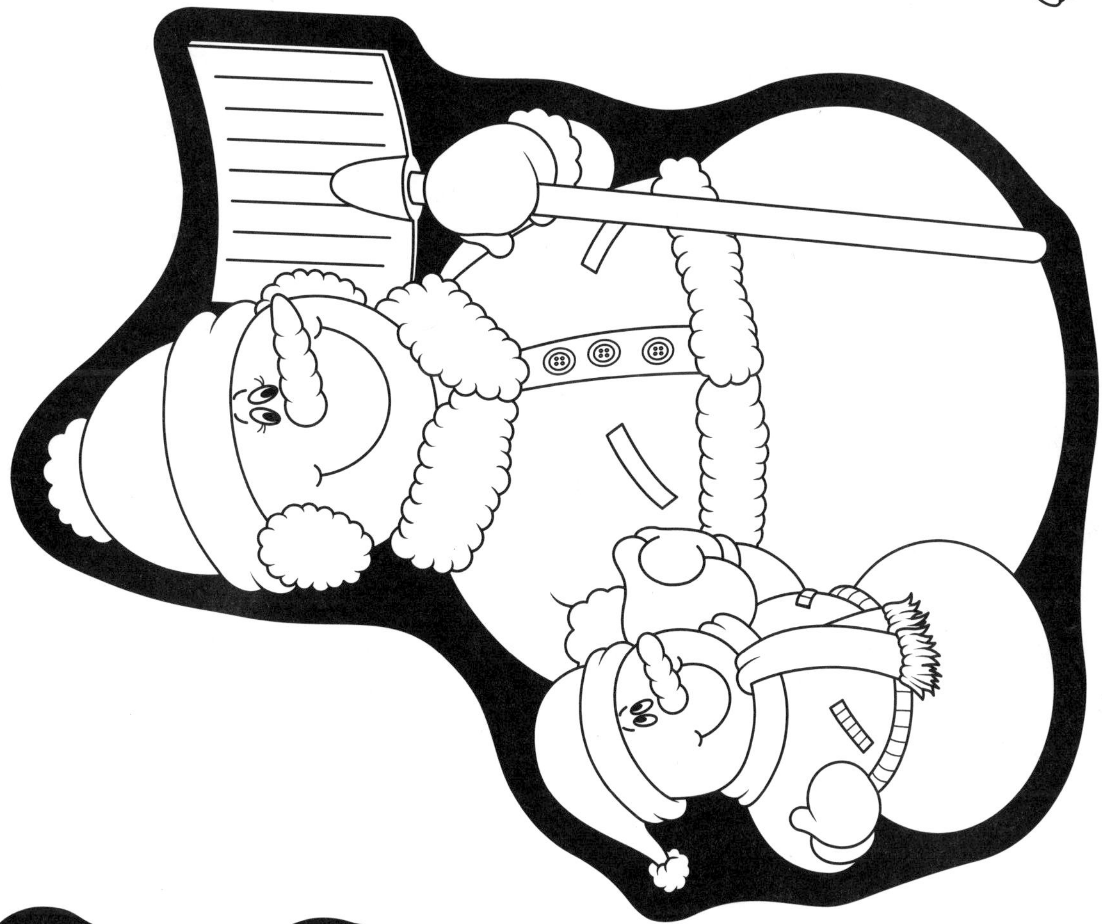

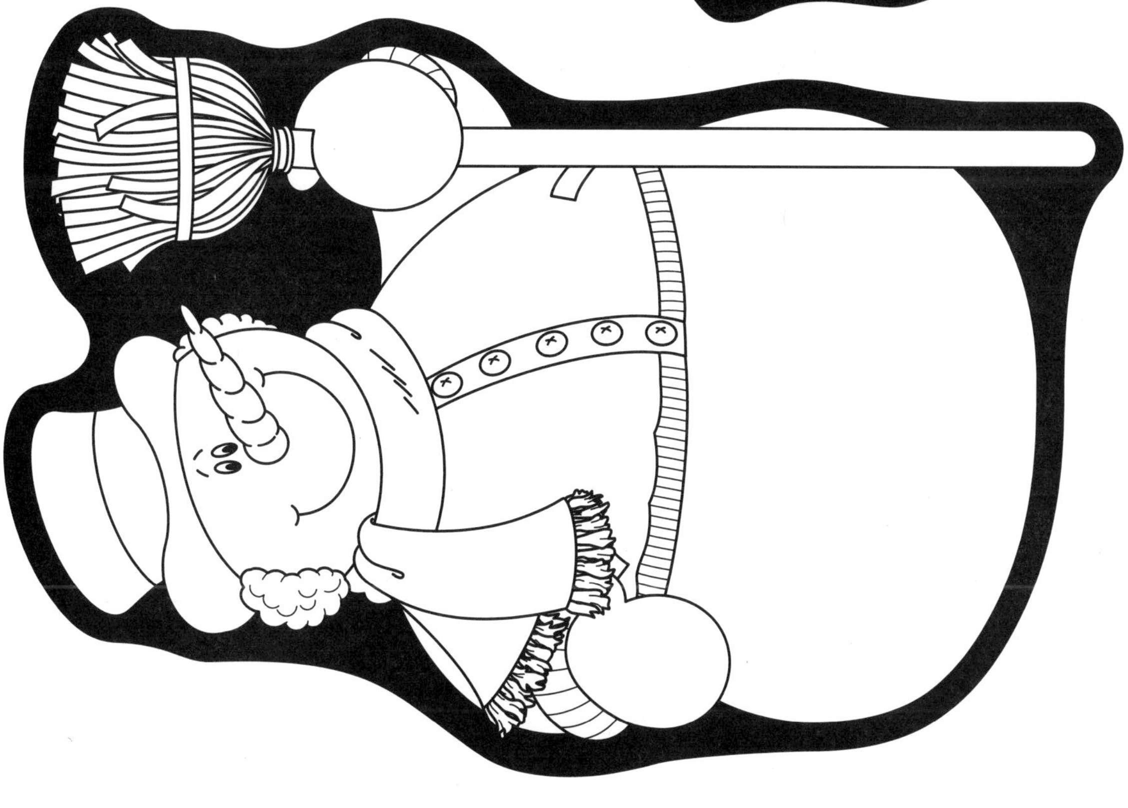

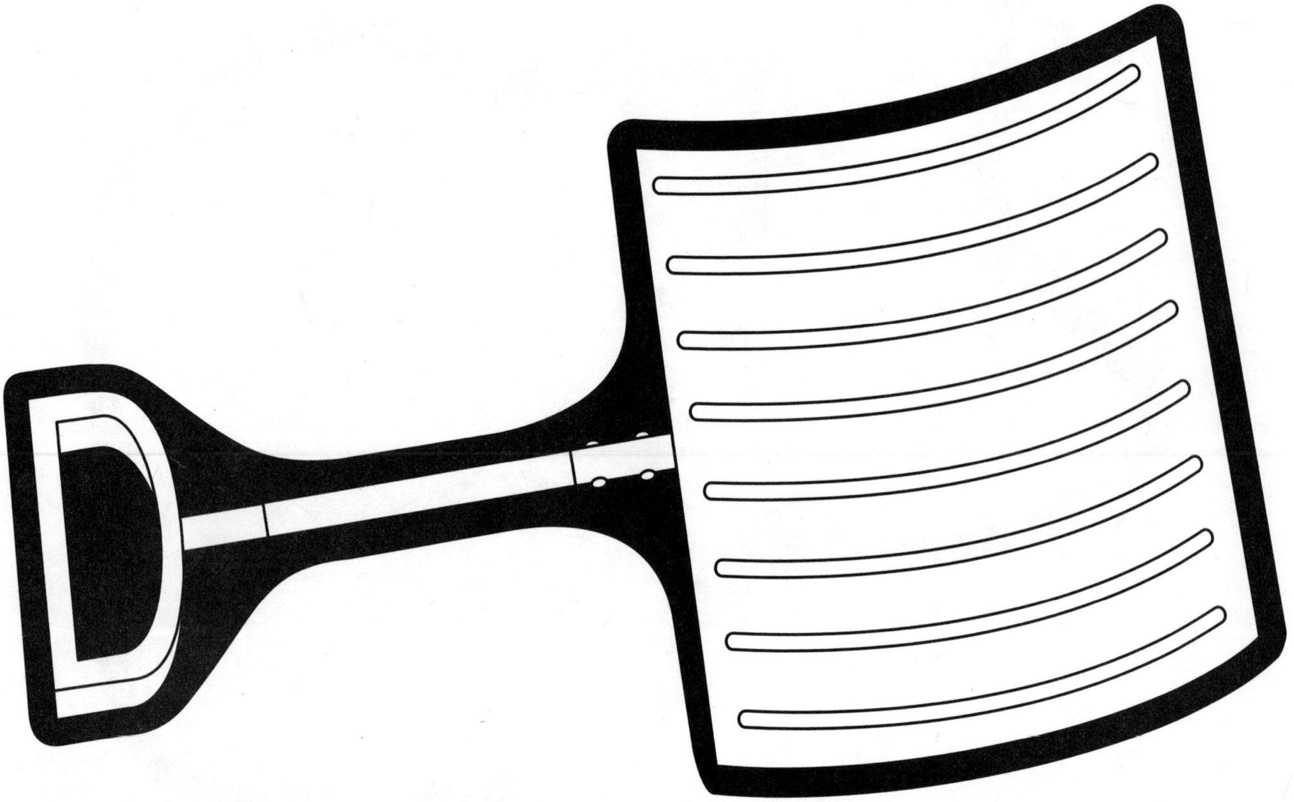

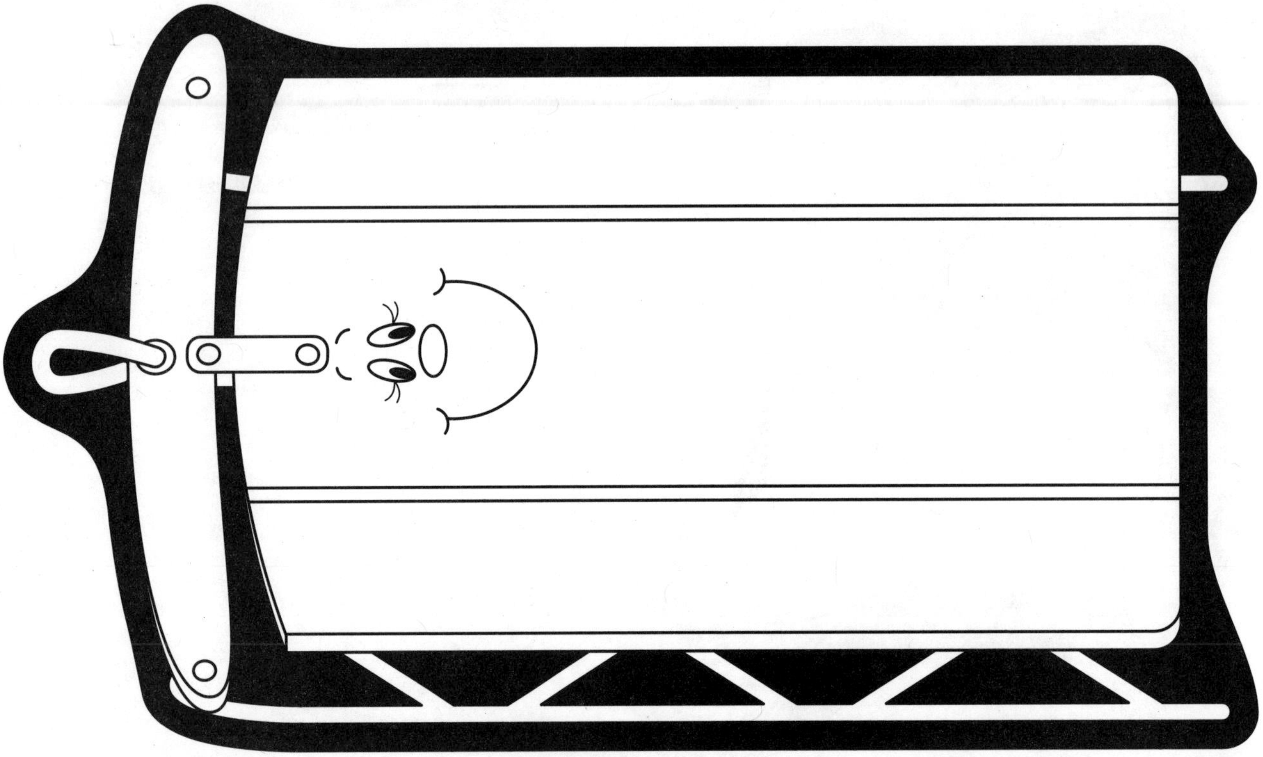

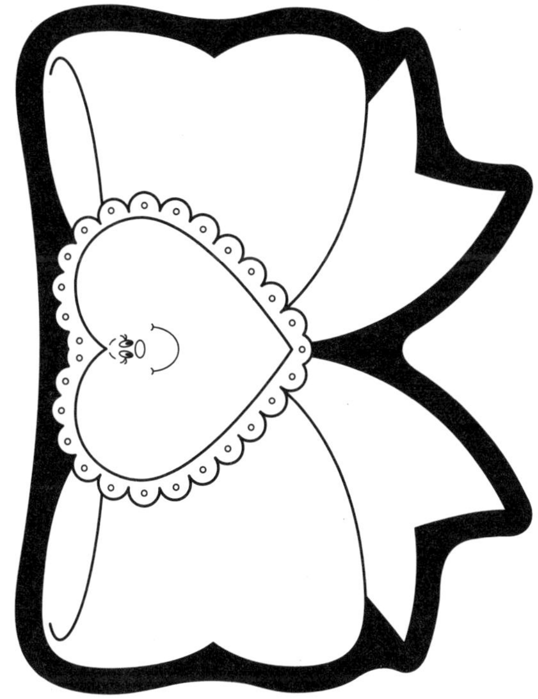

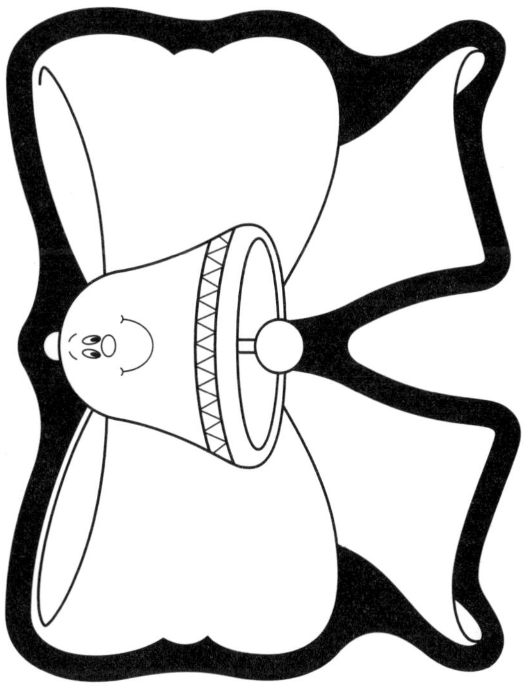

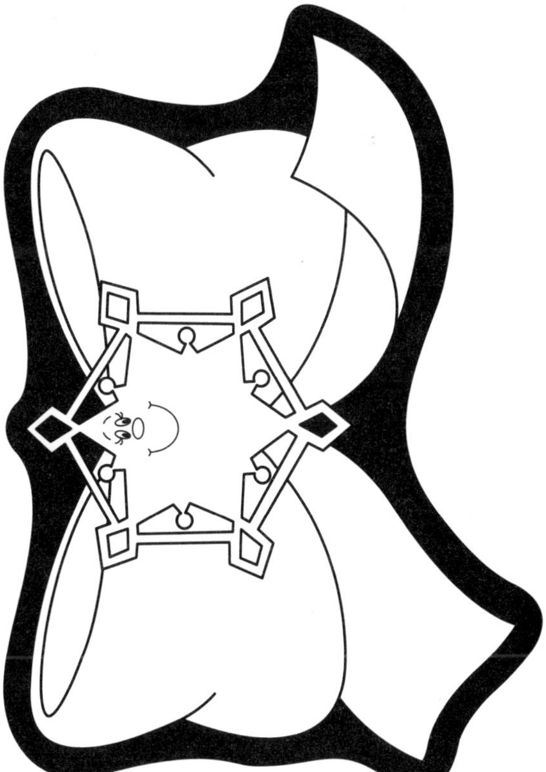

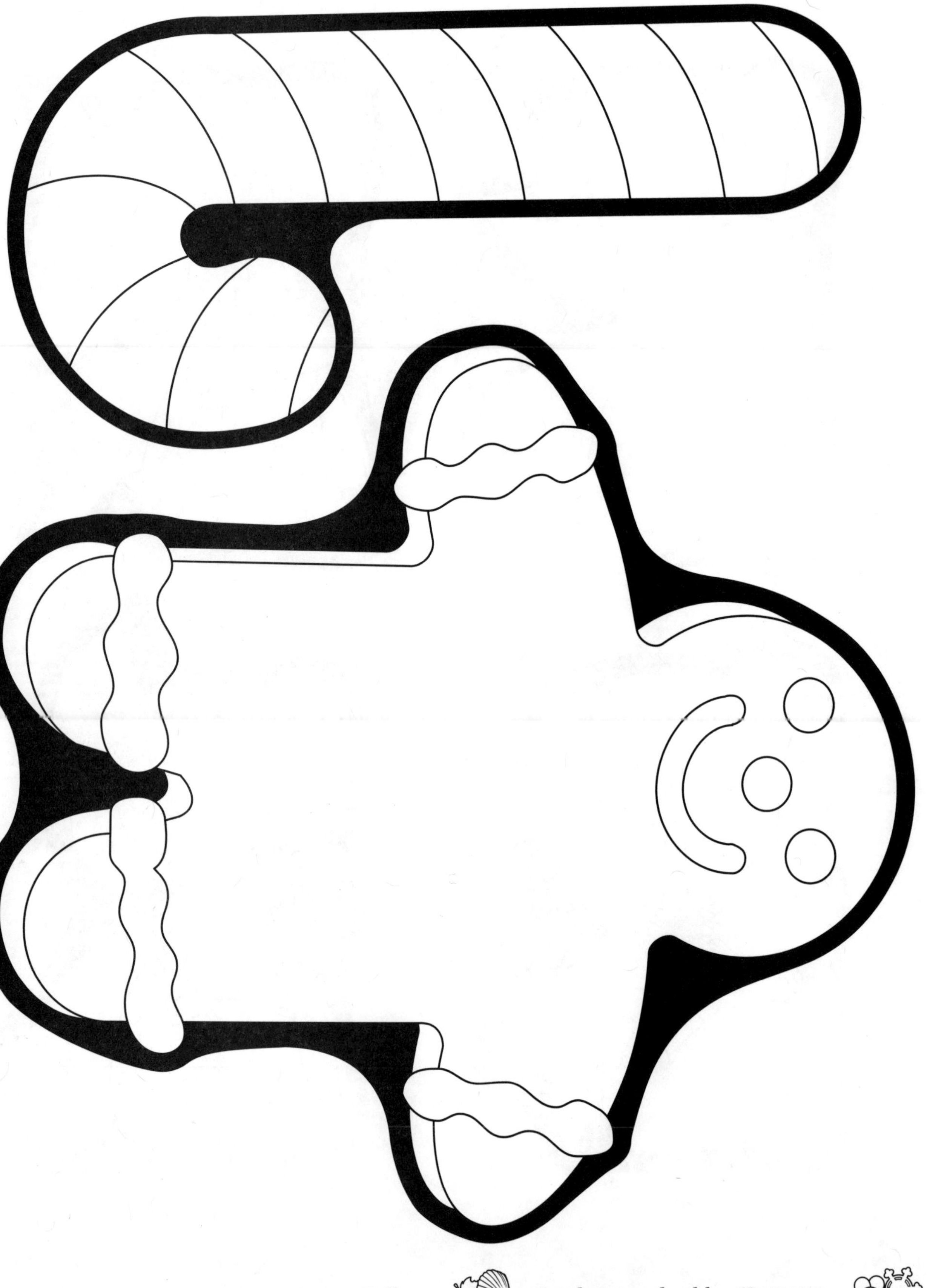

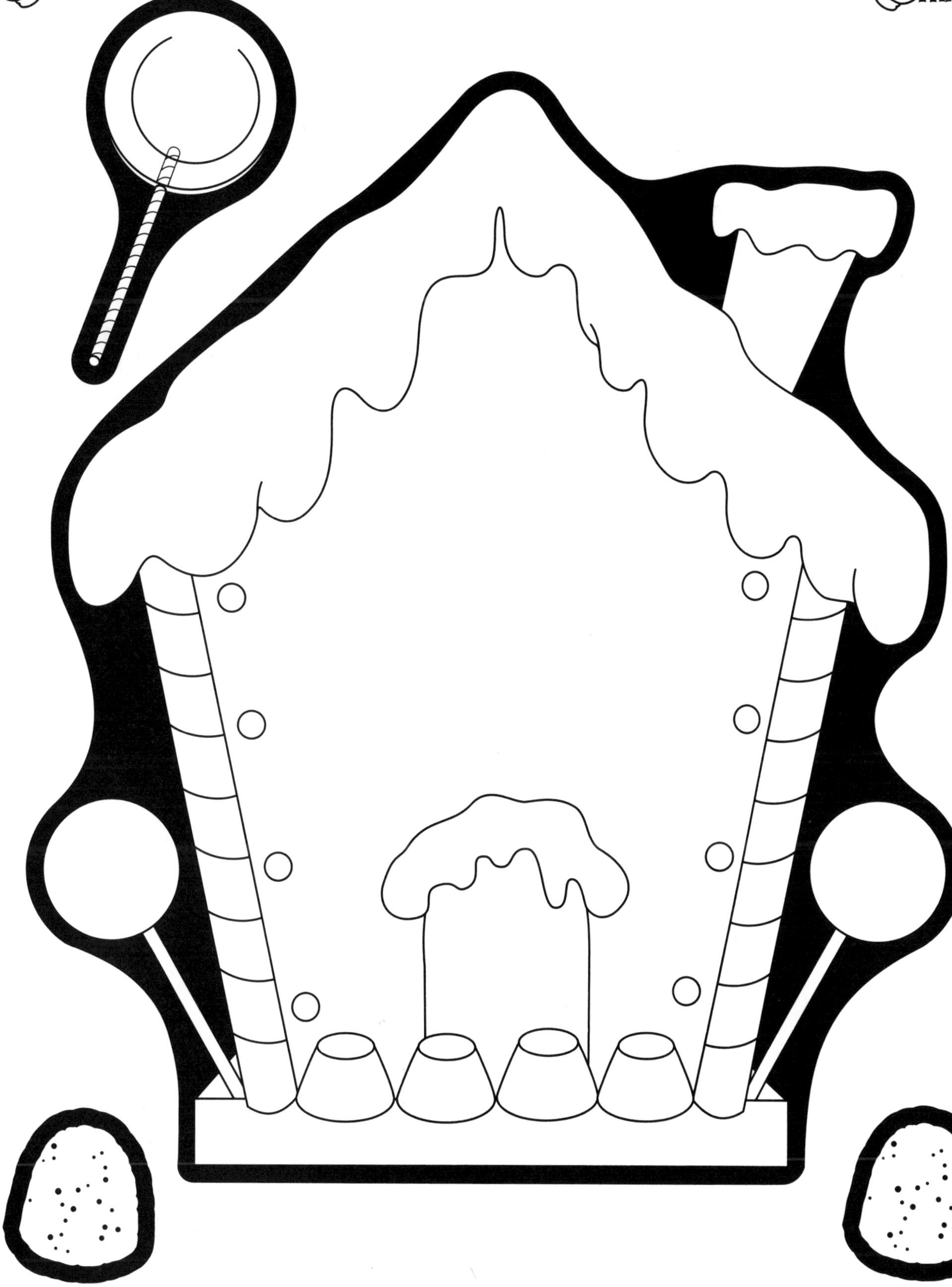

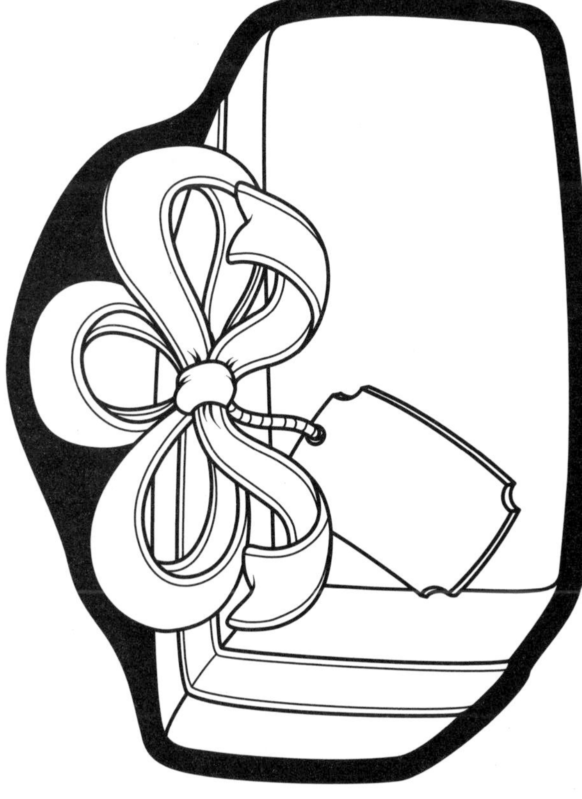

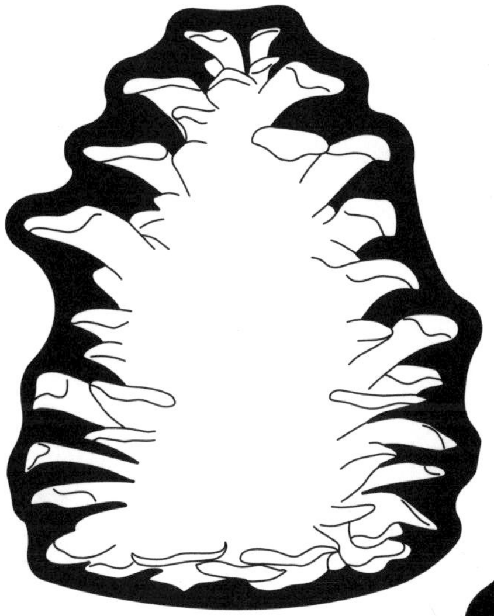

Spring

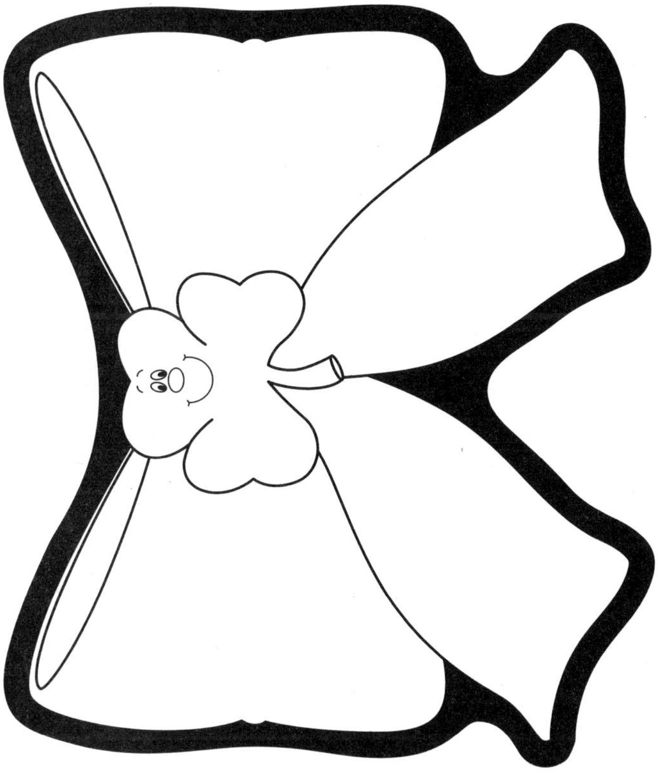

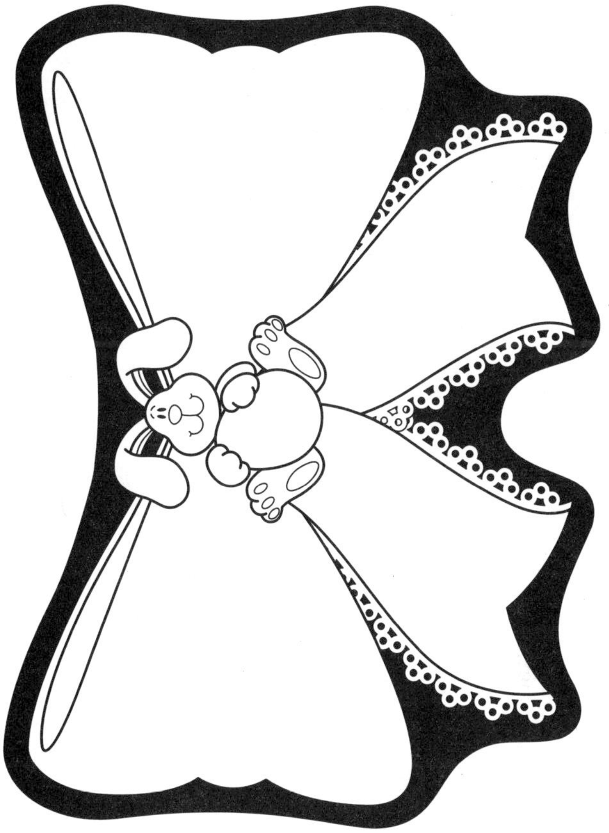

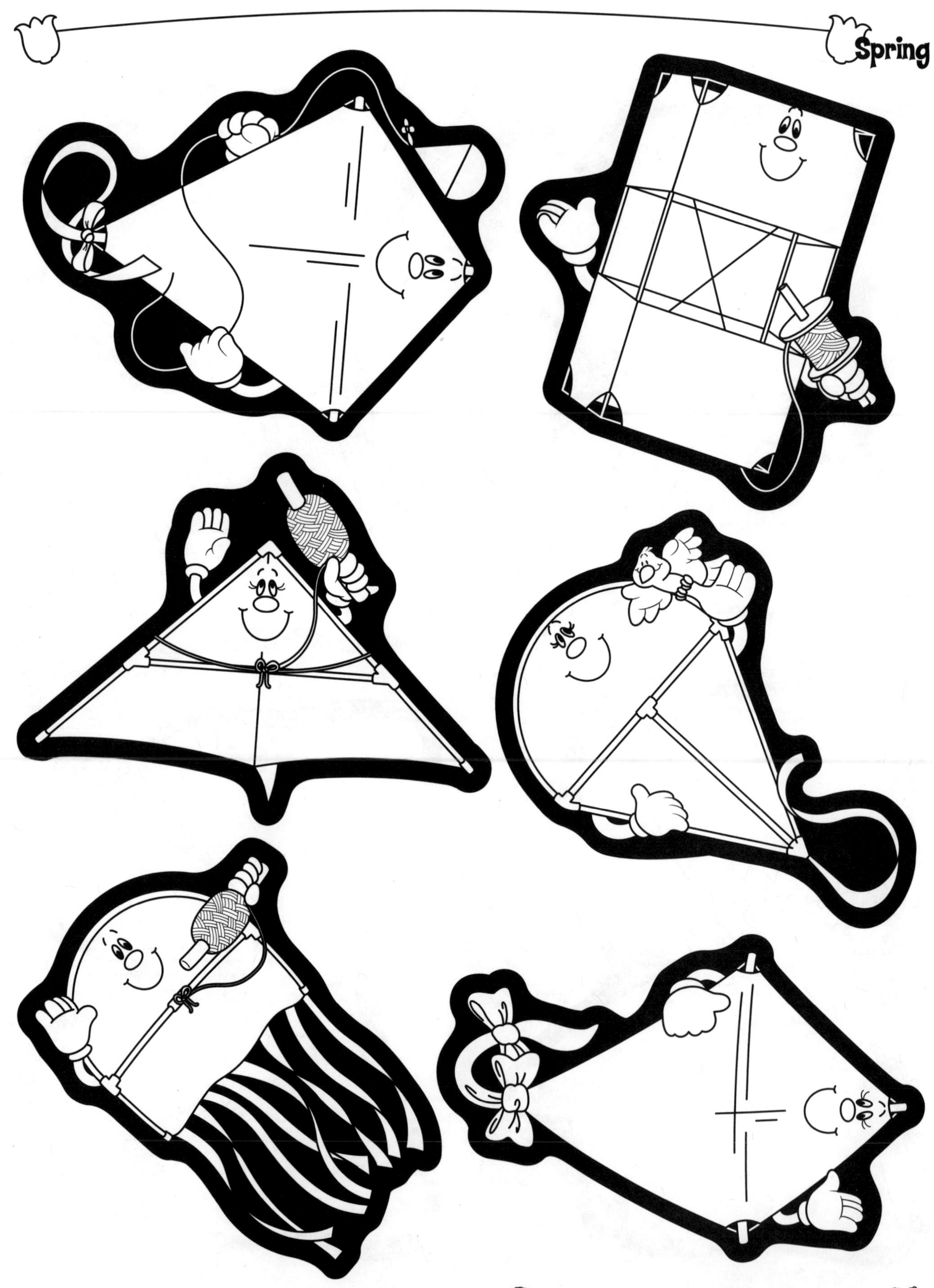

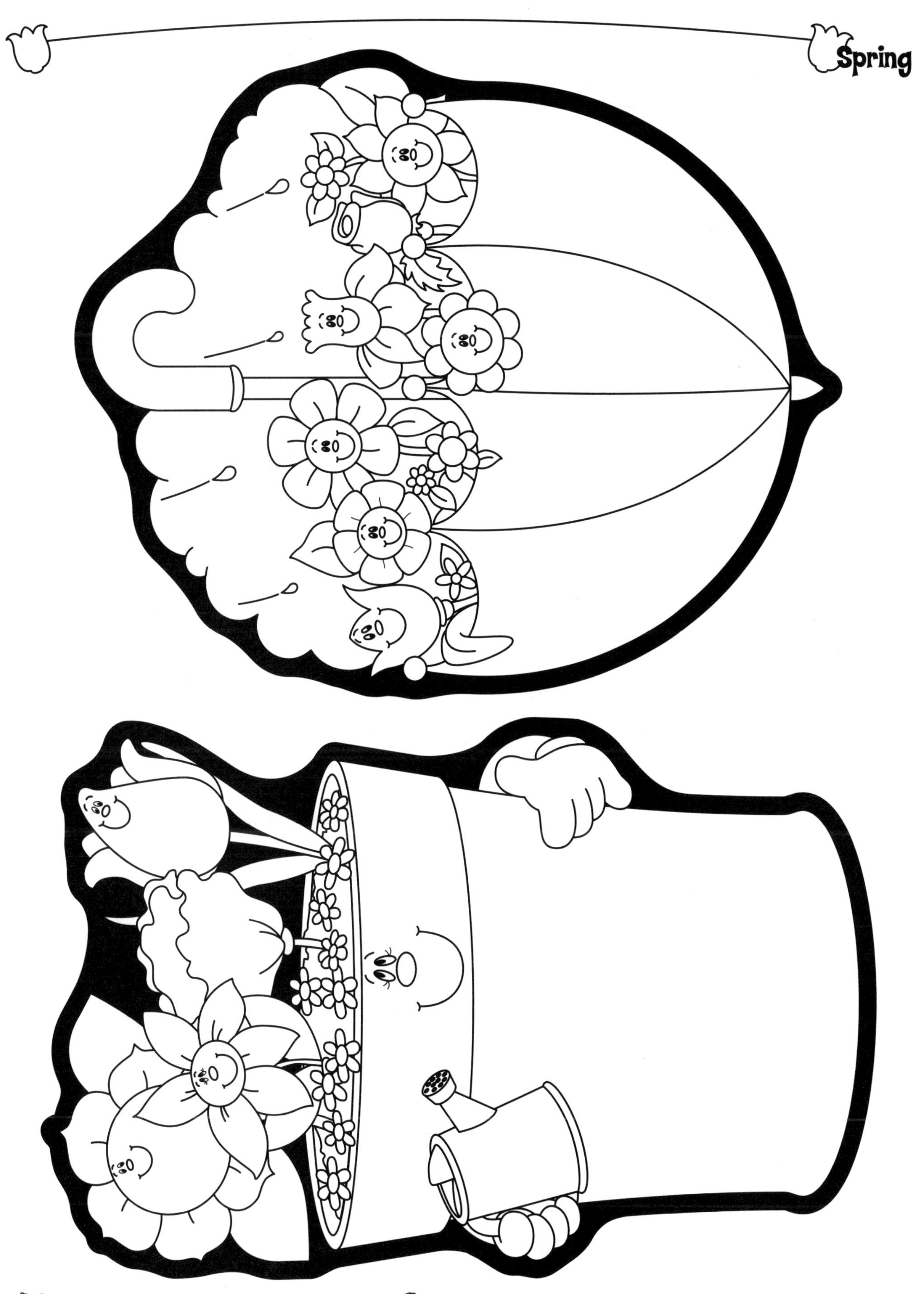

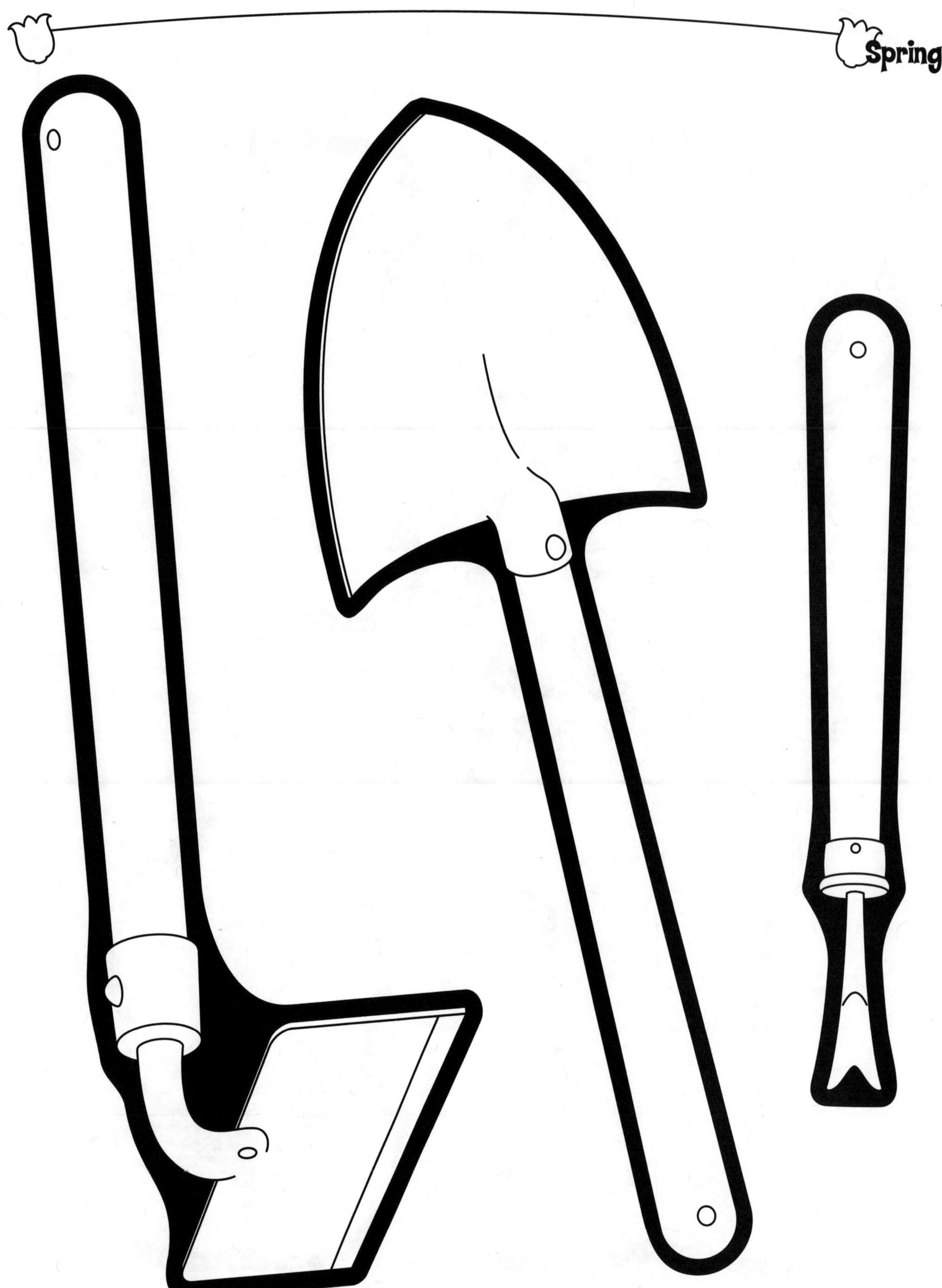

Summer

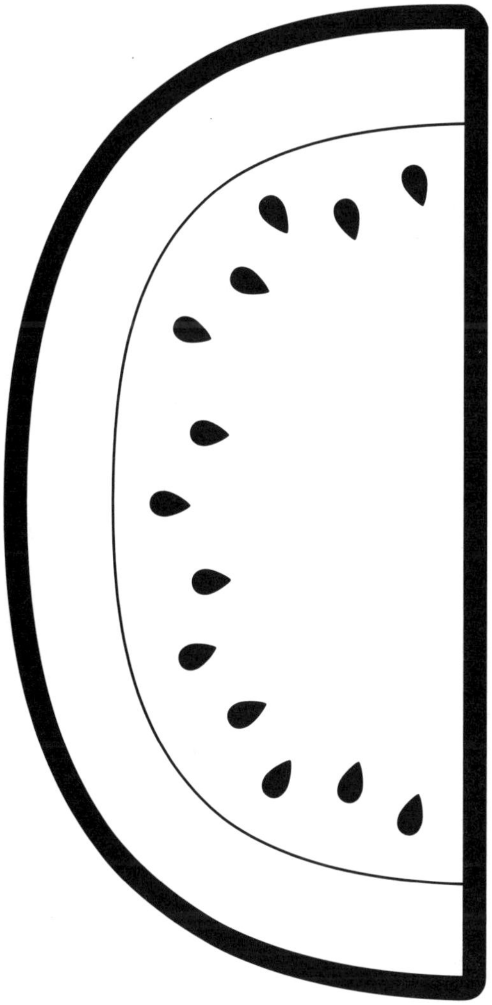

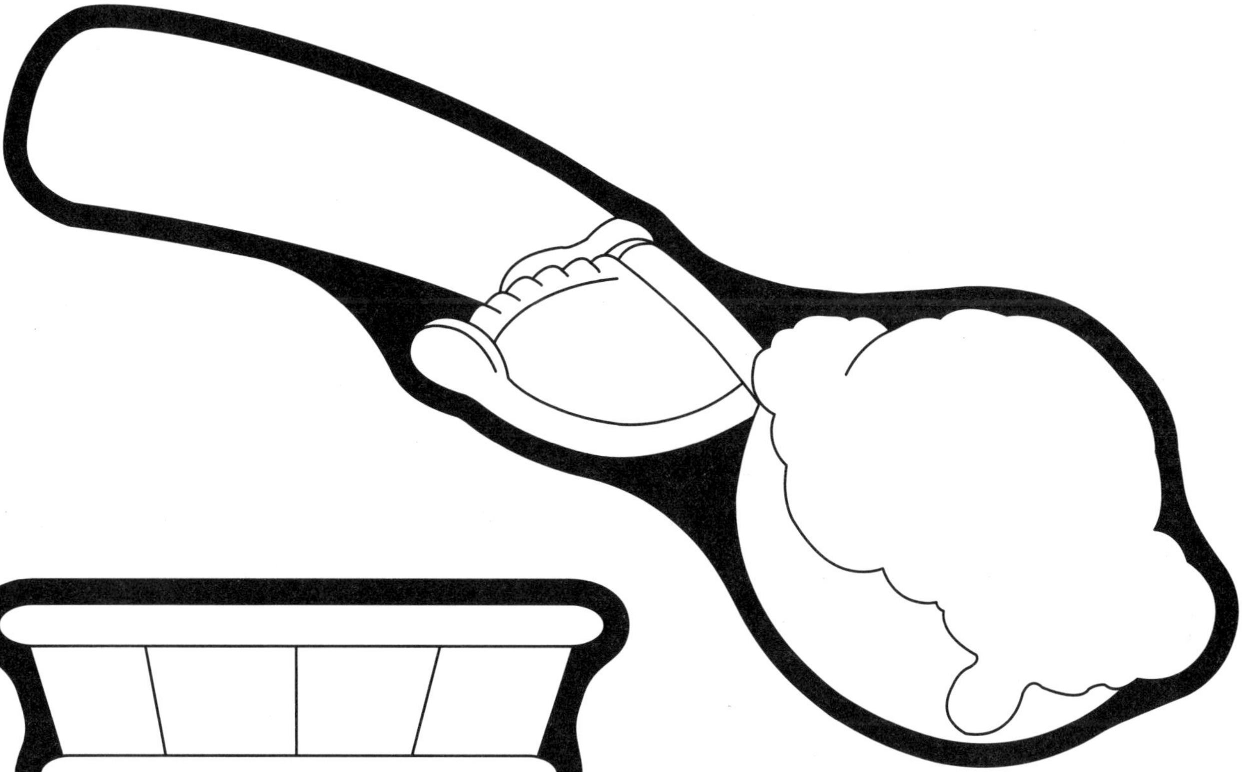

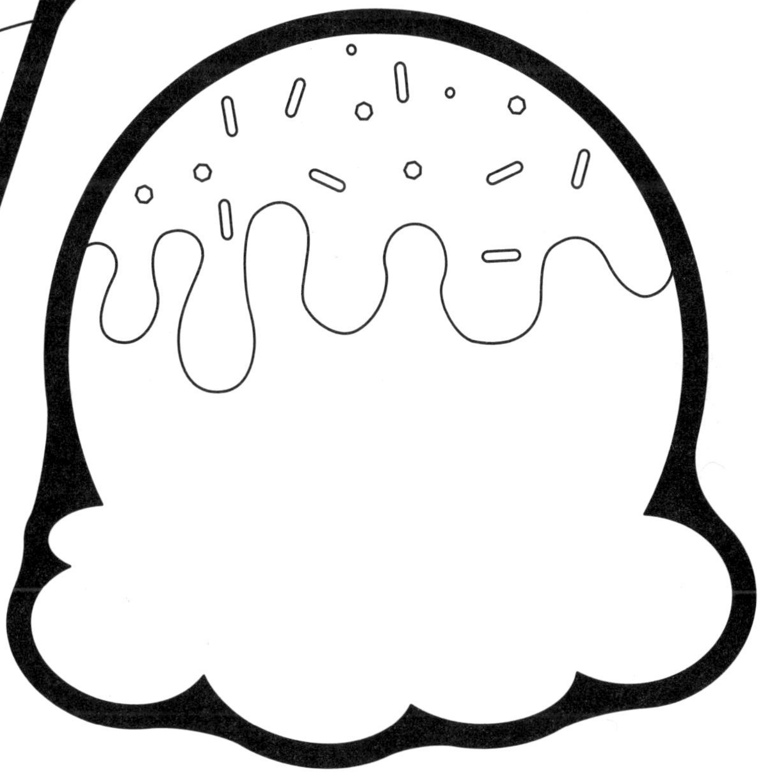

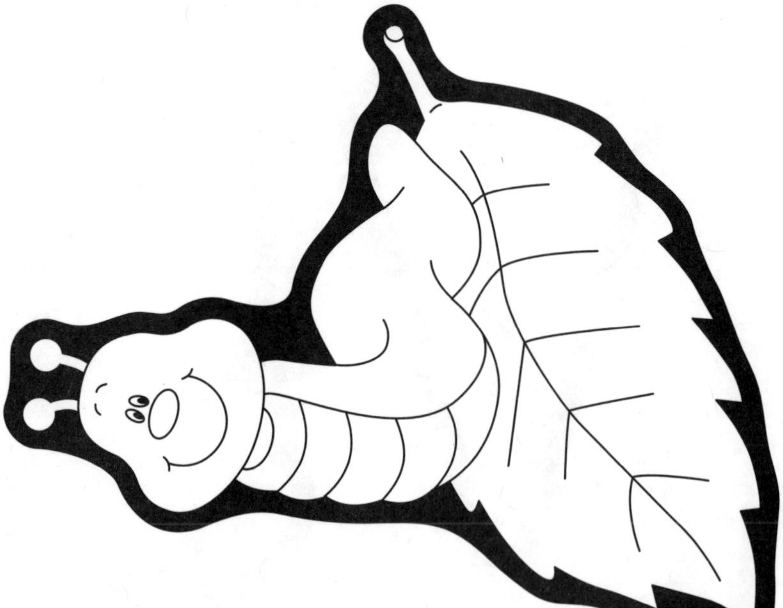

Fall

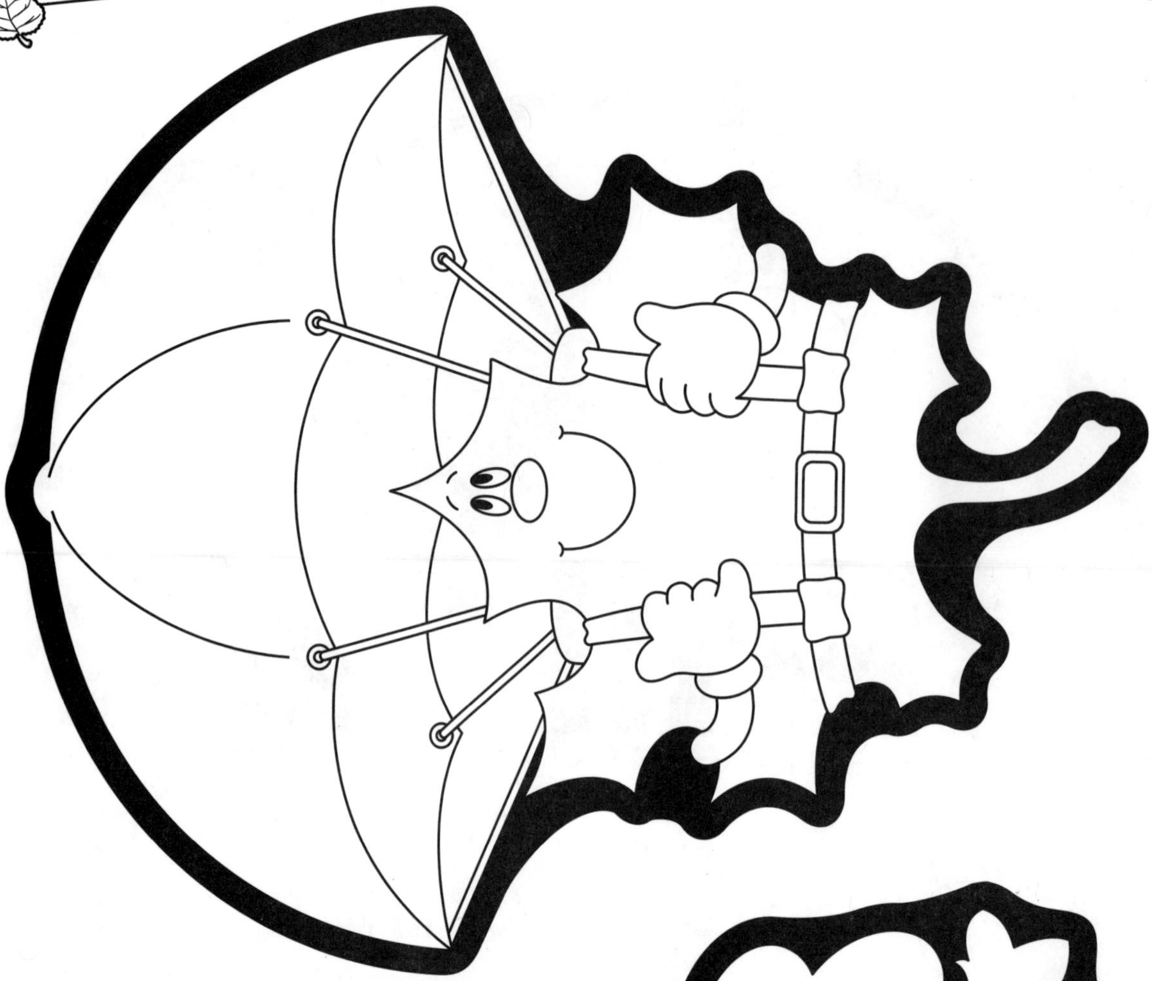

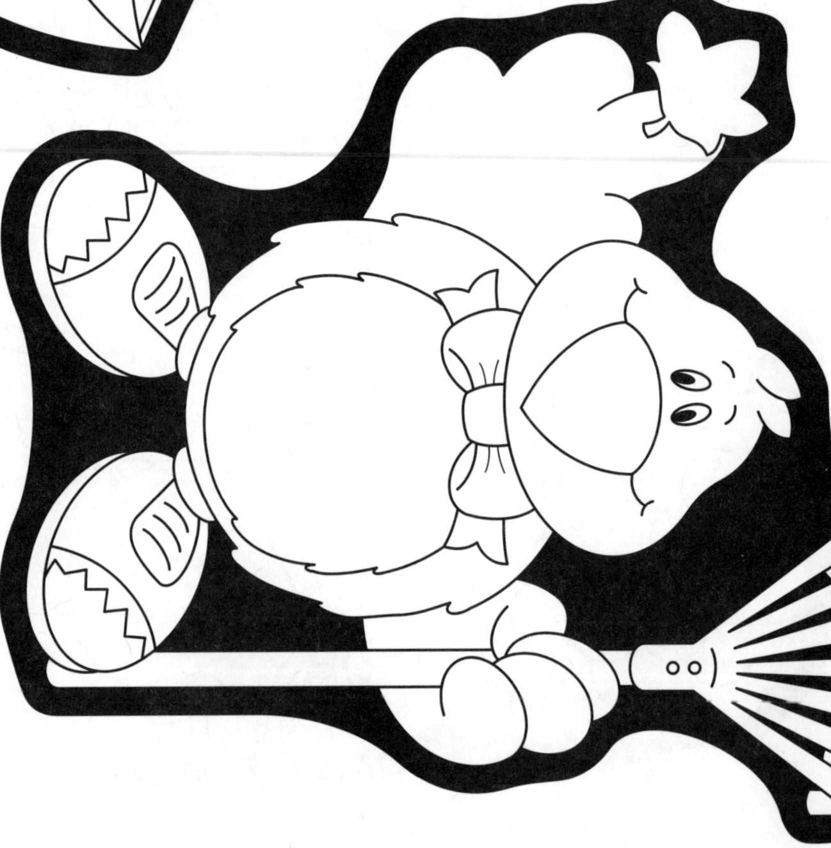

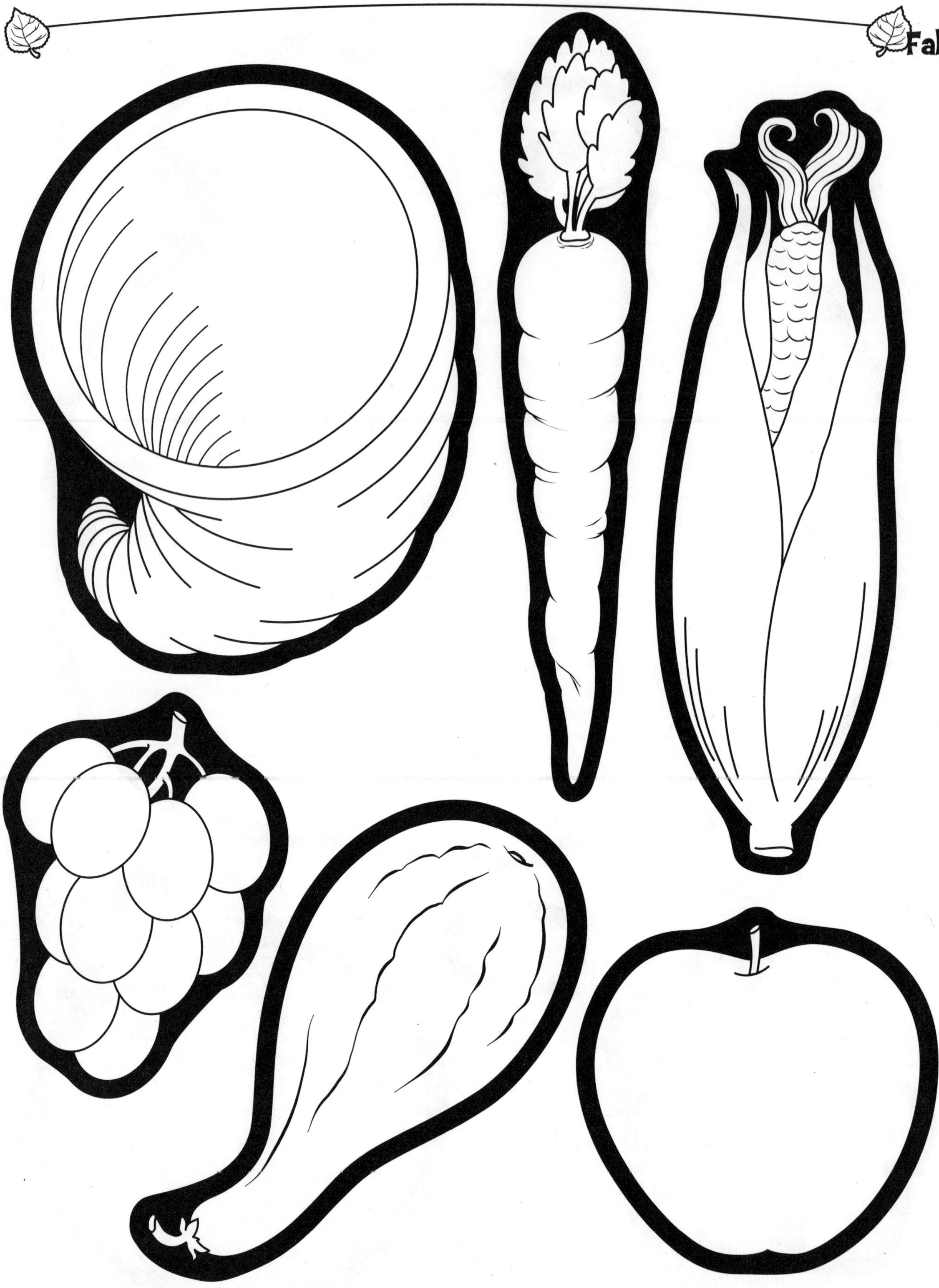

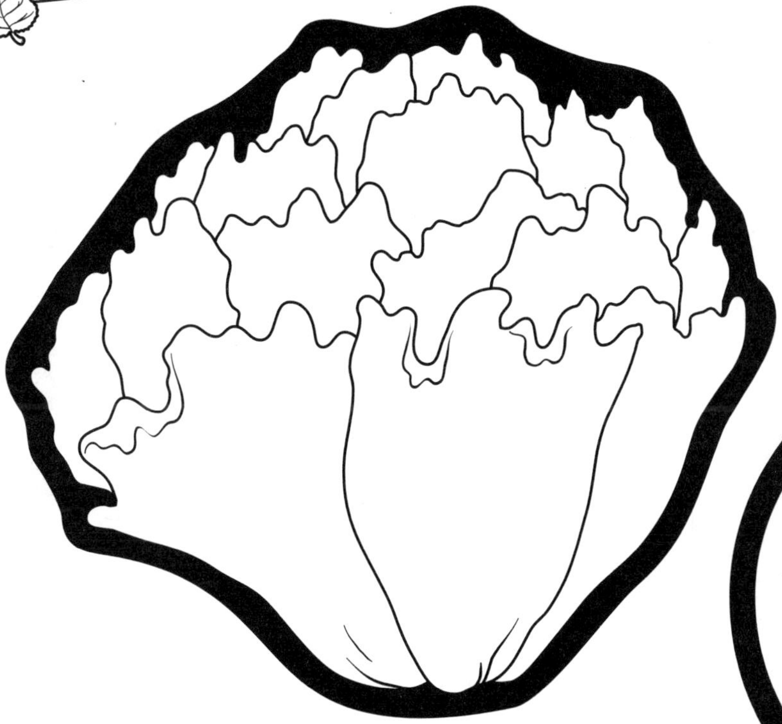

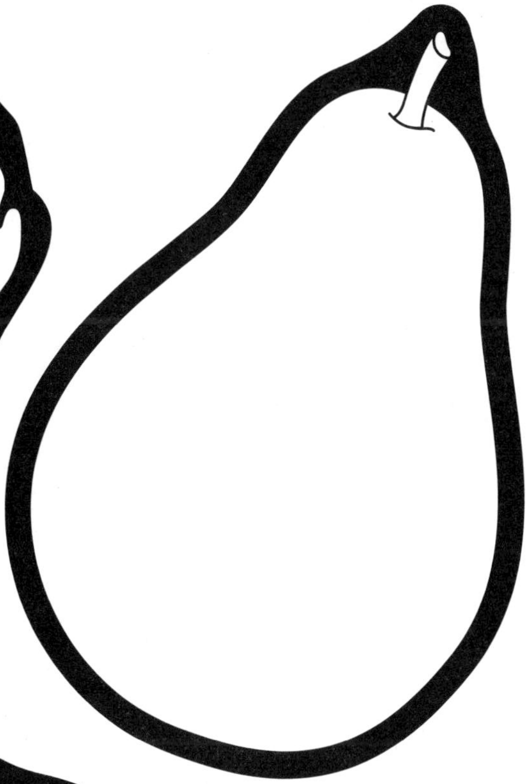

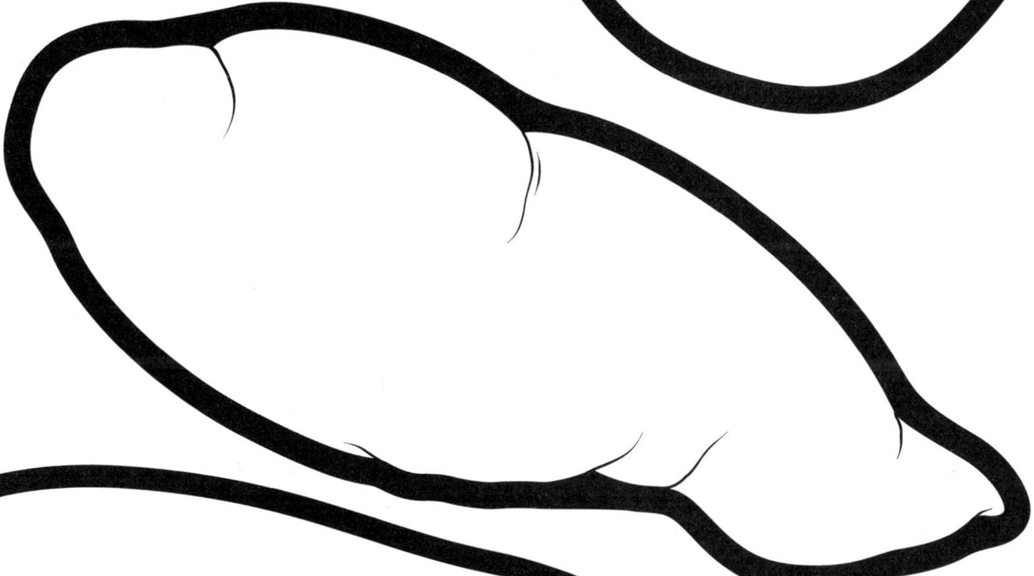

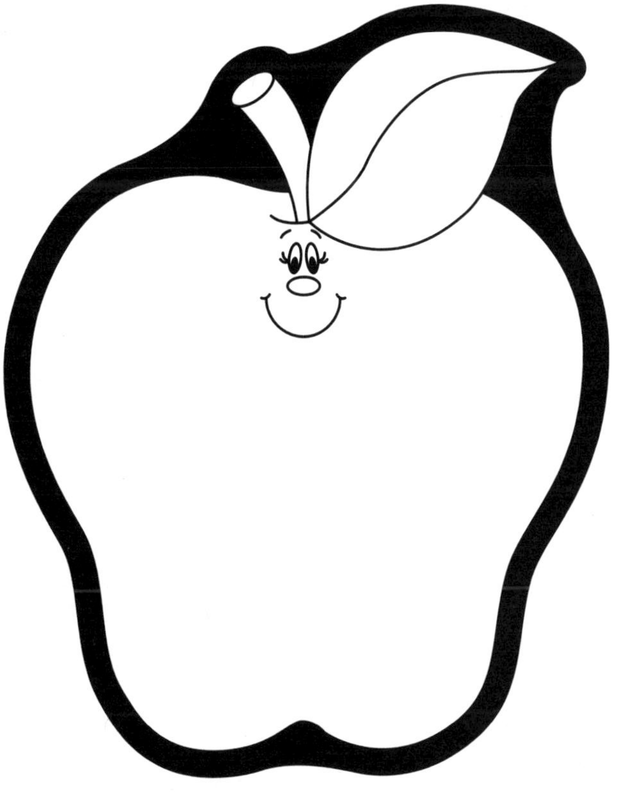

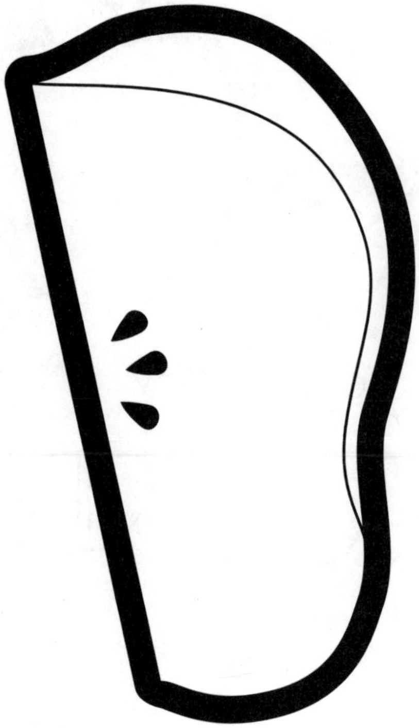

All About Me

ALL ABOUT ME LITERATURE SELECTIONS

All About You by Laurence Anholt (Puffin, 1994)

Dandelion by Don Freeman (Puffin, 1977)

Dumpy La Rue by Elizabeth Winthrop (Henry Holt & Company, Inc., 2001)

Horton Hears a Who! by Dr. Seuss (Random House Books for Young Readers, 1954)

How Are You Peeling? by Saxton Freymann (Arthur A. Levine, 1999)

I Like Me! by Nancy Carlson (Penguin Putnam Books for Young Readers, 1990)

I'm Gonna Like Me: Letting Off a Little Self-Esteem by Jamie Lee Curtis (Joanna Cotler, 2002)

I'm Terrific by Marjorie Weinman Sharmat (Holiday House, 1992)

It's Okay to Be Different by Todd Parr (Megan Tingley, 2001)

My Many Colored Days by Dr. Seuss (Knopf Books for Young Readers, 1996)

Olivia by Ian Falconer (Atheneum, 2000)

We're Different, We're the Same by Bobbi Kane Kates (Random House, 1992)

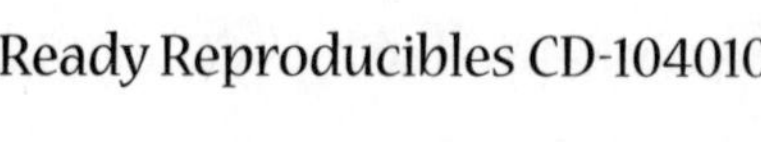

This is me when I was a baby.

This is me now.

This is my family.

I want to learn about ______________________.

I like to eat ______________________________.

I like to ________________________________.

Animals

ANIMAL LITERATURE SELECTIONS

Animals in Winter by Henrietta Bancroft (HarperTrophy, 1997)

Around the Pond: Who's Been Here? by Lindsay Barrett George (Greenwillow, 1996)

Click Clack Moo: Cows That Type by Doreen Cronin (Simon & Schuster Children's Publishing, 2000)

Edward the Emu by Sheena Knowles (HarperTrophy, 1998)

Feathers for Lunch by Lois Ehlert (Voyager Books, 1996)

If My Mom Were A Platypus: Animal Babies and Their Mothers by Dia L. Michels (Platypus Media, 2001)

In My World by Lois Ehlert (Harcourt, 2002)

In the Woods: Who's Been Here? by Lindsay Barrett George (HarperTrophy, 1998)

I See Animals Hiding by Jim Arnosky (Scholastic, 2000)

No One Told the Aardvark by Deborah Eaton (Charlesbridge Publishing, 1997)

Officer Buckle and Gloria by Peggy Rathmann (Putnam Publishing Group, 1995)

Where Are the Night Animals? by Mary Ann Fraser (HarperTrophy, 1999)

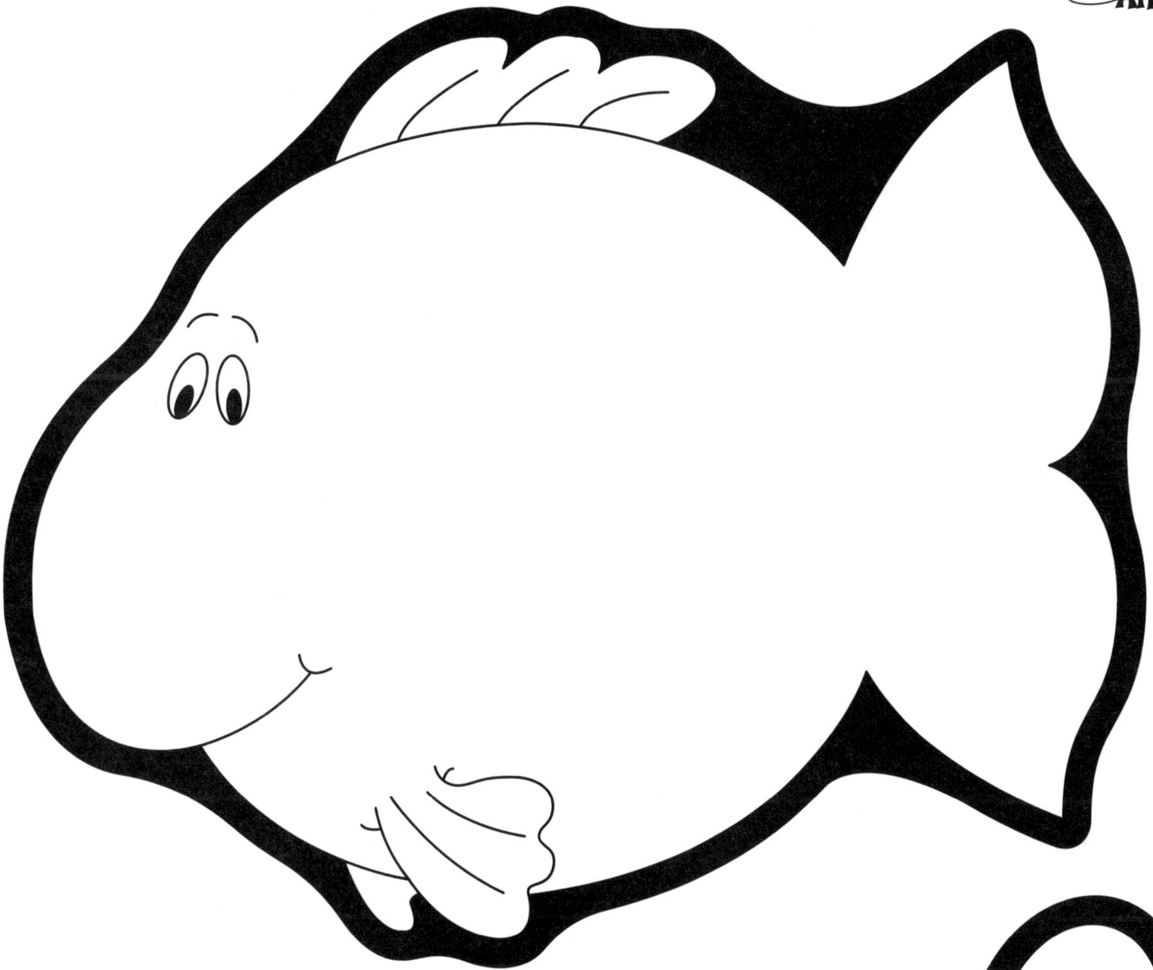

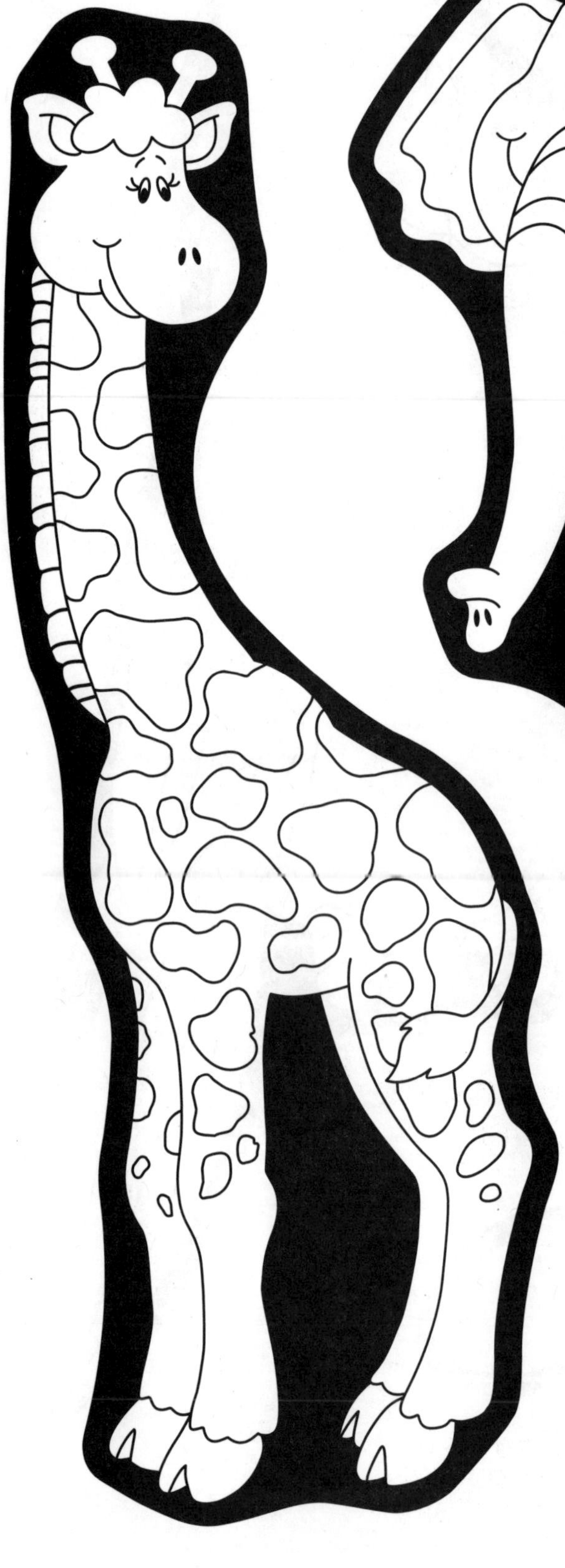

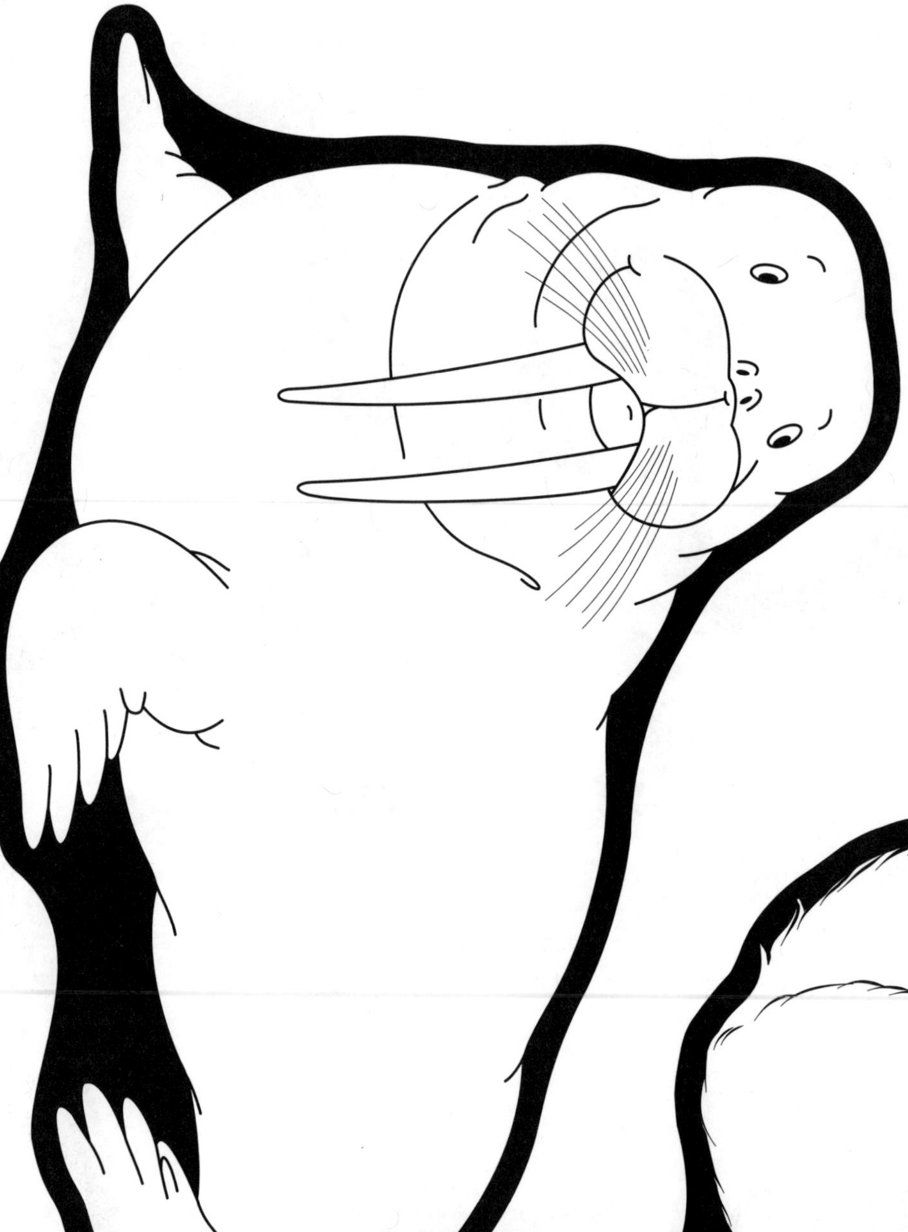

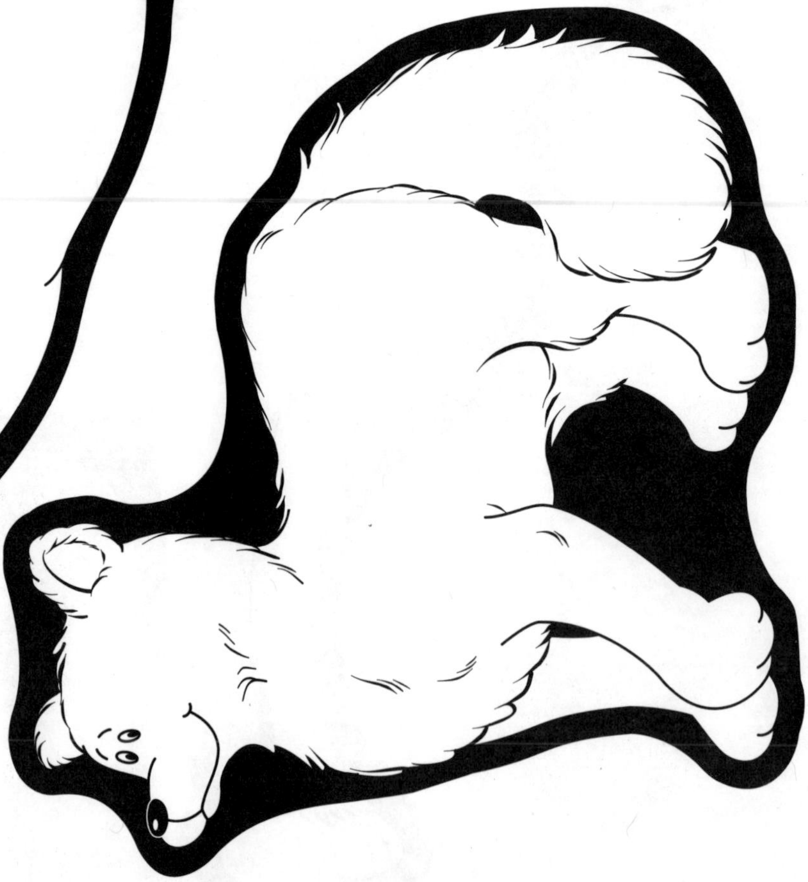

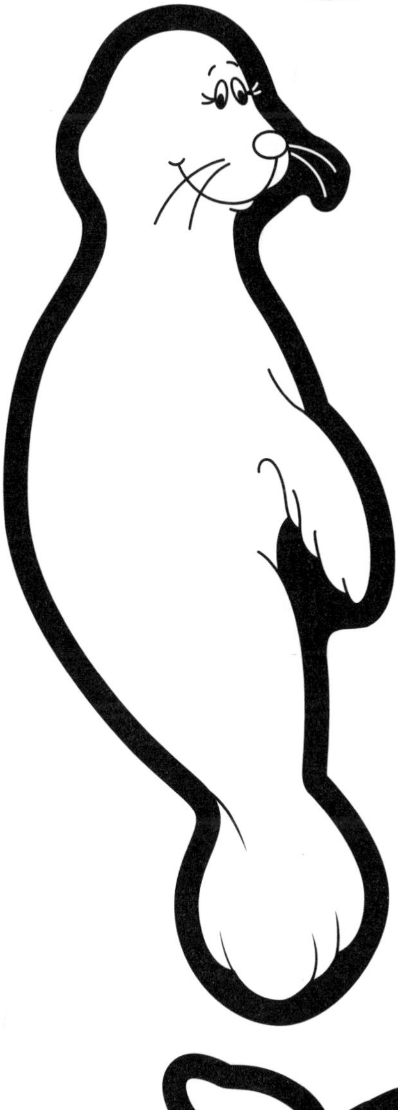

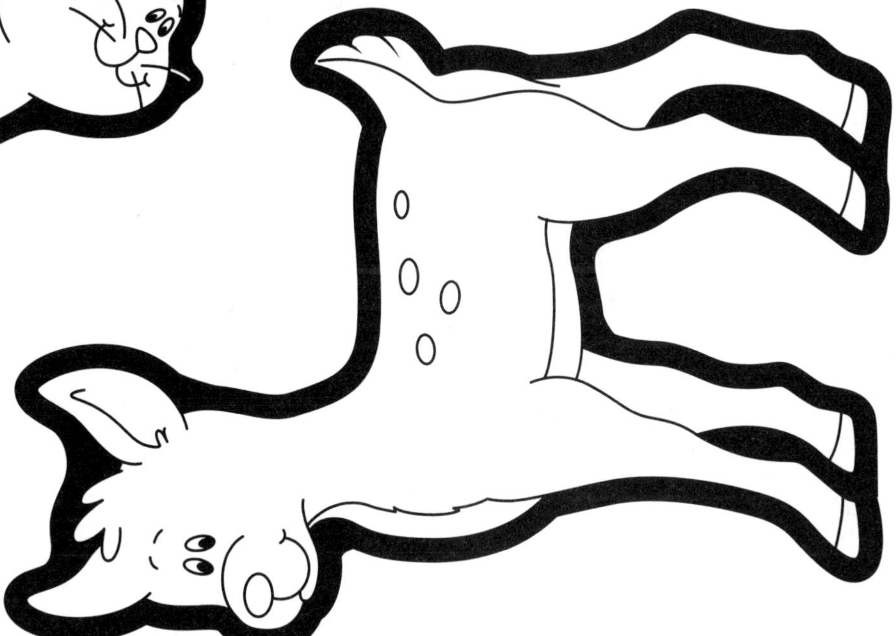

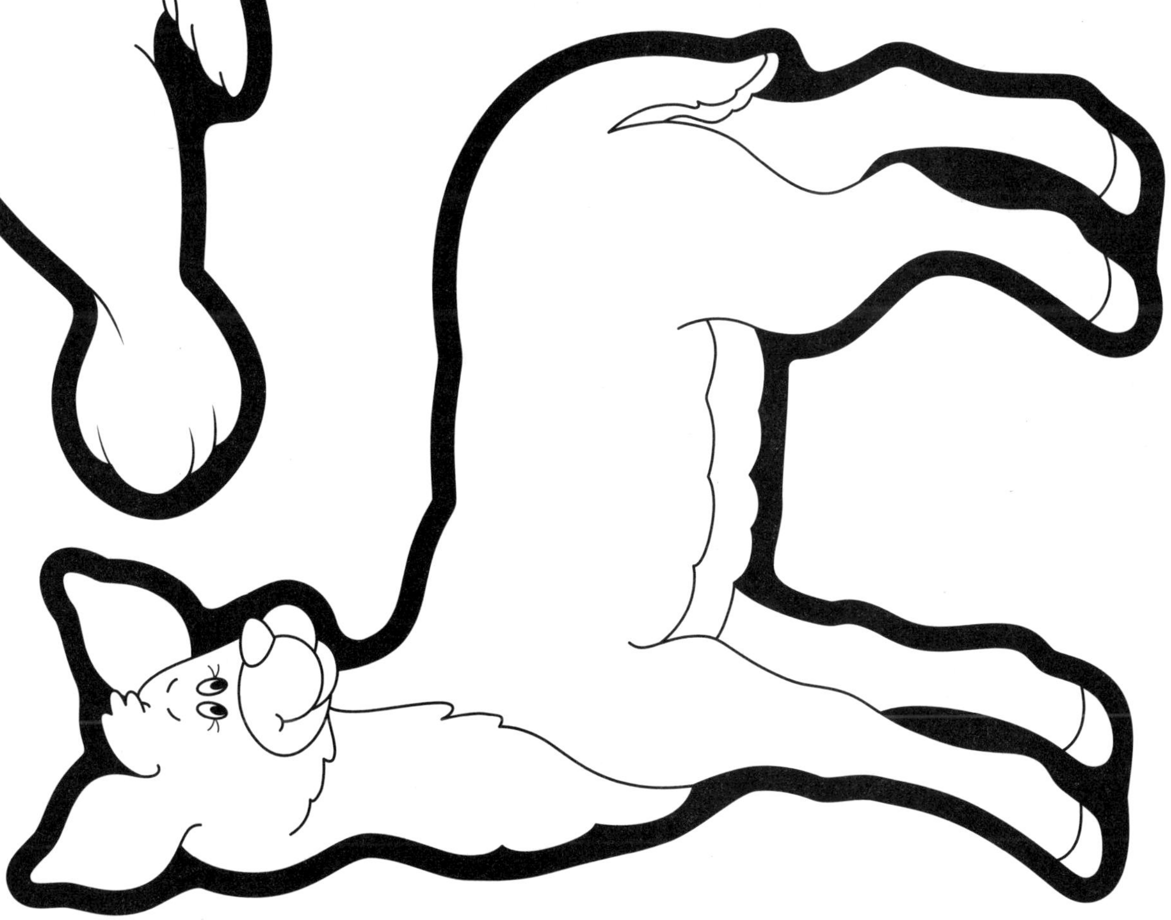

The Arts

THE ARTS LITERATURE SELECTIONS

Angelina on Stage by Katharine Holabird (Pleasant Company Publications, 2002)

Babar's Museum of Art by Laurent De Brunhoff (Harry N. Abrams, 2003)

Ben's Trumpet by Rachel Isadora (HarperTrophy, 1991)

Clap Your Hands by Lorinda Bryan Cauley (Putnam Publishing Group, 1997)

Dance! by Bill T. Jones (Hyperion Press, 1998)

Dance on a Sealskin by Barbara Winslow (Alaska Northwest Books, 2002)

The Dot by Peter H. Reynolds (Candlewick Press, 2003)

Katie Meets the Impressionists by James Mayhew (Orchard Books, 1999)

Max by Rachel Isadora (Aladdin Library, 1984)

Music, Music for Everyone by Vera B. Williams (HarperTrophy, 1988)

My Family Plays Music by Judy Cox (Holiday House, 2003)

Squeaking of Art: The Mice Go To the Museum by Monica Wellington (Dutton Books, 2000)

Zin! Zin! Zin! A Violin by Lloyd Moss (Aladdin Library, 2000)

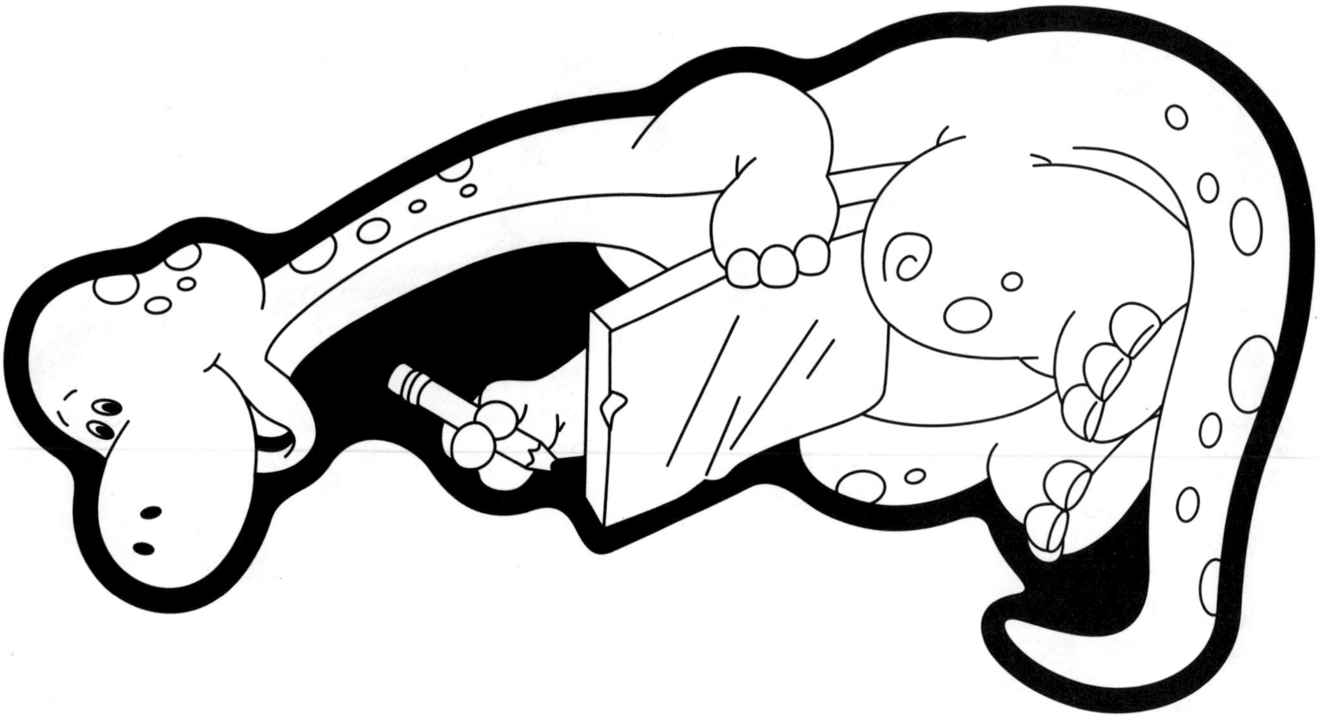

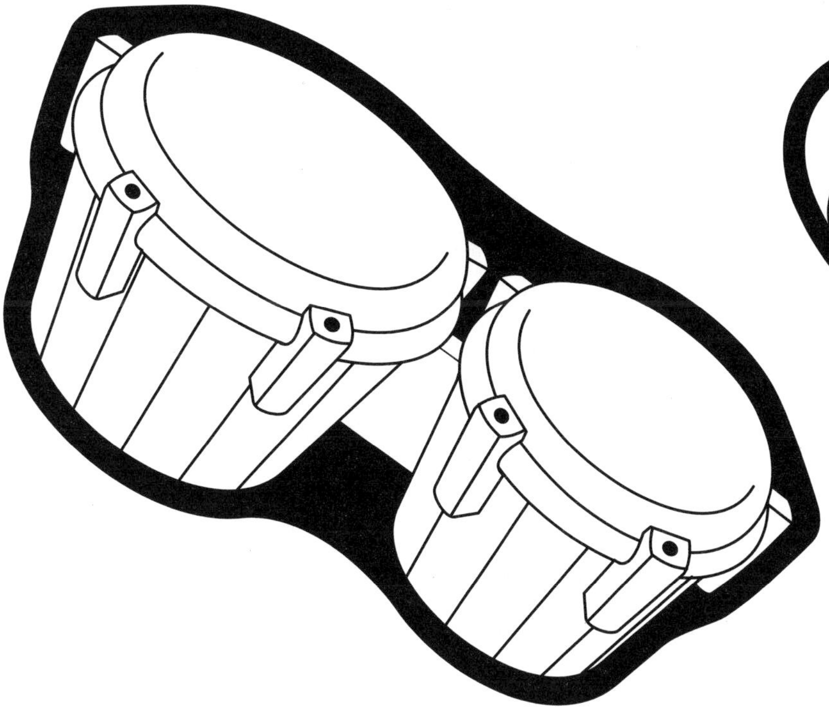

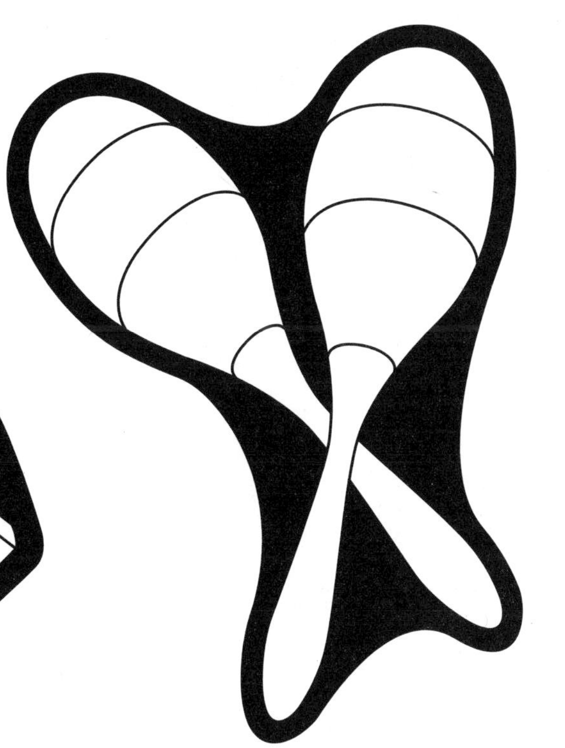

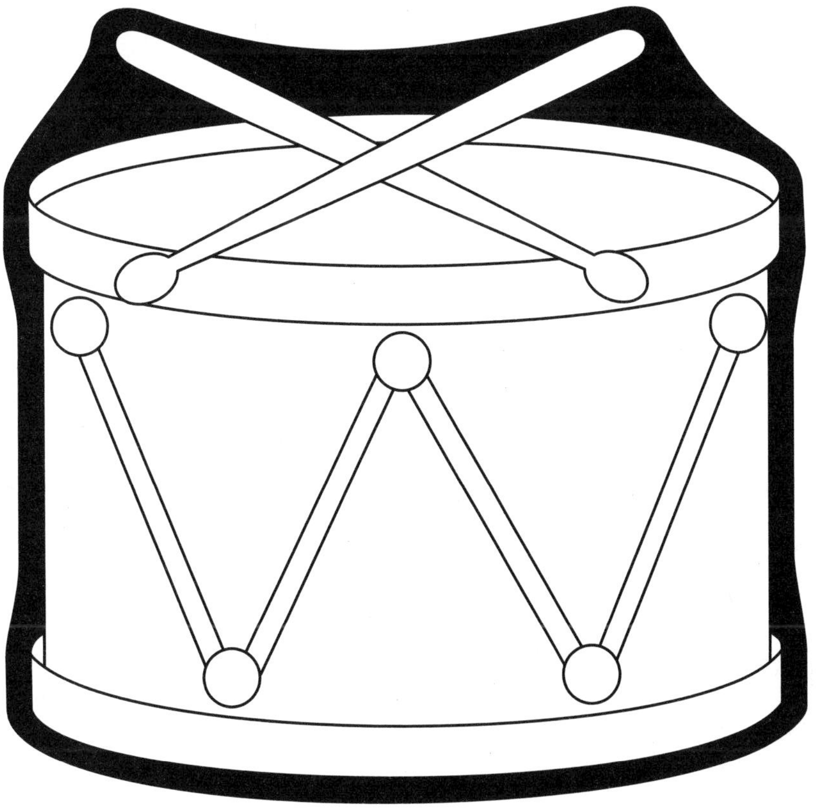

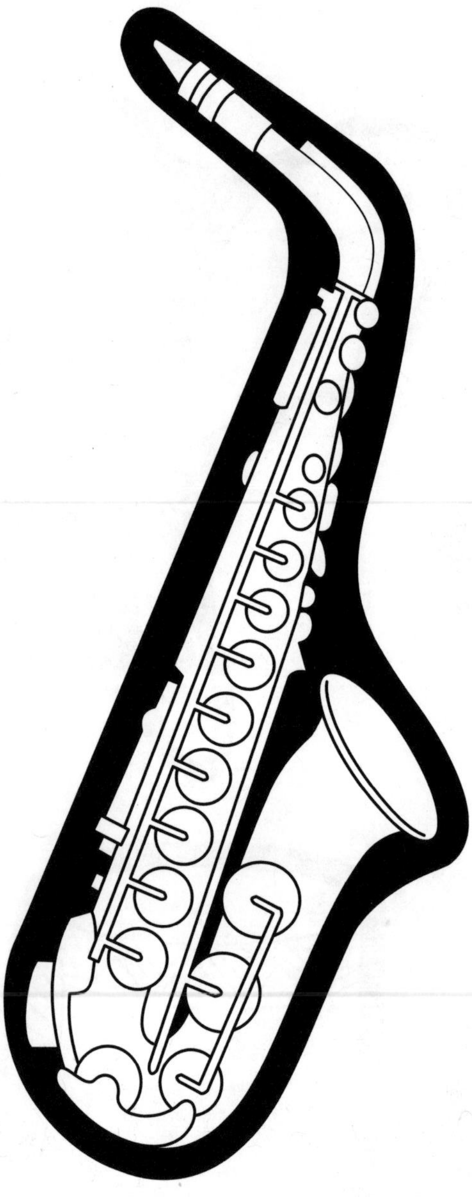

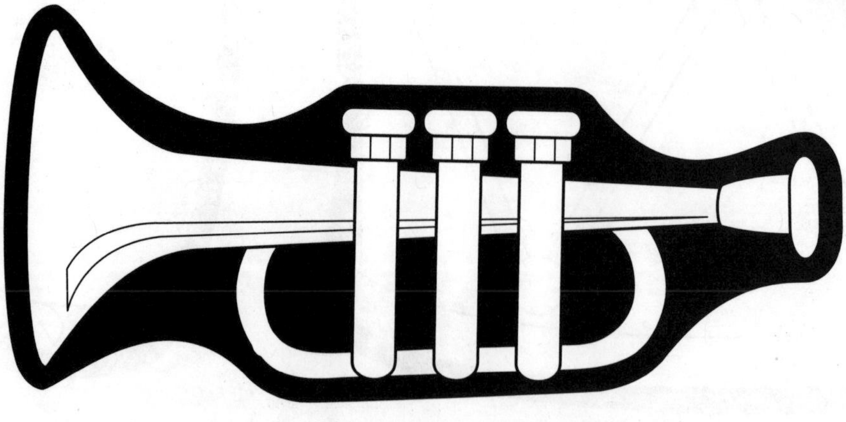

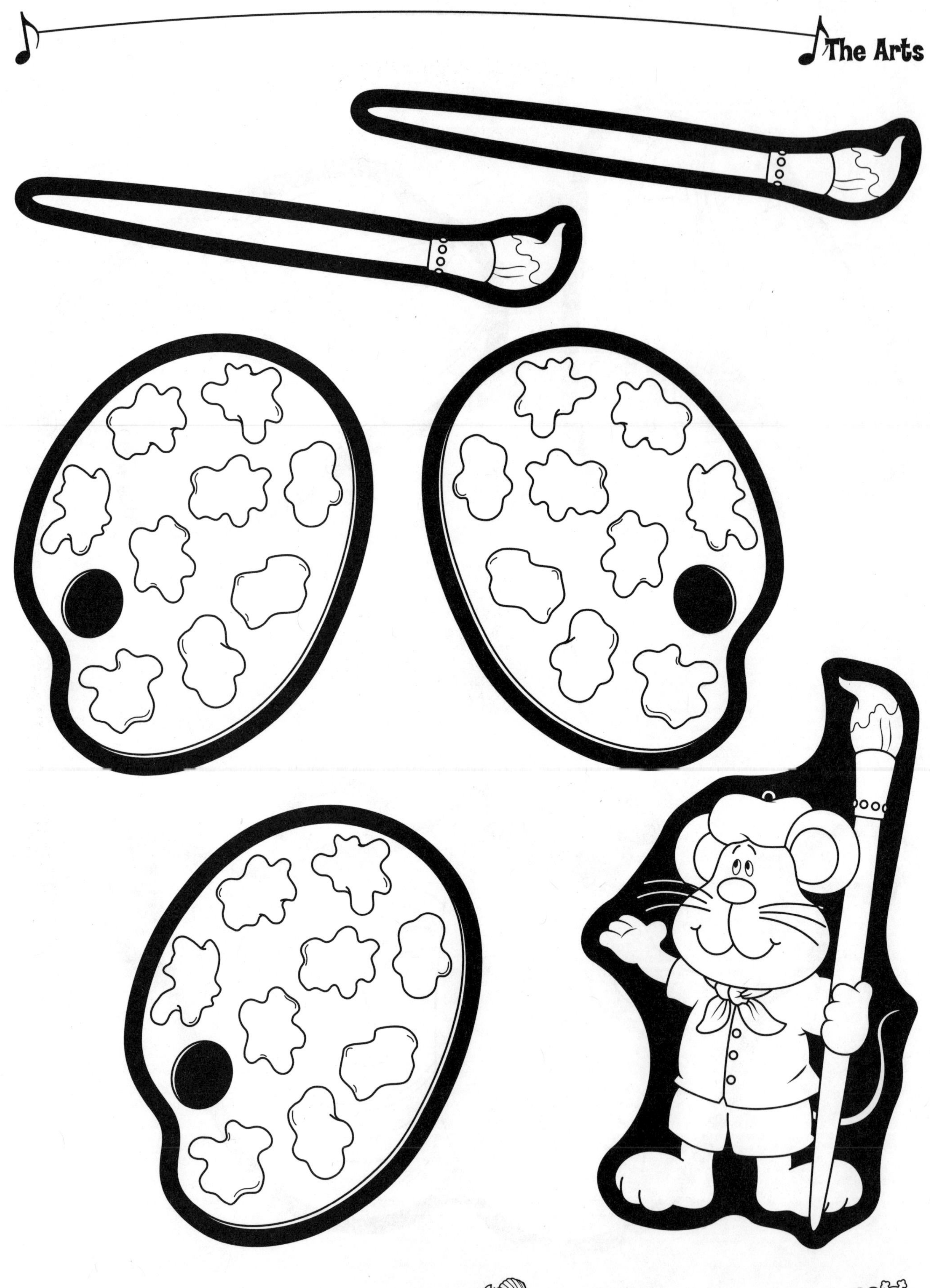

AWARDS

NICE MOVE!

AWESOME!

WOW!

WAY TO GO!

1

3

2

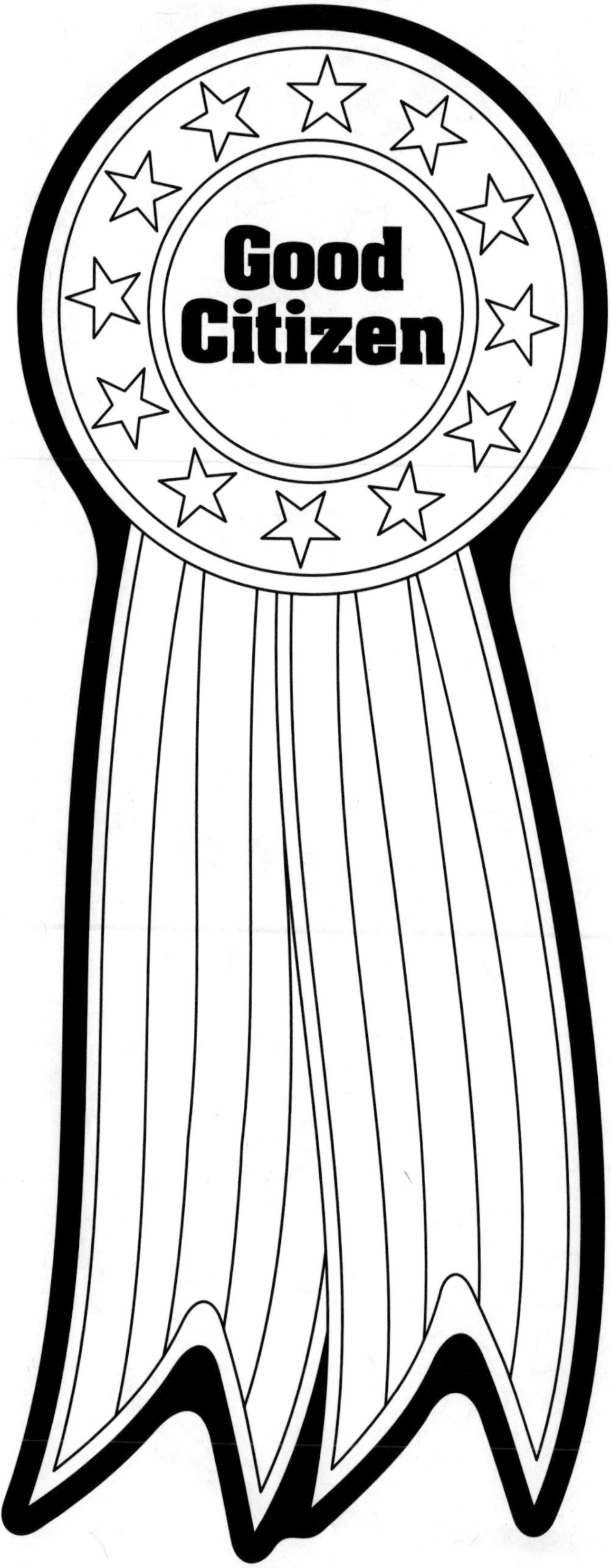

Good Citizen

Happy Birthday!

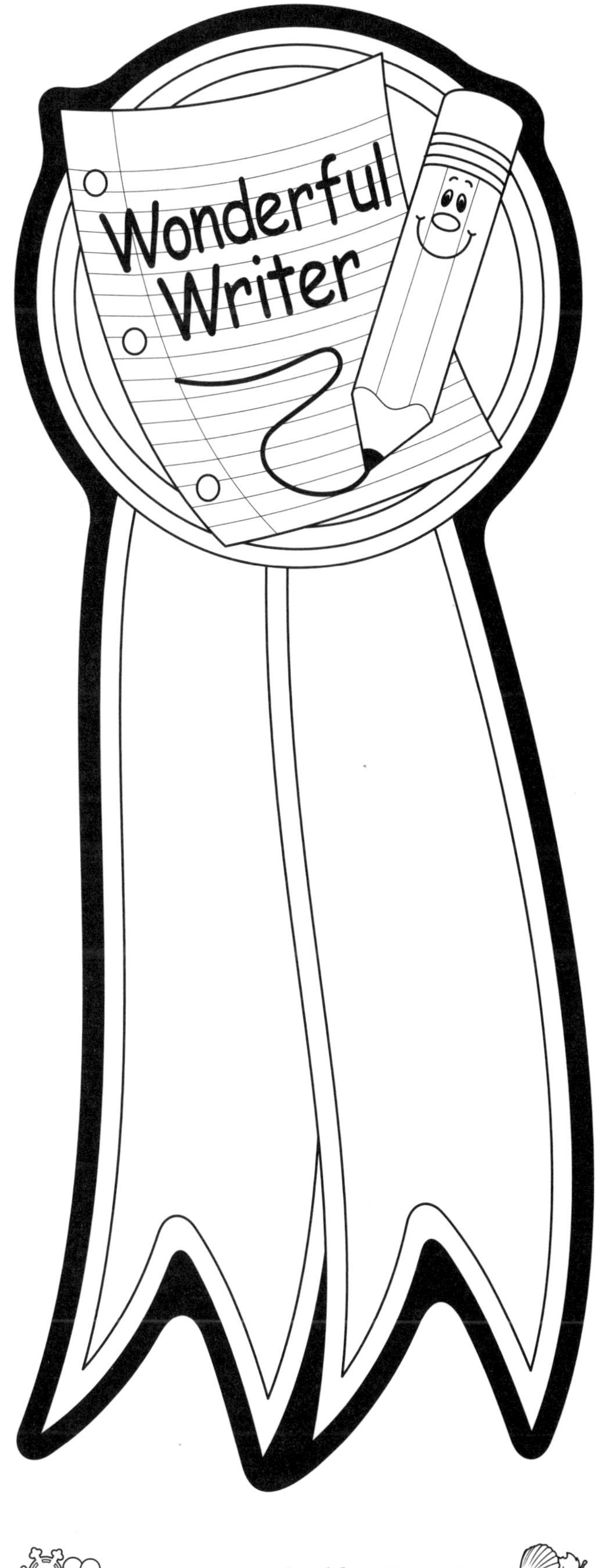

Wonderful Writer

STAR STUDENT

Thumbs up for

Way to read!

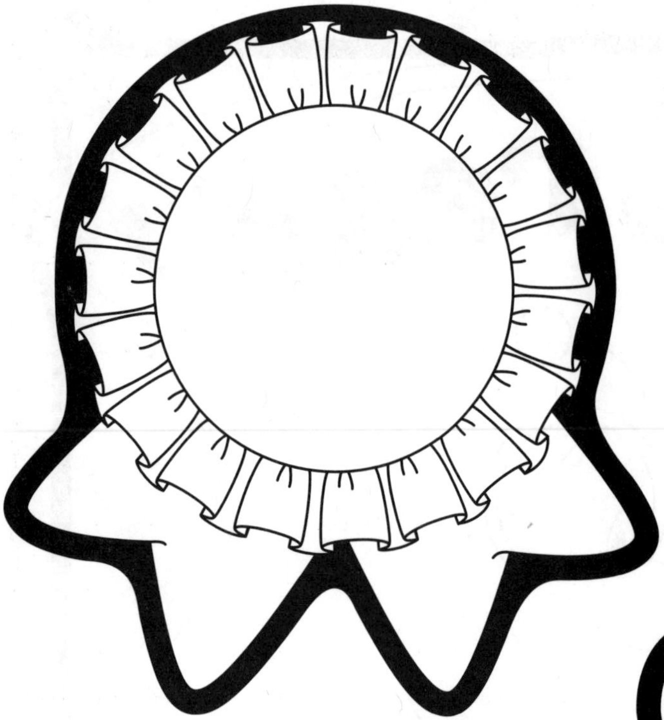

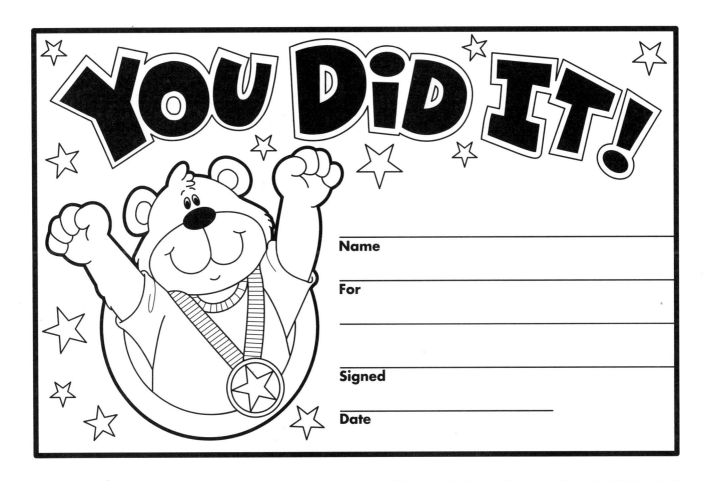

YOU DID IT!

Name

For

Signed

Date

THREE CHEERS FOR YOU!

Cheers!

Cheers!

Cheers!

Name

Signed

Date

______________________________ shows

Tremendous Teamwork!

Signed ______________________ Date ______________

Thanks For Your Helping Hand!

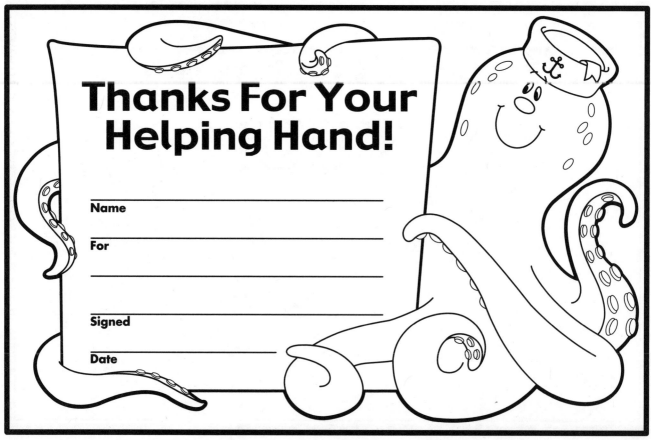

____
Name

____
For

____

____
Signed

____
Date

Reading Makes Me Hoppy

Name

Signed

Date

Congratulations Young Author!

Title

Author

Publication Date

THANKS FOR LENDING A PAIR OF HELPFUL HANDS!

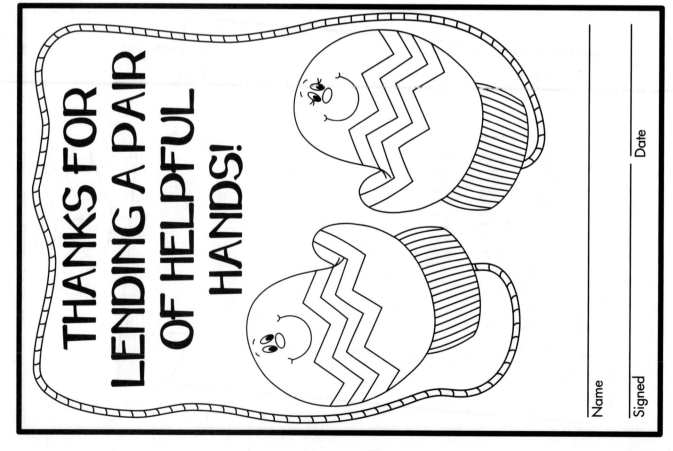

Name

Signed

Date

You are Unique

because

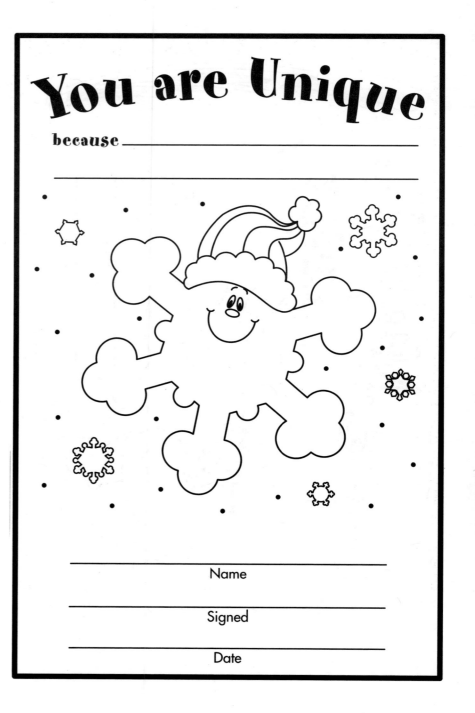

Name

Signed

Date

For ______________________________

WOW

GREAT JOB

NICE WORK

Signed ____________________________

Date ______________________________

WOW!

____
Name

HAD A GOOD DAY!

Signed ______________ Date ______________

______________________ turned in a Shower of Good Work

Signed ______________________

Date ______________________

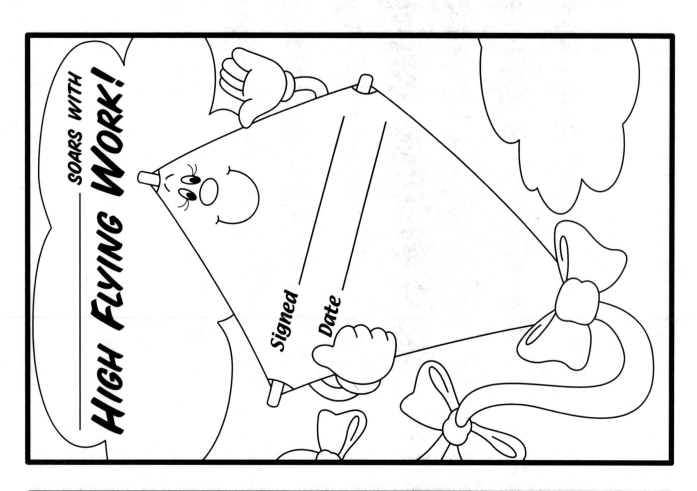

______________________ SOARS WITH

HIGH FLYING WORK!

Signed ______________________

Date ______________________

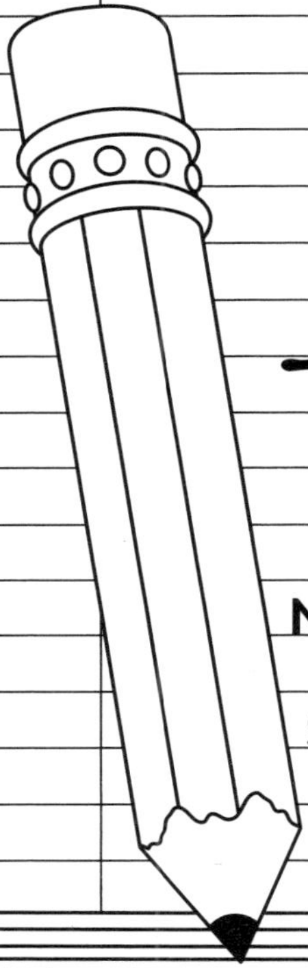

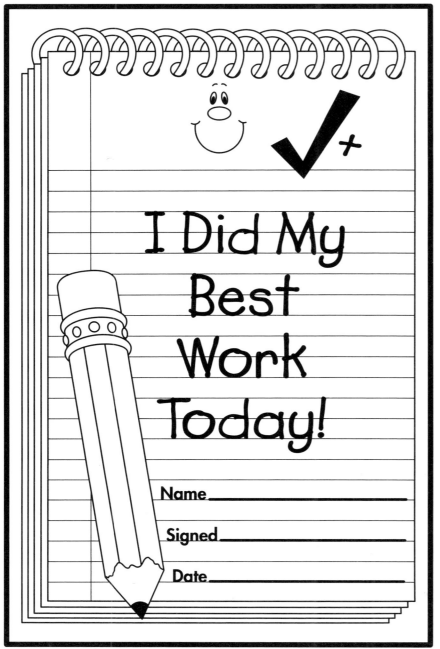

I Did My Best Work Today!

Name ____________________

Signed ____________________

Date ____________________

____________________ does

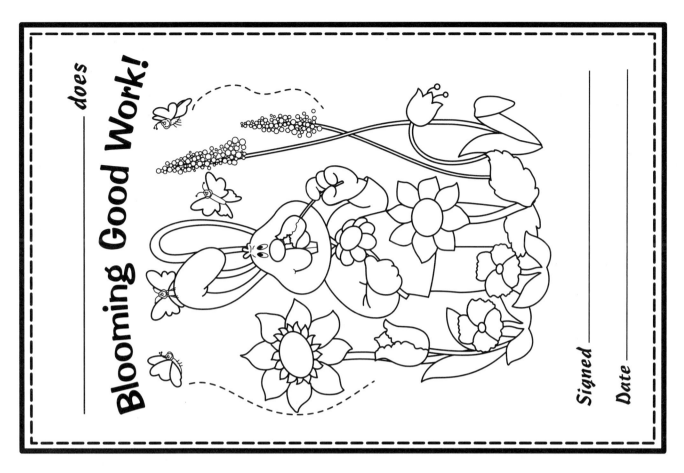

Blooming Good Work!

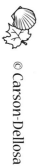

Signed ____________________

Date ____________________

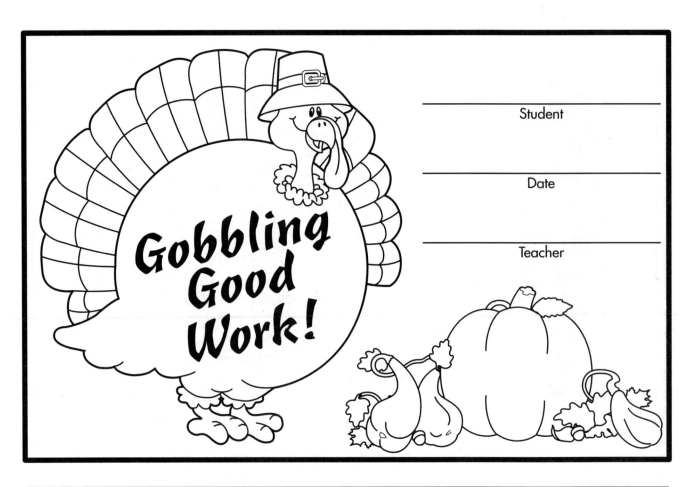

Gobbling Good Work!

Student

Date

Teacher

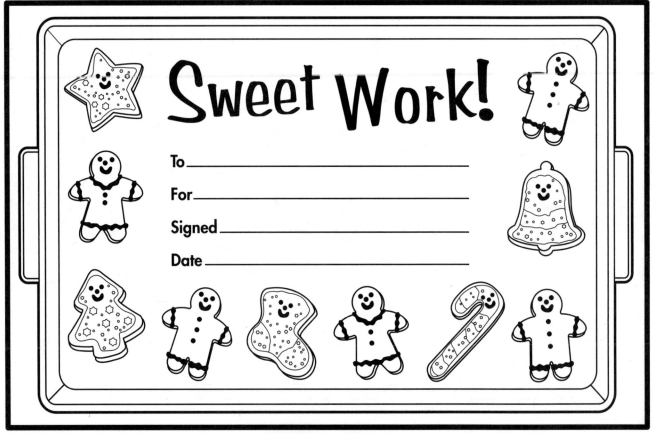

Sweet Work!

To ______________________________

For ______________________________

Signed ______________________________

Date ______________________________

BACK TO SCHOOL!

SCHOOL

WELCOME

BACK-TO-SCHOOL LITERATURE SELECTIONS

Don't Eat the Teacher! by Nick Ward (Scholastic, 2000)

First Day, Hooray! by Nancy Poydar (Holiday House, 2000)

First Day Jitters by Julie Danneberg (Charlesbridge Publishing, 2000)

Frog and Toad Are Friends by Arnold Lobel (HarperTrophy, 1979)

George and Martha by James Marshall (Houghton Mifflin Co., 1974)

Hello School!: A Classroom Full of Poems by Dee Lillegard (Dragonfly, 2003)

Miss Bindergarten Gets Ready for Kindergarten by Joseph Slate (Puffin, 2001)

Miss Malarkey Doesn't Live in Room 10 by Judy Finchler (Walker & Co., 1996)

The Teeny Tiny Teacher by Stephanie Calmenson (Scholastic, 2002)

This is the Way We Go To School by Edith Baer (Scholastic, 1992)

Yo! Yes? by Chris Raschka (Orchard Books, 1998)

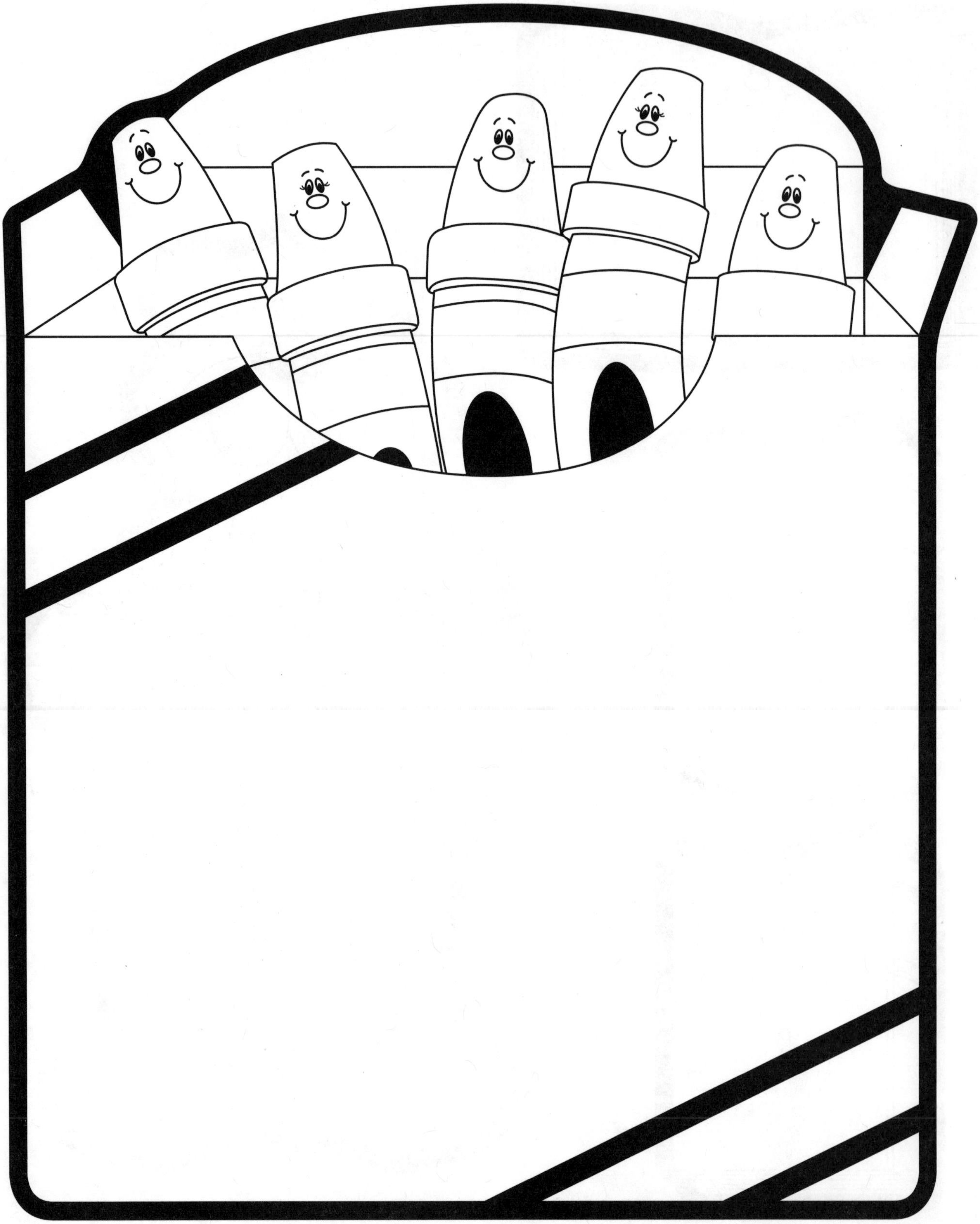

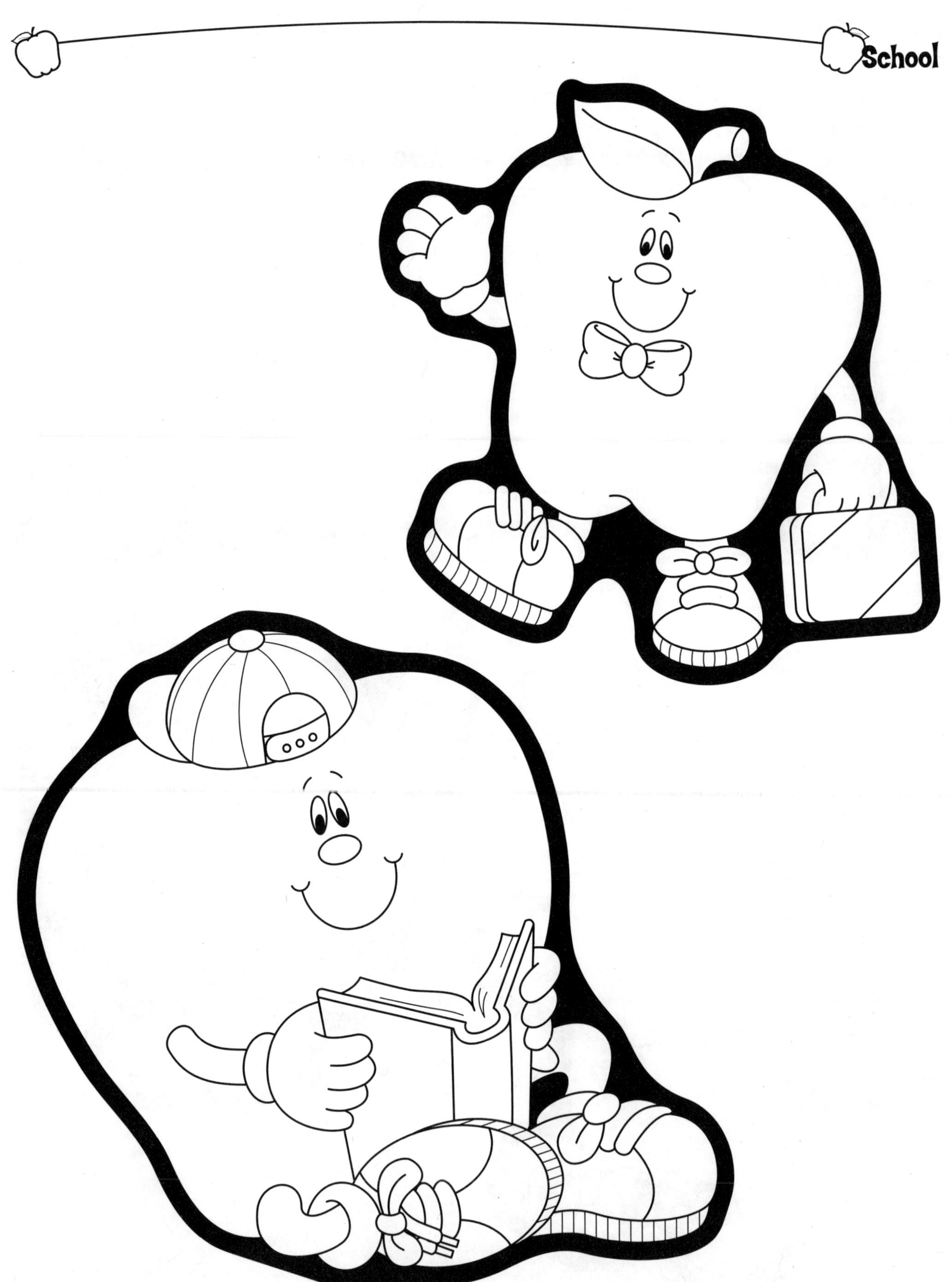

Bees, Bugs, and Butterflies

BEES, BUGS, AND BUTTERFLIES LITERATURE SELECTIONS

The Bee (Animal Close-Ups) edited by Elena Dworkin Wright (Charlesbridge Publishing, 1993)

The Bee Tree by Patricia Polacco (Putnam Juvenile, 1998)

The Big Bug Search by Caroline Young (Usborne Books, 1997)

Bugs by Joan Richards Wright (HarperTrophy, 1988)

Bugs A to Z by Terri Degezelle (Capstone Press, 2000)

Bugs! Bugs! Bugs! by Bob Barner (Chronicle Books, 1999)

The Butterfly House by Eve Bunting (Scholastic, 1999)

Butterfly Story by Anca Hariton (Dutton Books, 1995)

Caterpillars, Bugs and Butterflies by Mel Boring (Northword Press, 1999)

How Bees Be by Alison Boyle (Milet Publishing, 2003)

Monarch Butterfly by Gail Gibbons (Holiday House, 1991)

The Very Hungry Caterpillar by Eric Carle (Scholastic, 1994)

Waiting for Wings by Lois Ehlert (Harcourt Children's Books, 2001)

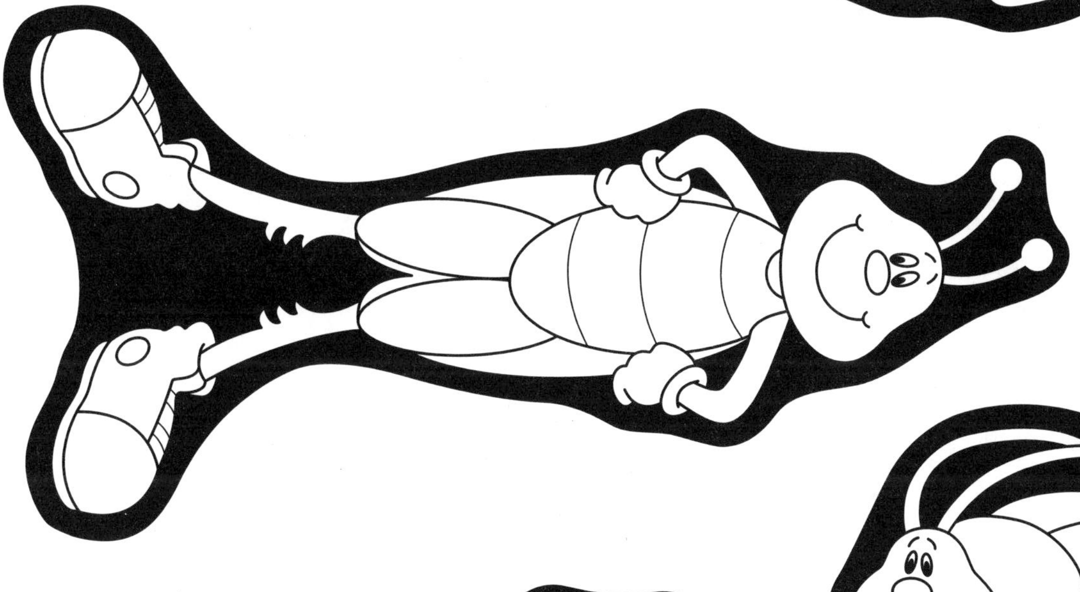

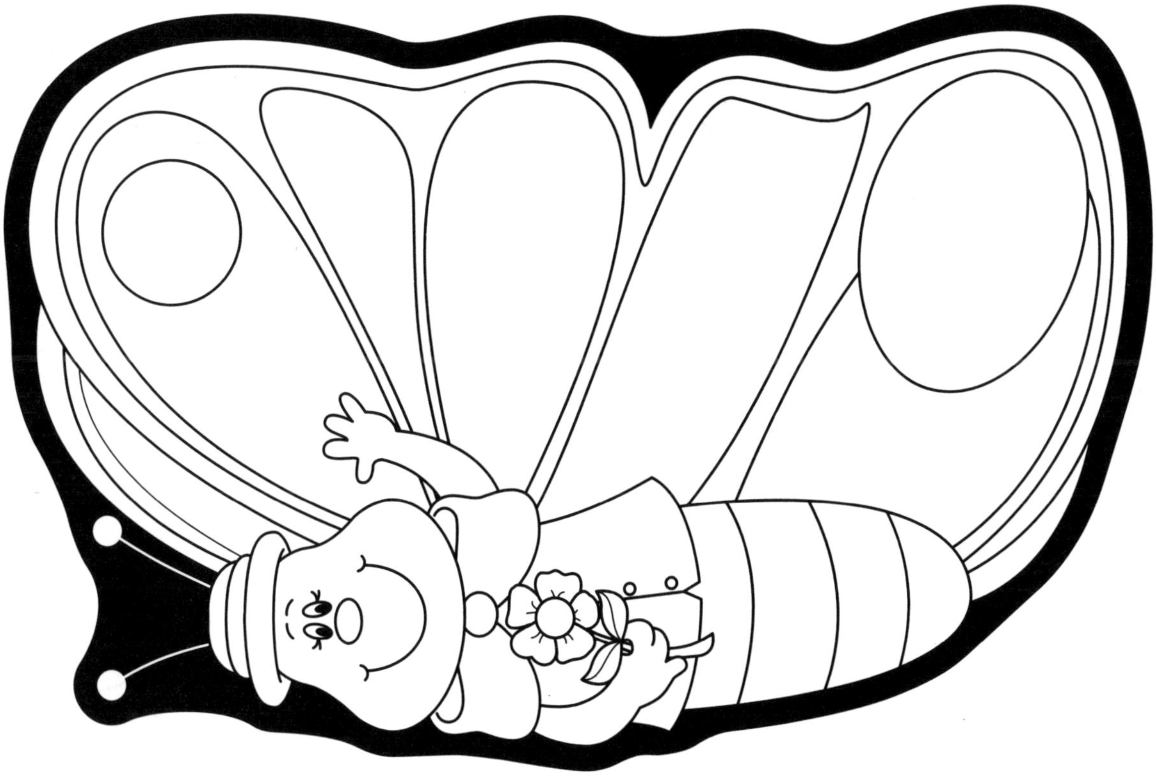

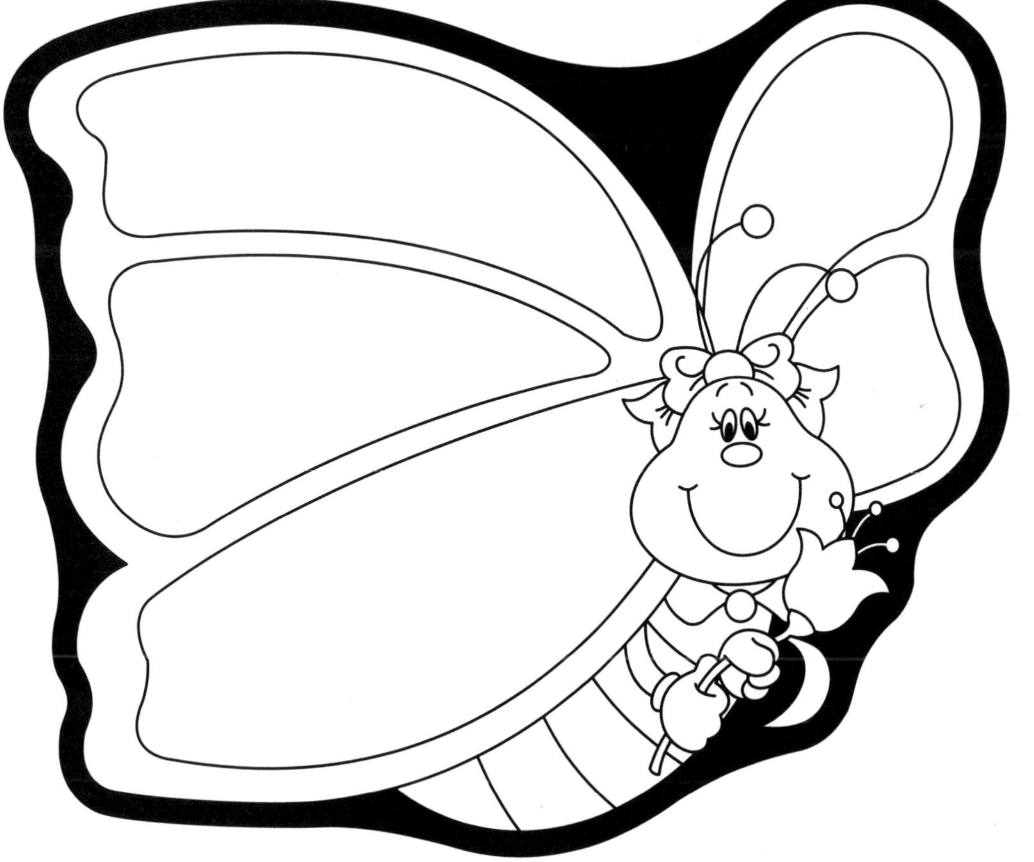

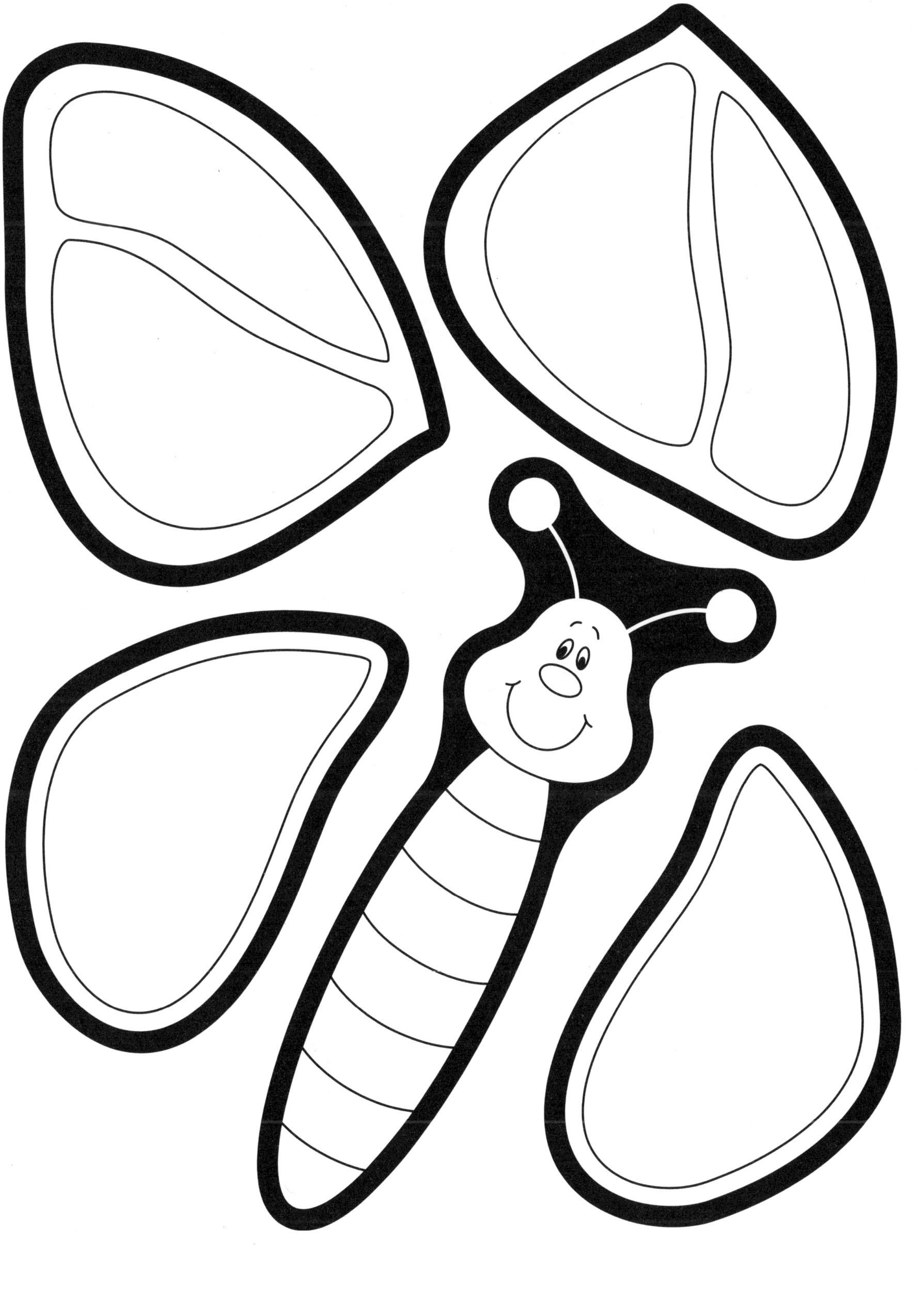

Community Helpers

COMMUNITY HELPERS LITERATURE SELECTIONS

Career Day by Anne Rockwell (HarperCollins, 2000)

Community Helpers from A to Z by Bobbie Kalman (Crabtree Publishing, 1997)

Curious George Takes a Job by H. A. Rey (Houghton Mifflin Co., 1973)

Does a Dinosaur Check Your Teeth? Learn About Community Helpers by Viki Woodworth (Child's World, 1996)

Garbage Collectors (In My Neighborhood) by Paulette Bourgeois (Kids Can Press, 2000)

I Want To Be a Doctor by Daniel Liebman (Firefly Books, 2000)

I Want To Be a Police Officer by Daniel Liebman (Firefly Books, 2000)

Jobs People Do by Christopher Maynard (Penguin Books, Ltd., 1997)

Pig Pig Gets a Job by David McPhail (Dutton Books, 1990)

Whose Shoe? by Margaret Miller (Greenwillow, 1991)

Who Uses This? by Margaret Miller (Morrow, William & Co., 1999)

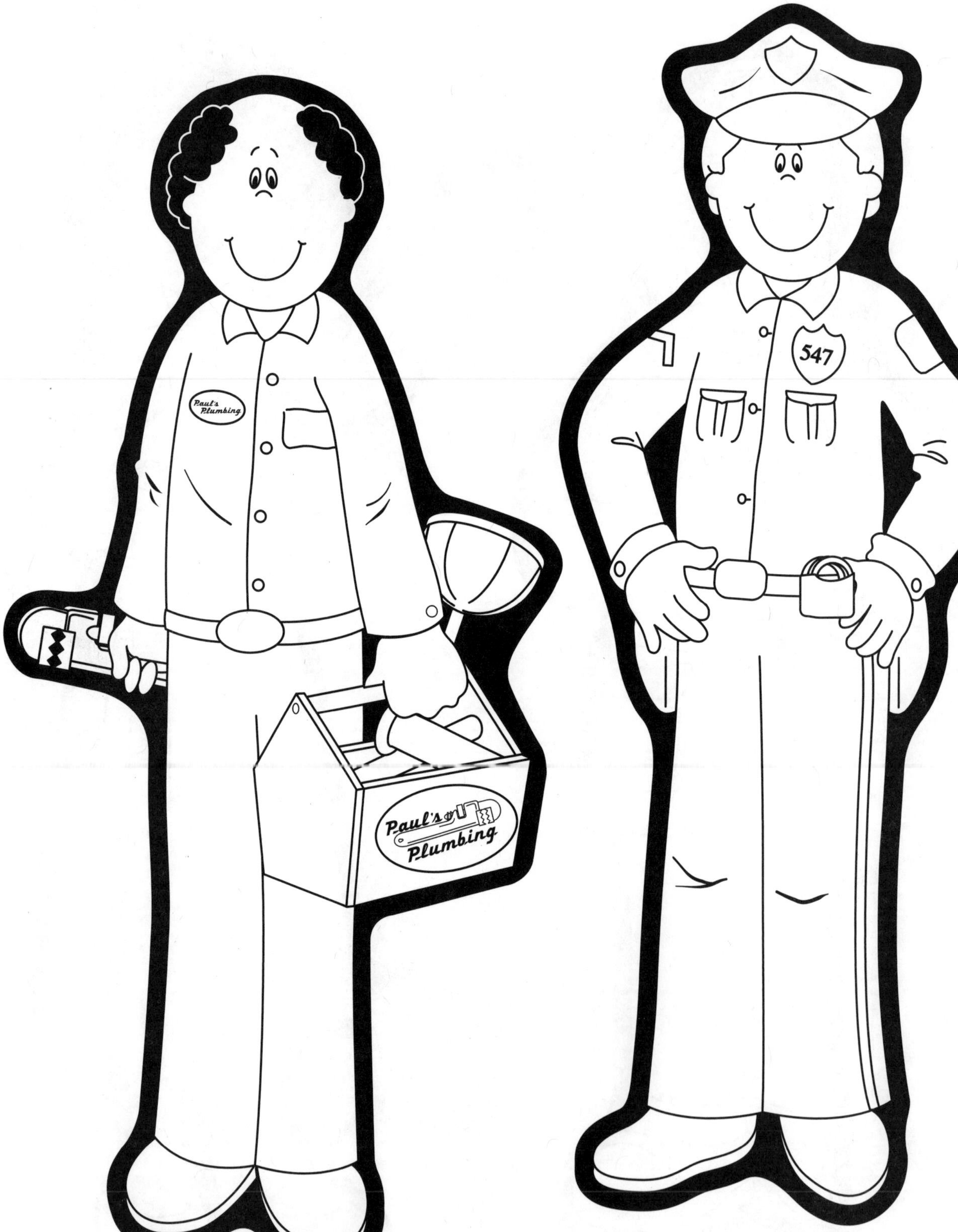
Paul's Plumbing
Paul's Plumbing
547

US MAIL

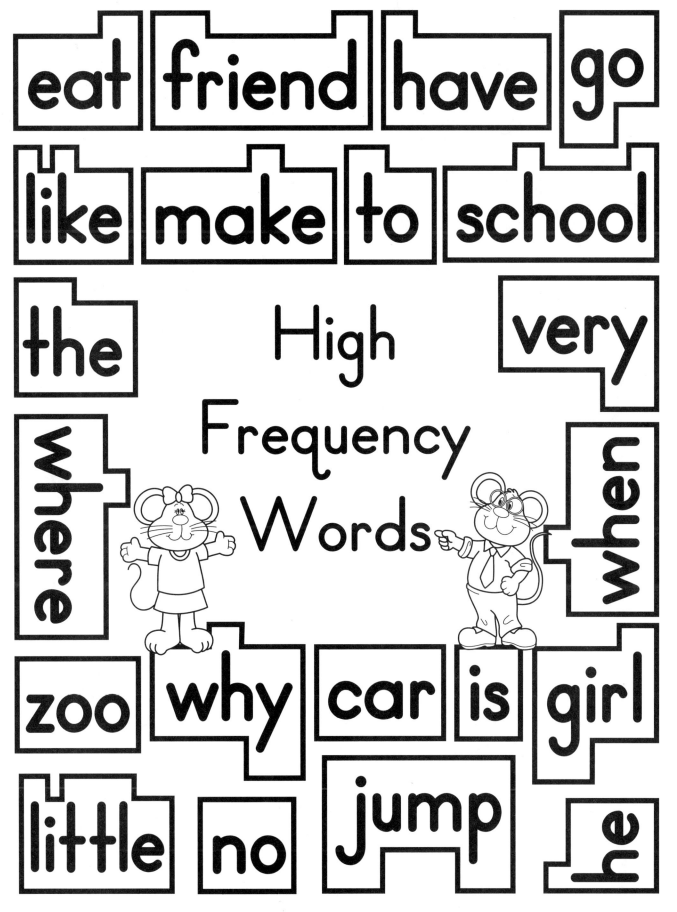

High Frequency Words

eat friend have go

like make to school

the very

where when

zoo why car is girl

little no jump he

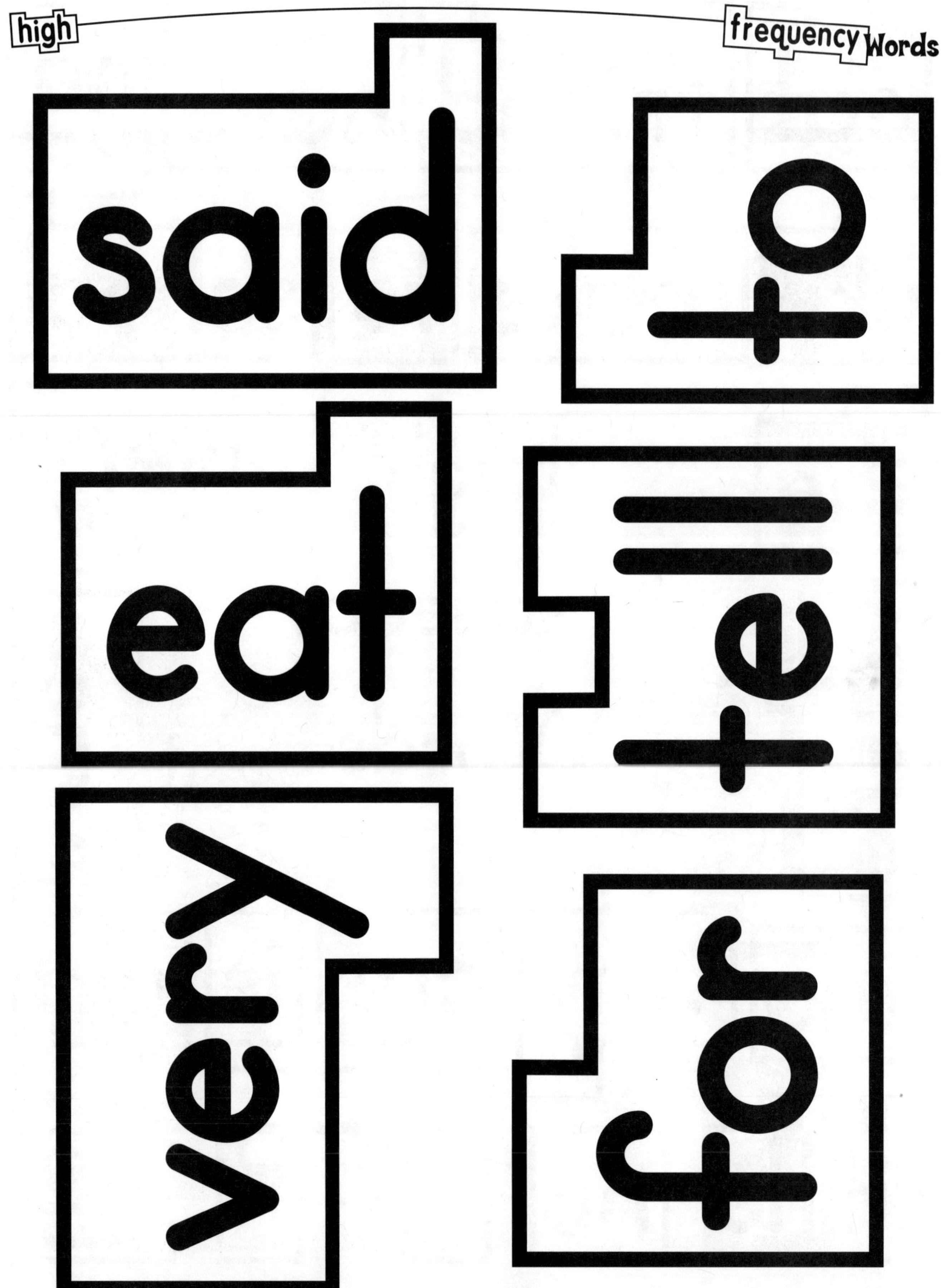
said
to
eat
tell
very
for

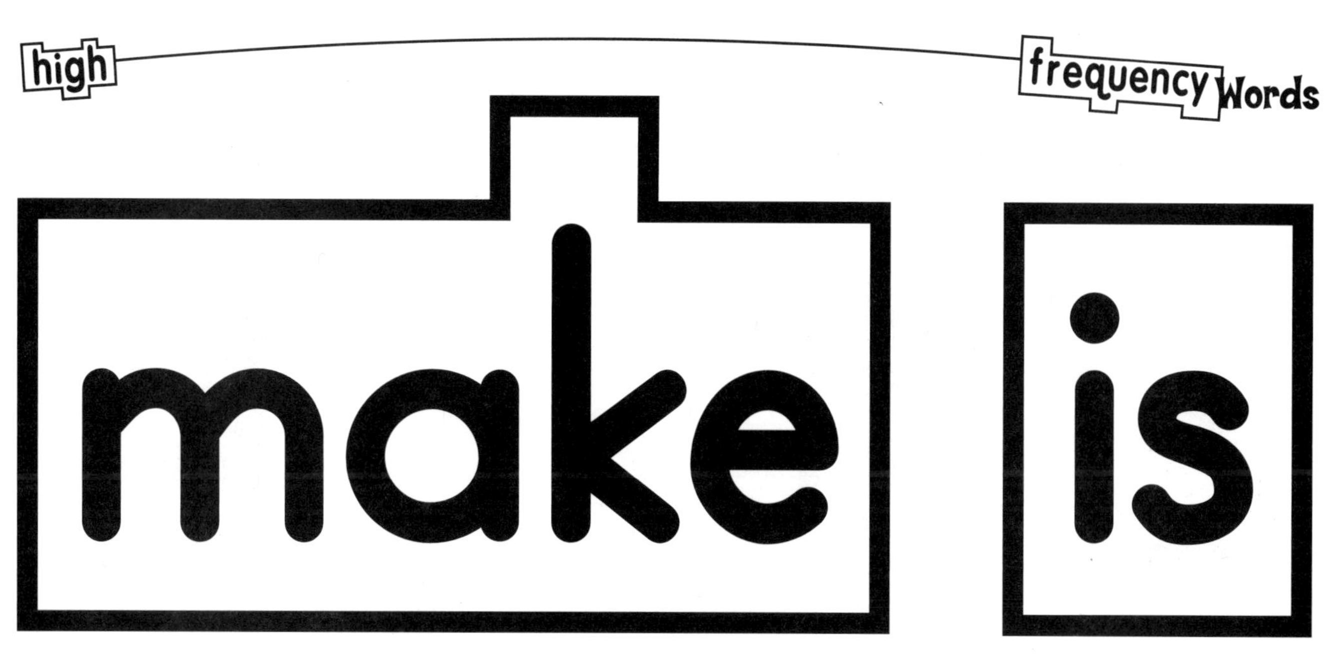

I

he

am

house

old

friend

in

it

on

we

me

has

look

jump

ride

where

to

and

zoo

can

what

boy

do

the

my

him

see

she

you

her

off

girl
they
will
fun
school

like

be

when

down

car

new

have

up

good

no

did

play

go

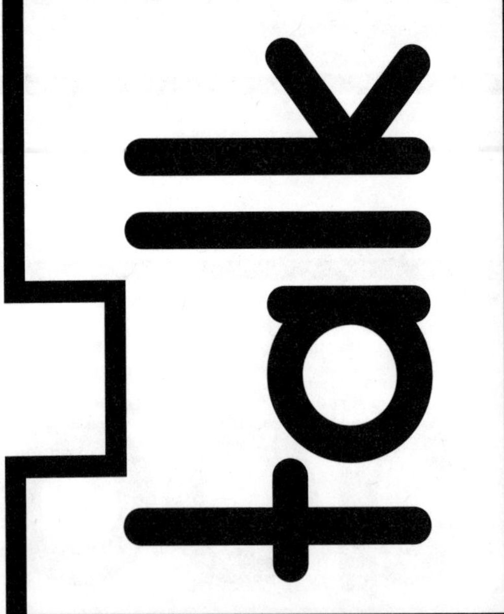

little

Notes for Home

Notes for Home

Notes for Home

Journal

GLUE

THANK YOU!

Good Work!

Time to Celebrate!

GLUE
GLUE
GLUE

OPEN HOUSE

SCHOOL

WELCOME

ABC
123

Date and Time

Teacher/Room Number

Name

LOST A TOOTH!

Signed

Date

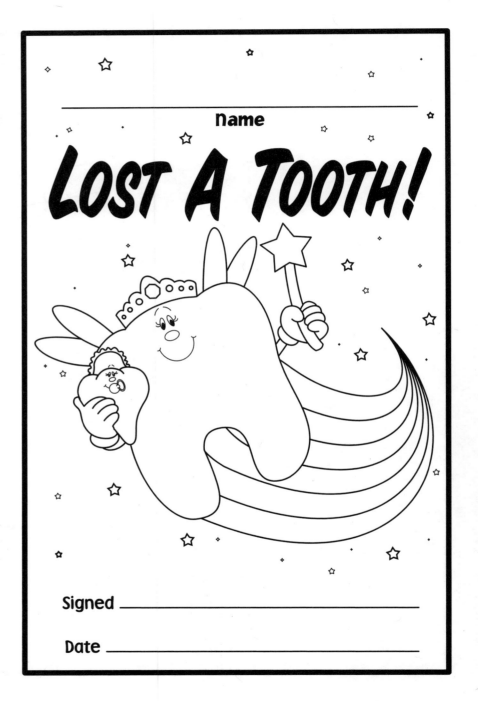

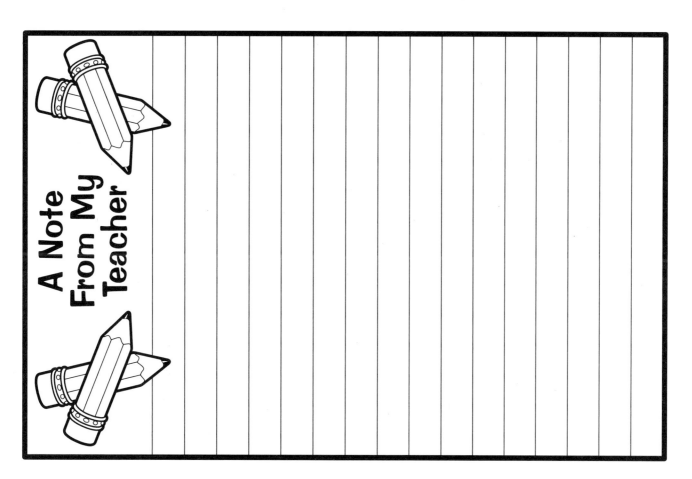

A Note From My Teacher

Nursery
Rhymes

NURSERY RHYMES LITERATURE SELECTIONS

Best Mother Goose Ever illustrated by Richard Scarry (Golden Books, 1970)

Grandmother's Nursery Rhymes/ Las Nanas de Abuelita by Nelly Palacio Jaramillo (Henry Holt & Company, 1996)

The Itsy Bitsy Spider illustrated by Iza Trapani (Charlesbridge Publishing, 1997)

It's Raining, It's Pouring by Kin Eagle (Charlesbridge Publishing, 1997)

The Movable Mother Goose by Robert Sabuda (Little Simon, 1999)

Mother Goose Remembers illustrated by Clare Beaton (Barefoot Books, 2000)

My Very First Mother Goose edited by Iona Opie (Walker Books, 2001)

Over the Candlestick: Classic Nursery Rhymes and the Real Stories Behind Them edited by Michael and Wayne Montgomery (Peachtree Publishers, 2002)

The Real Mother Goose illustrated by Blanche Fisher Wright (Scholastic, 1994)

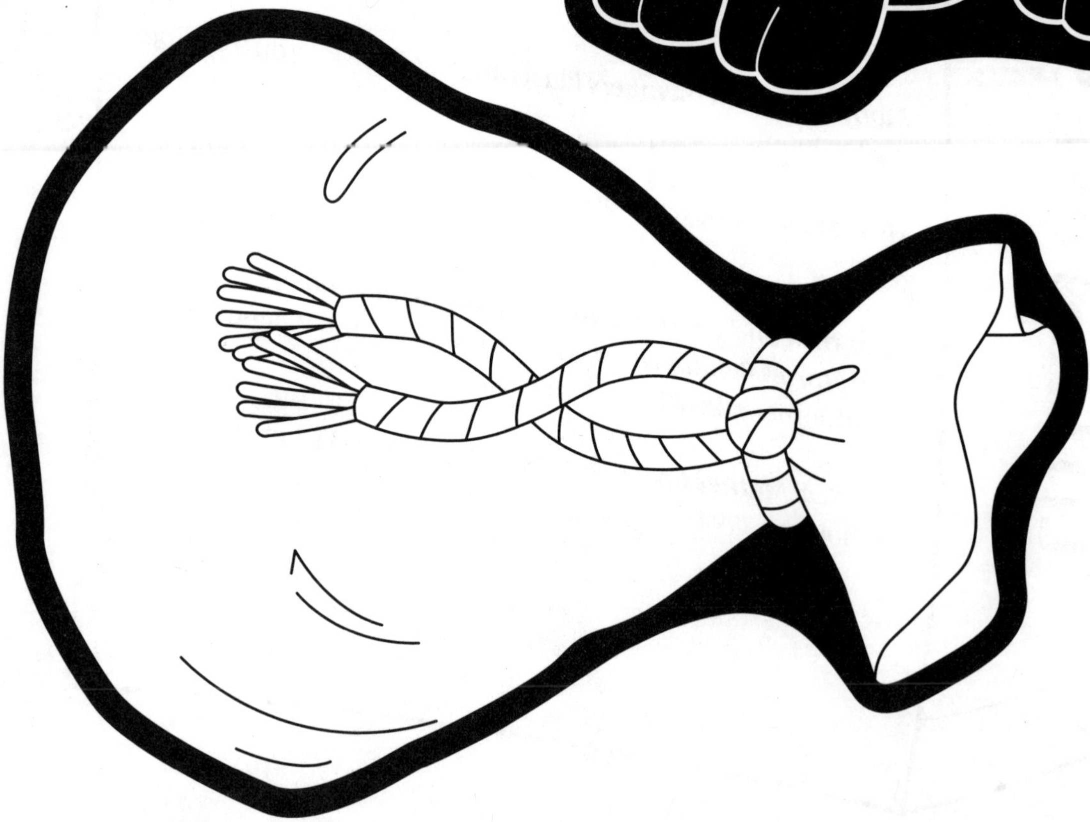

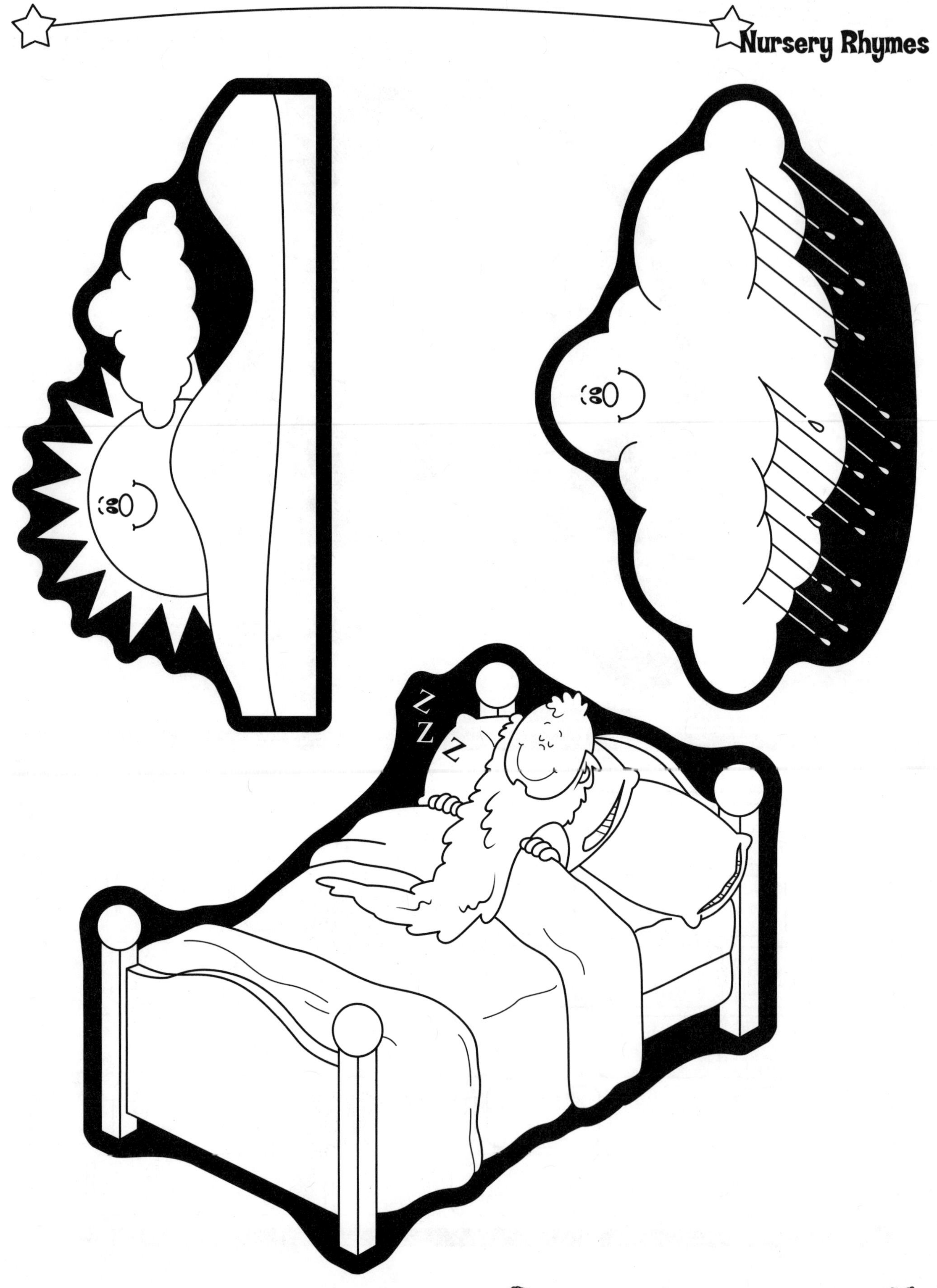
Z
Z
Z

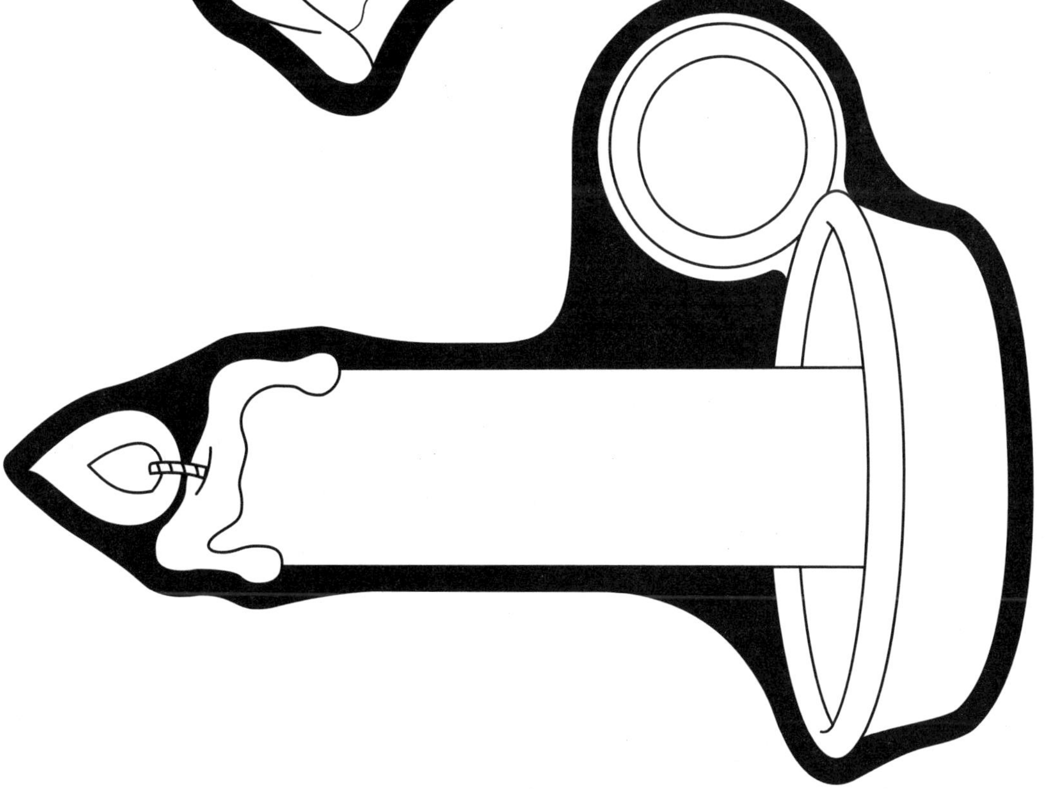

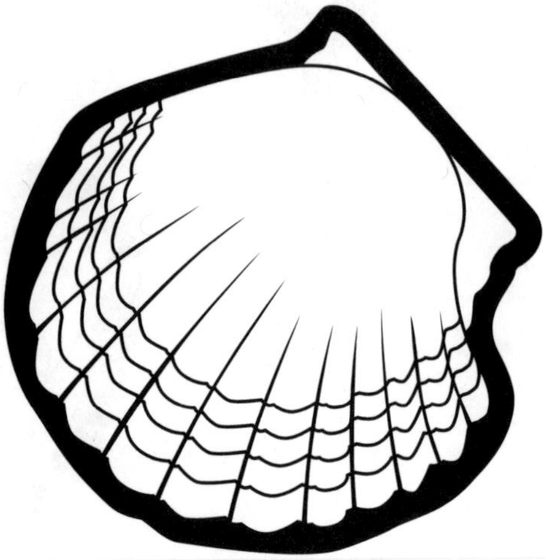

SCHOOL

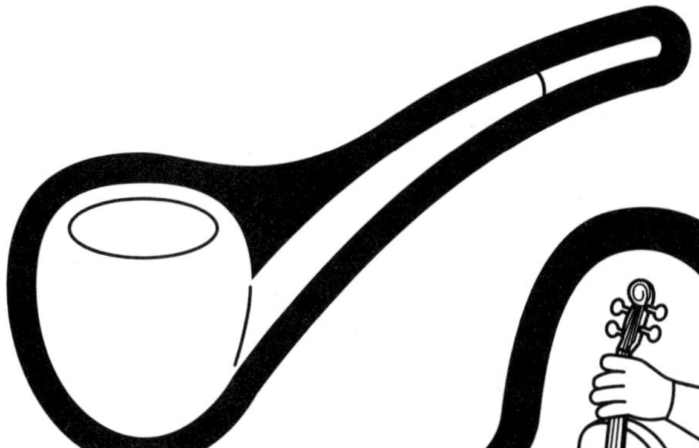

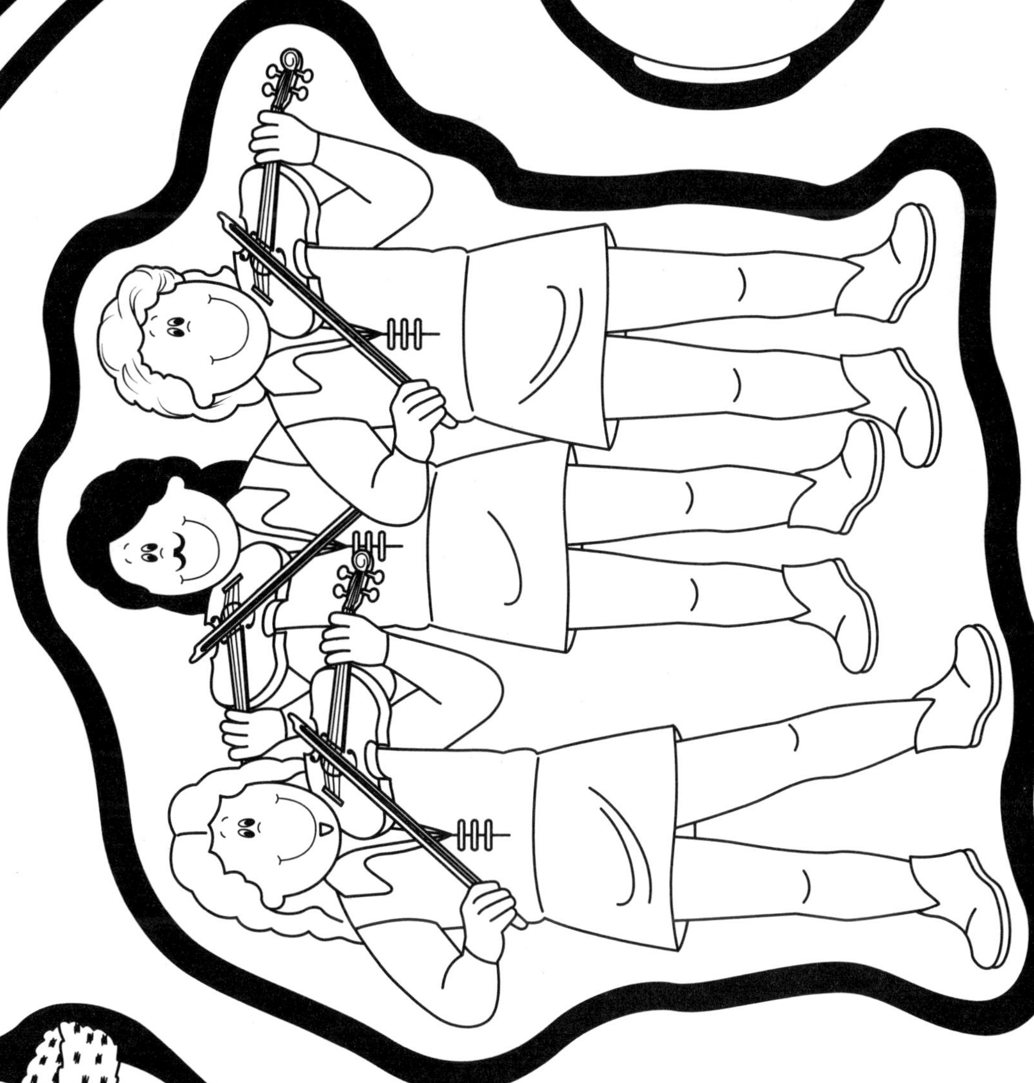

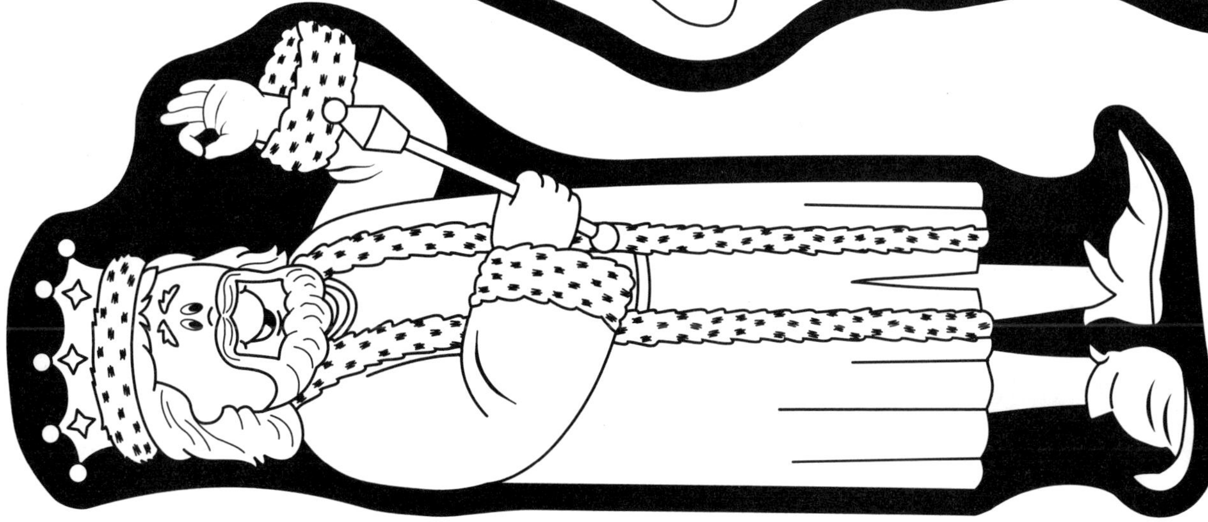

MARKET

Shapes

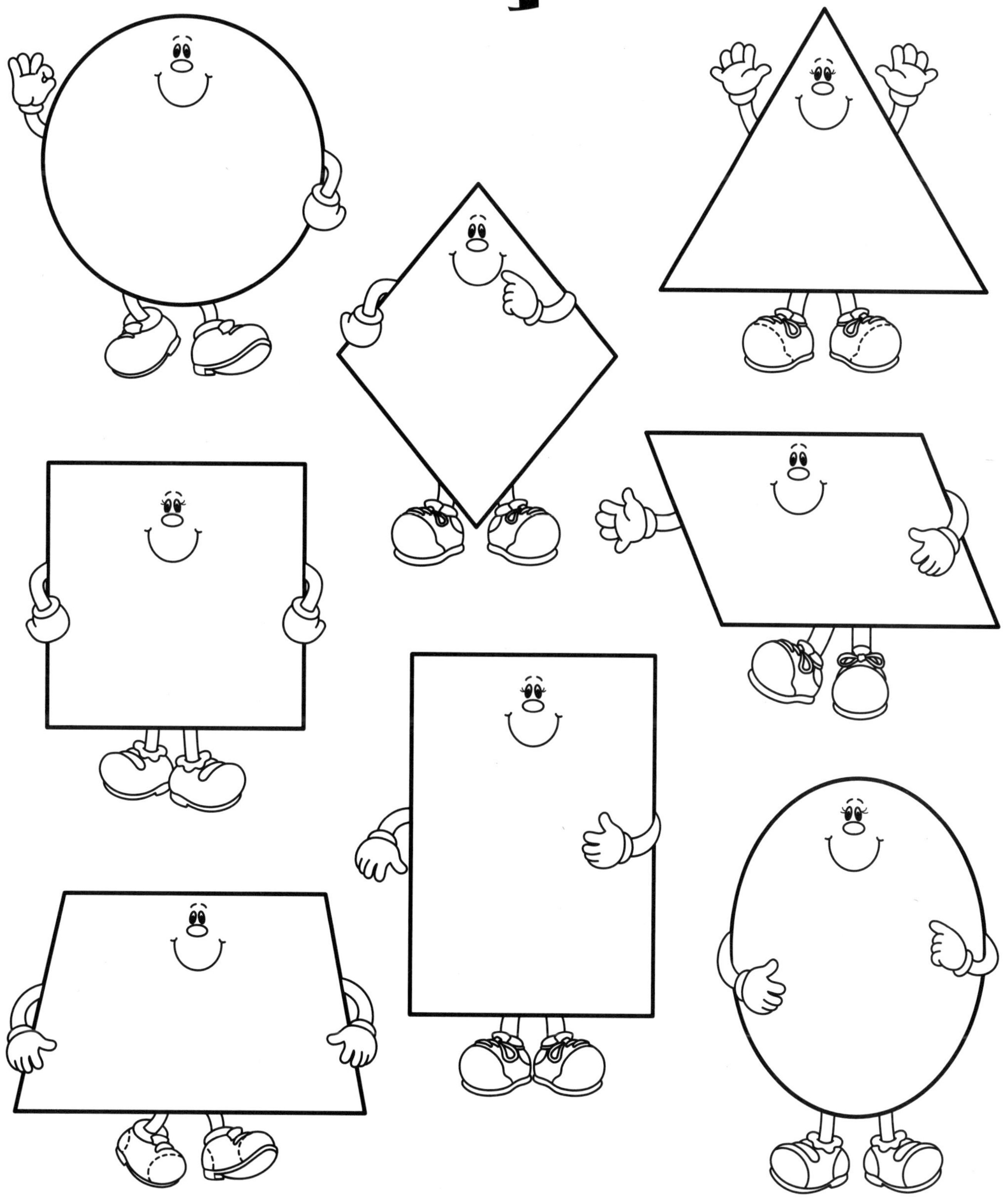

SHAPES LITERATURE SELECTIONS

Captain Invincible and the Space Shapes by Stuart J. Murphy (HarperTrophy, 2001)

Circles by Sarah L. Schuette (Pebble Books, 2002)

Color Zoo by Lois Ehlert (HarperCollins, 1989)

The Greedy Triangle by Marilyn Burns (Scholastic, 1995)

Ovals by Sarah L. Schuette (Pebble Books, 2002)

Rectangles by Sarah L. Schuette (Pebble Books, 2002)

The Shape of Me and Other Stuff by Dr. Seuss (Random House Children's Books, 1973)

The Shape of Things by Dayle Ann Dodds (Candlewick Press, 1996)

Shapes, Shapes, Shapes by Tana Hoban (HarperTrophy, 1996)

Shape Spotters (All Aboard Math Reader, Station Stop 1) by Megan E. Bryant (Grosset & Dunlap, 2002)

Squares by Sarah L. Schuette (Pebble Books, 2002)

Triangles by Sarah L. Schuette (Pebble Books, 2002)

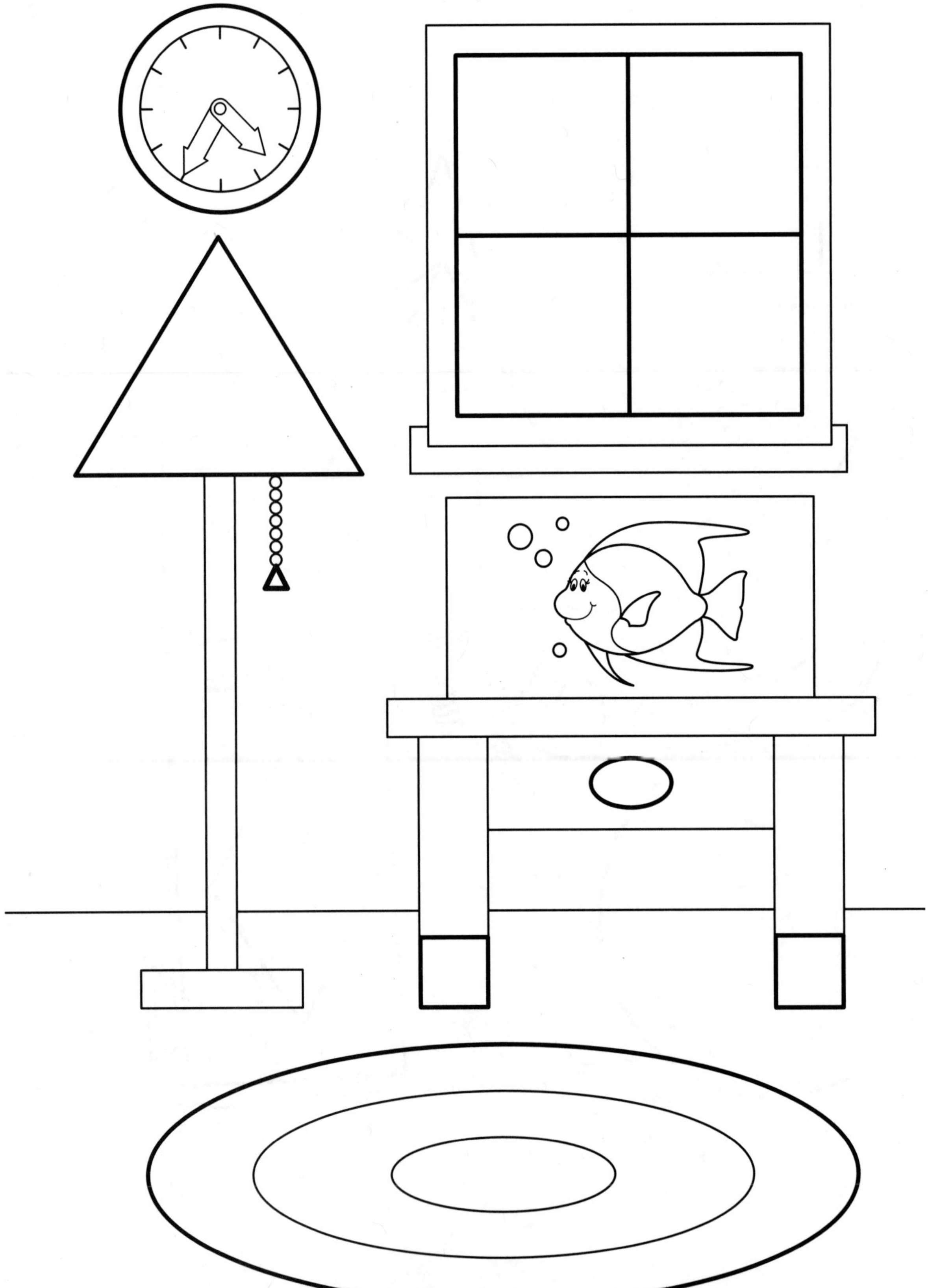

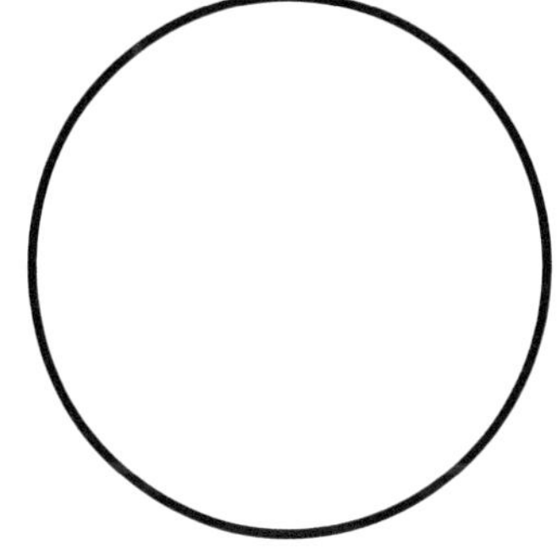

STOP

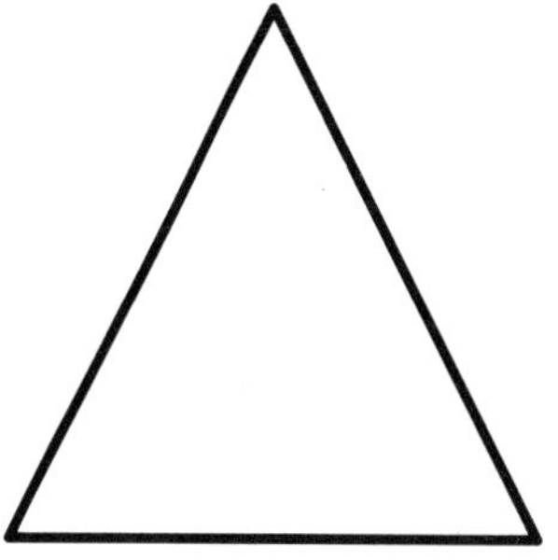

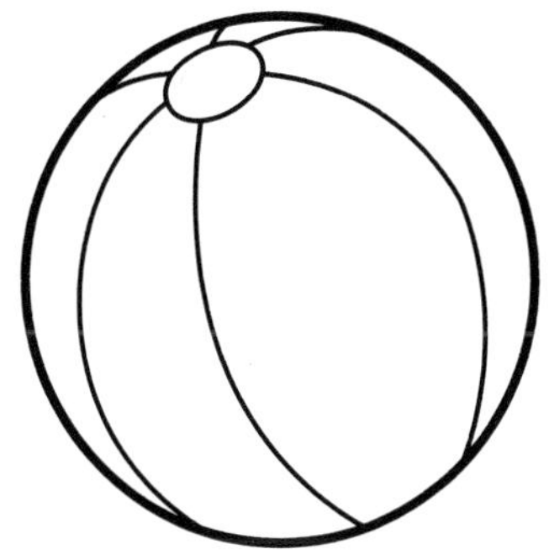

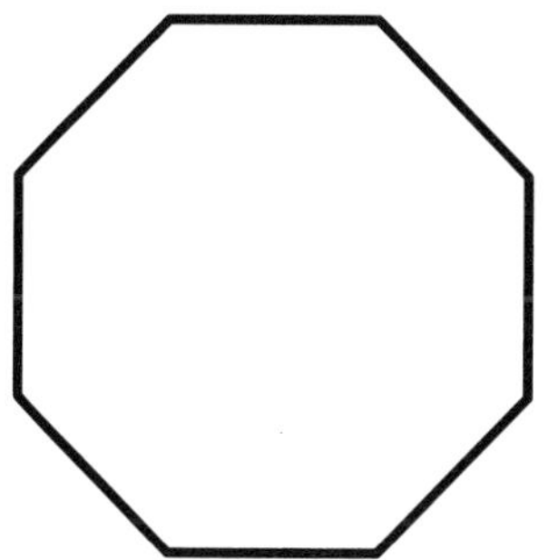

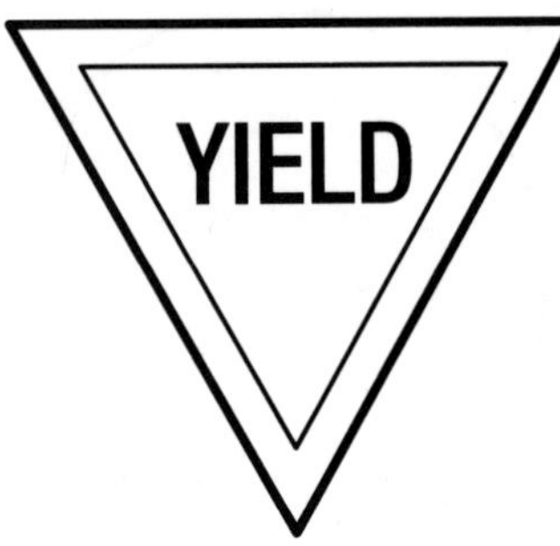
YIELD

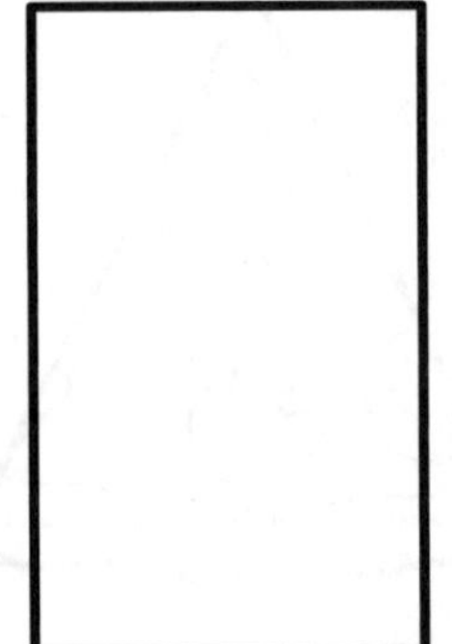

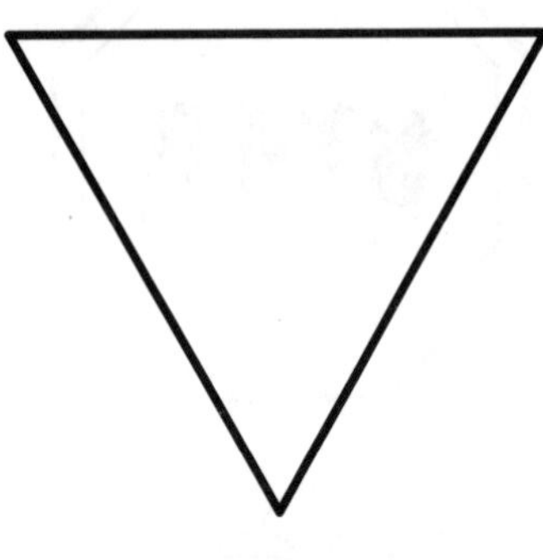

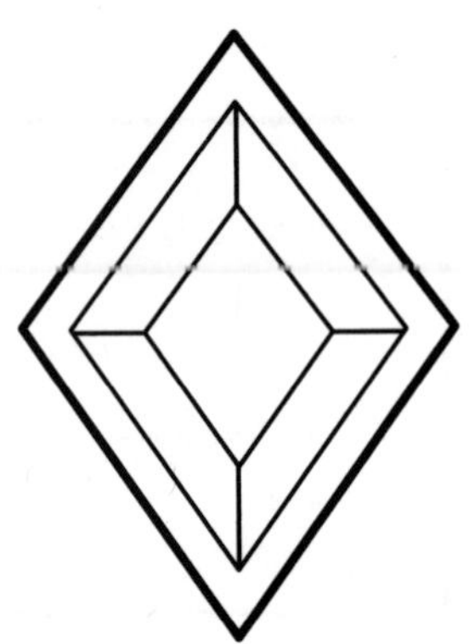

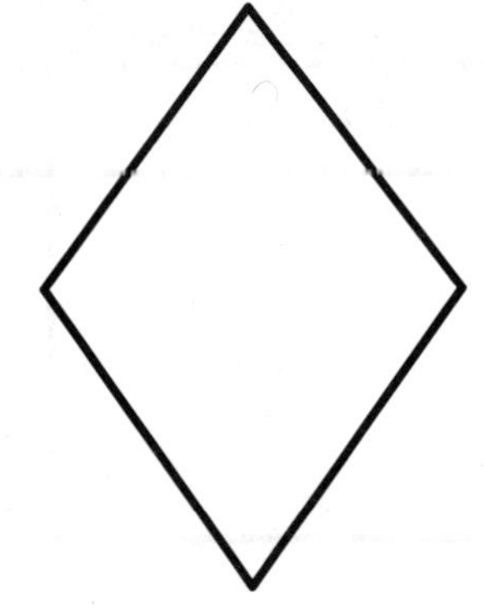

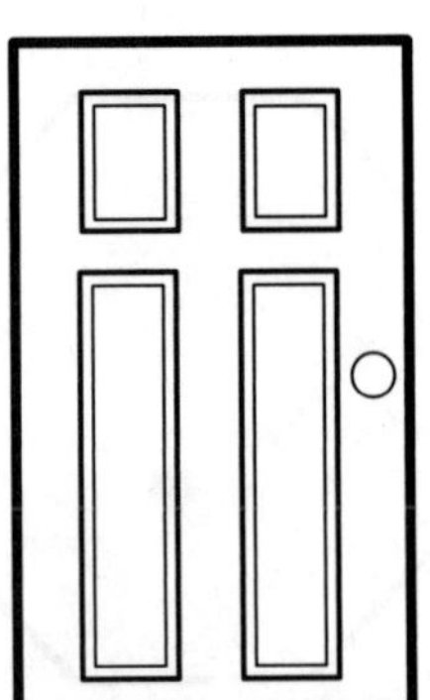

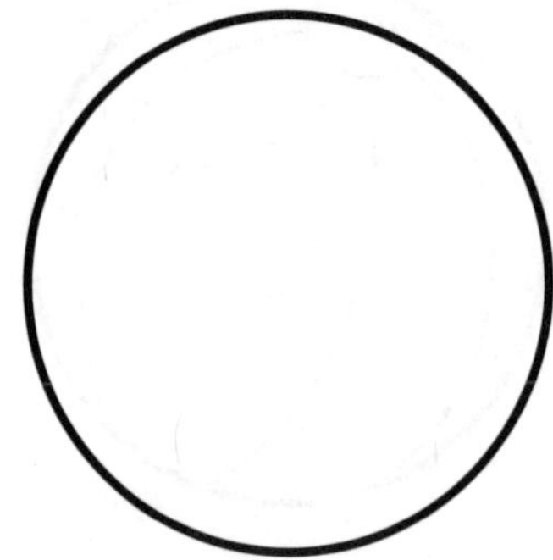

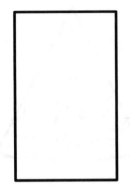

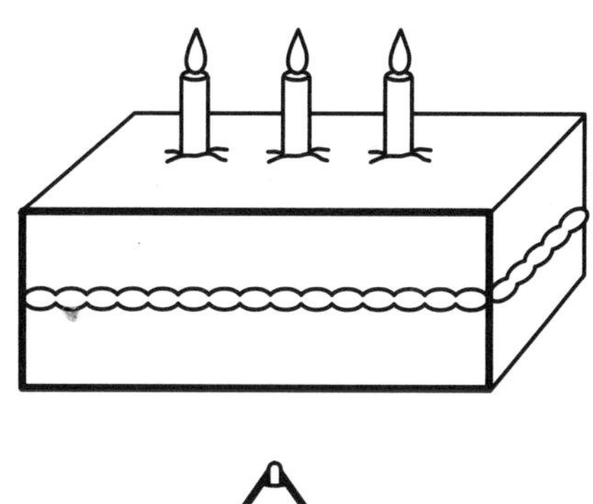

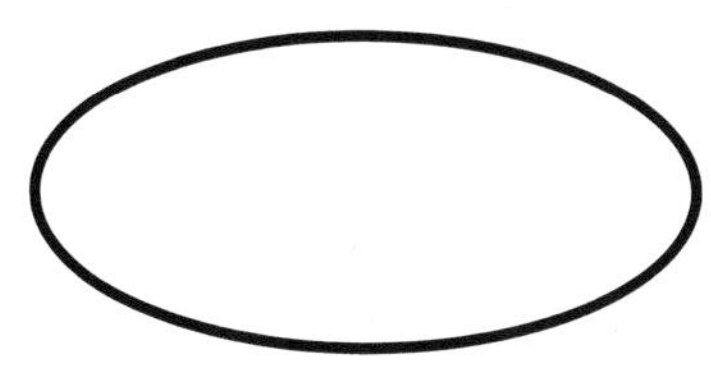

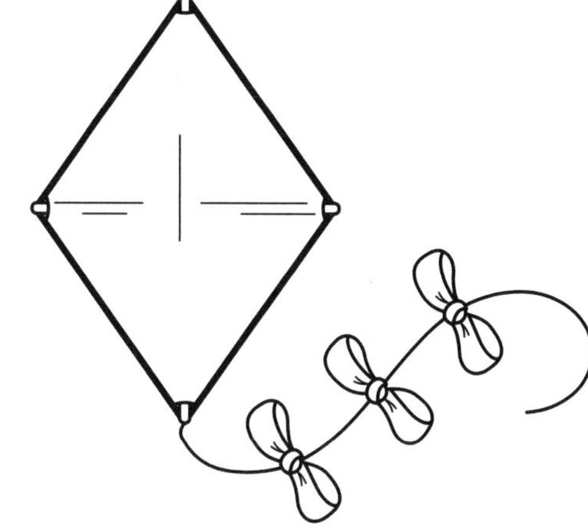

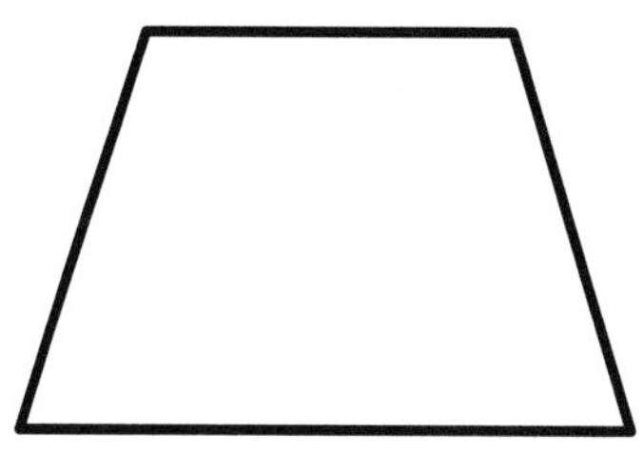

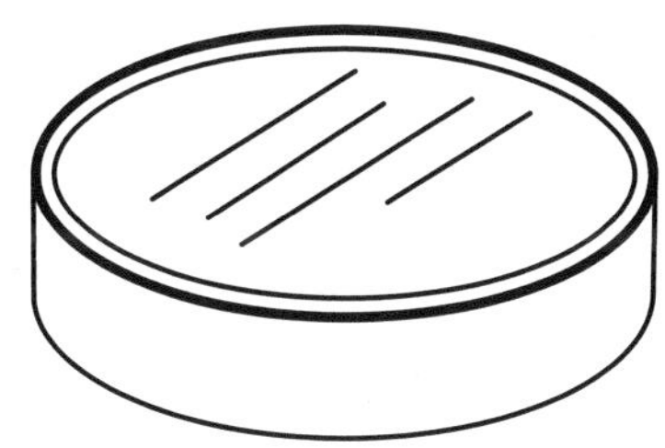

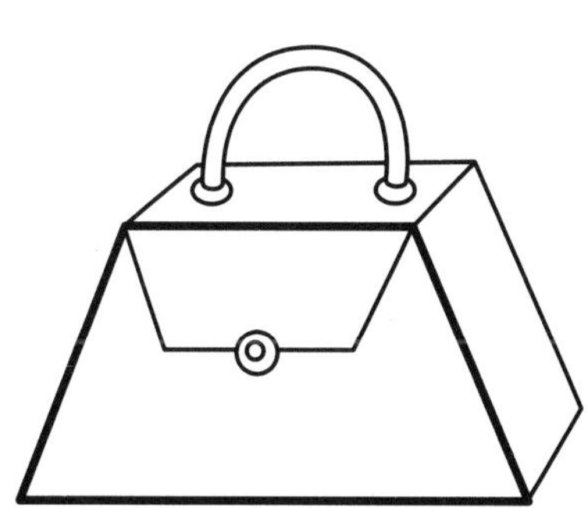

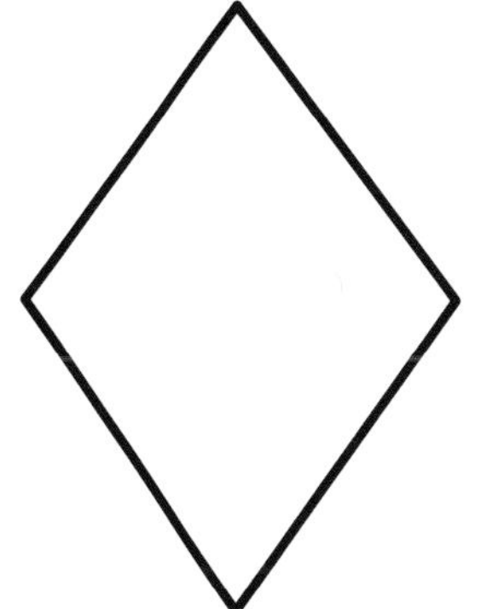

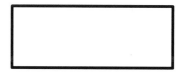

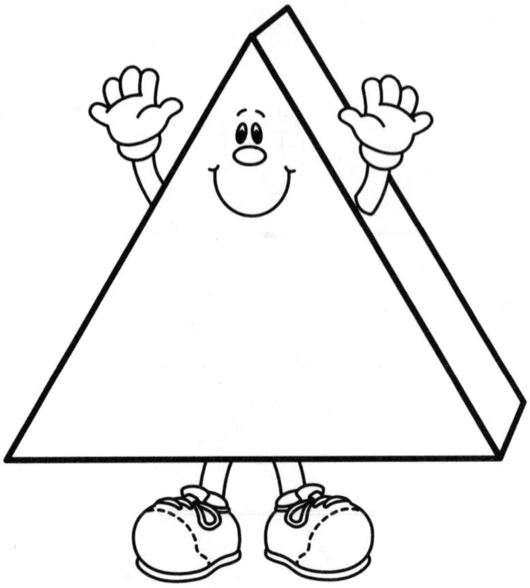

Sports

C

COMETS 2

SPORTS LITERATURE SELECTIONS

Allie's Basketball Dream by Barbara E. Barber (Lee & Low Books, 1998)

Balls (Rookie Readers Level A) by Melanie Davis Jones (Children's Press, 2003)

Basketball ABC: The NBA Alphabet by Florence Cassen Mayers (Harry N. Abrams, 1996)

Coach John and His Soccer Team by Alice K. Flanagan (Children's Press, 1999)

Home Run: The Story of Babe Ruth by Robert Burleigh (Voyager Books, 2003)

The Magic School Bus Plays Ball: A Book About Forces by Joanna Cole (Scholastic, 1998)

My Baseball Book by Gail Gibbons (HarperCollins, 2000)

My Basketball Book by Gail Gibbons (HarperCollins, 2000)

My Football Book by Gail Gibbons (HarperCollins, 2000)

My Soccer Book by Gail Gibbons (HarperCollins, 2000)

Play Ball by Mercer Mayer (Mercer Mayer First Readers, 2001)

Swish! by Bill Martin Jr. and Michael Sampson (Henry Holt & Company, Inc., 2000)

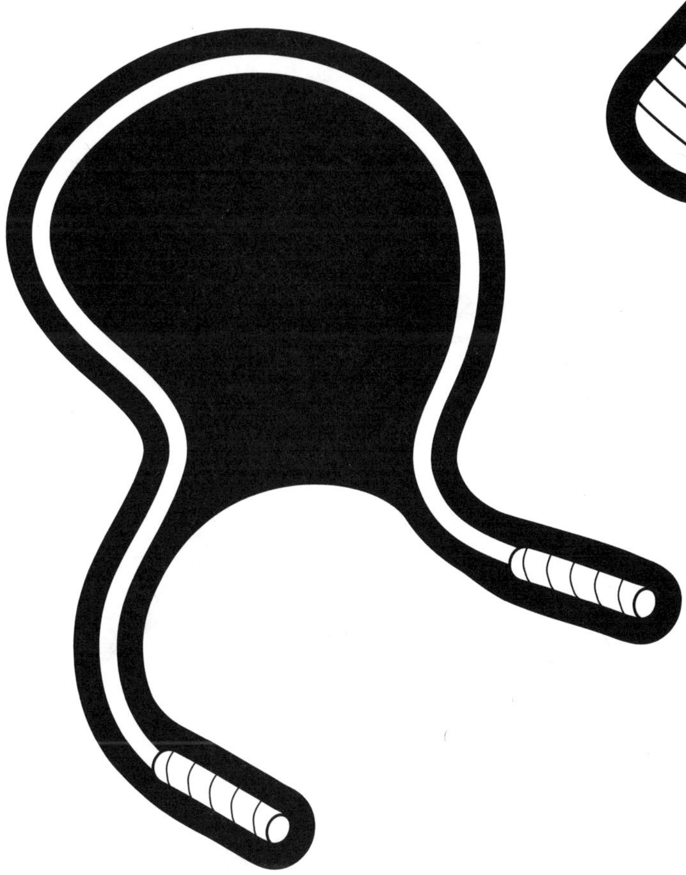

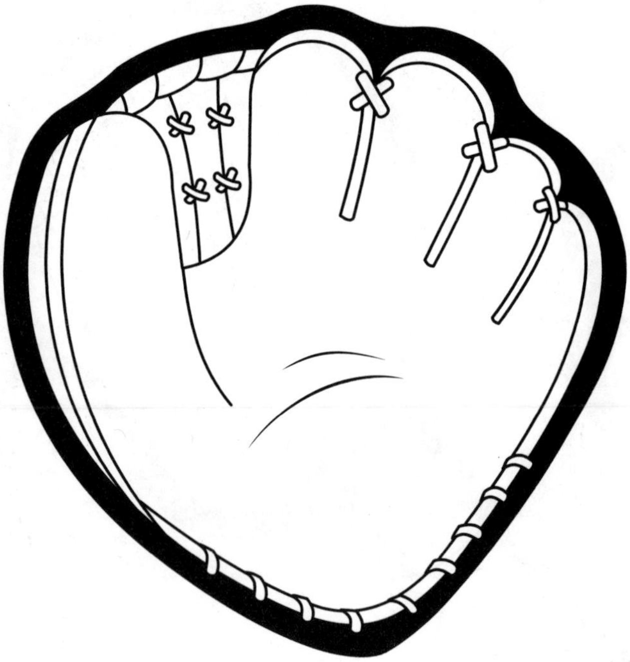

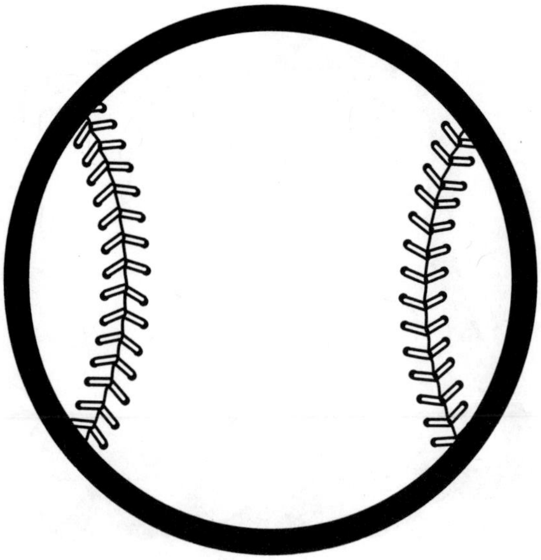

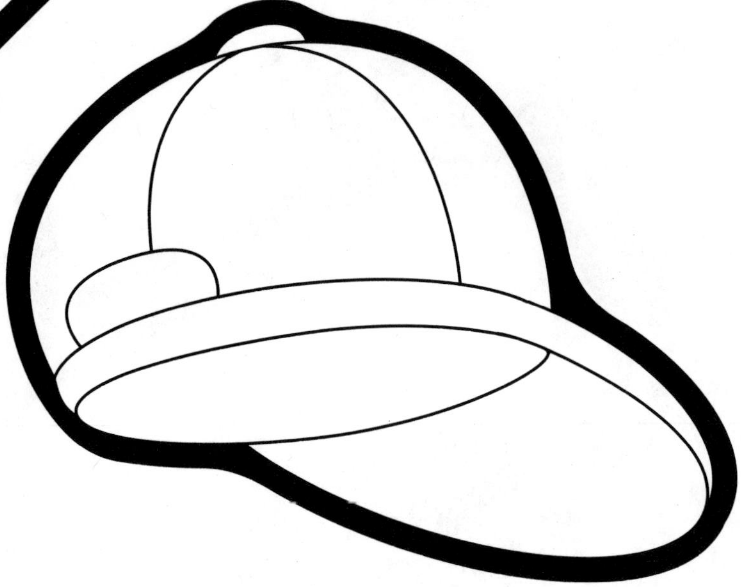

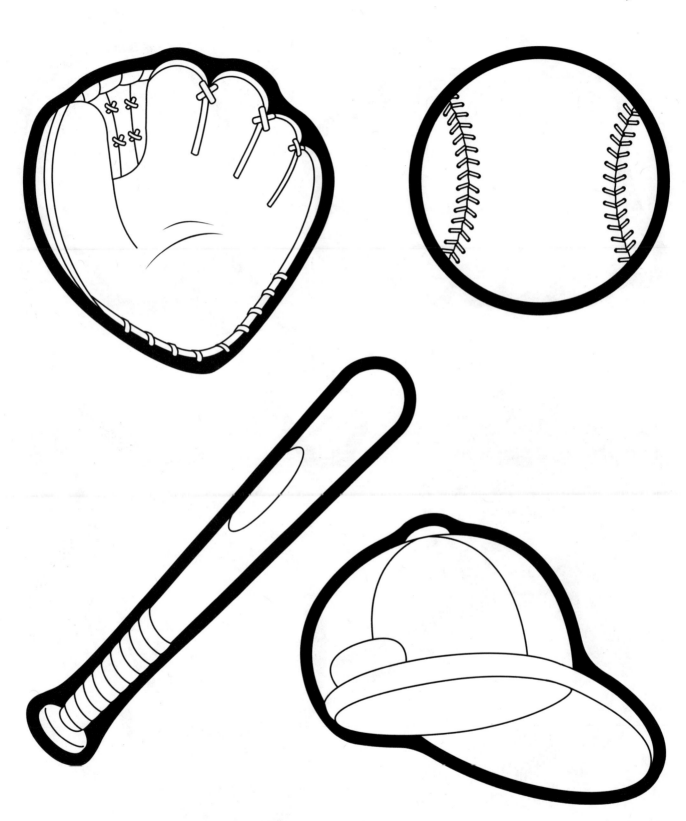

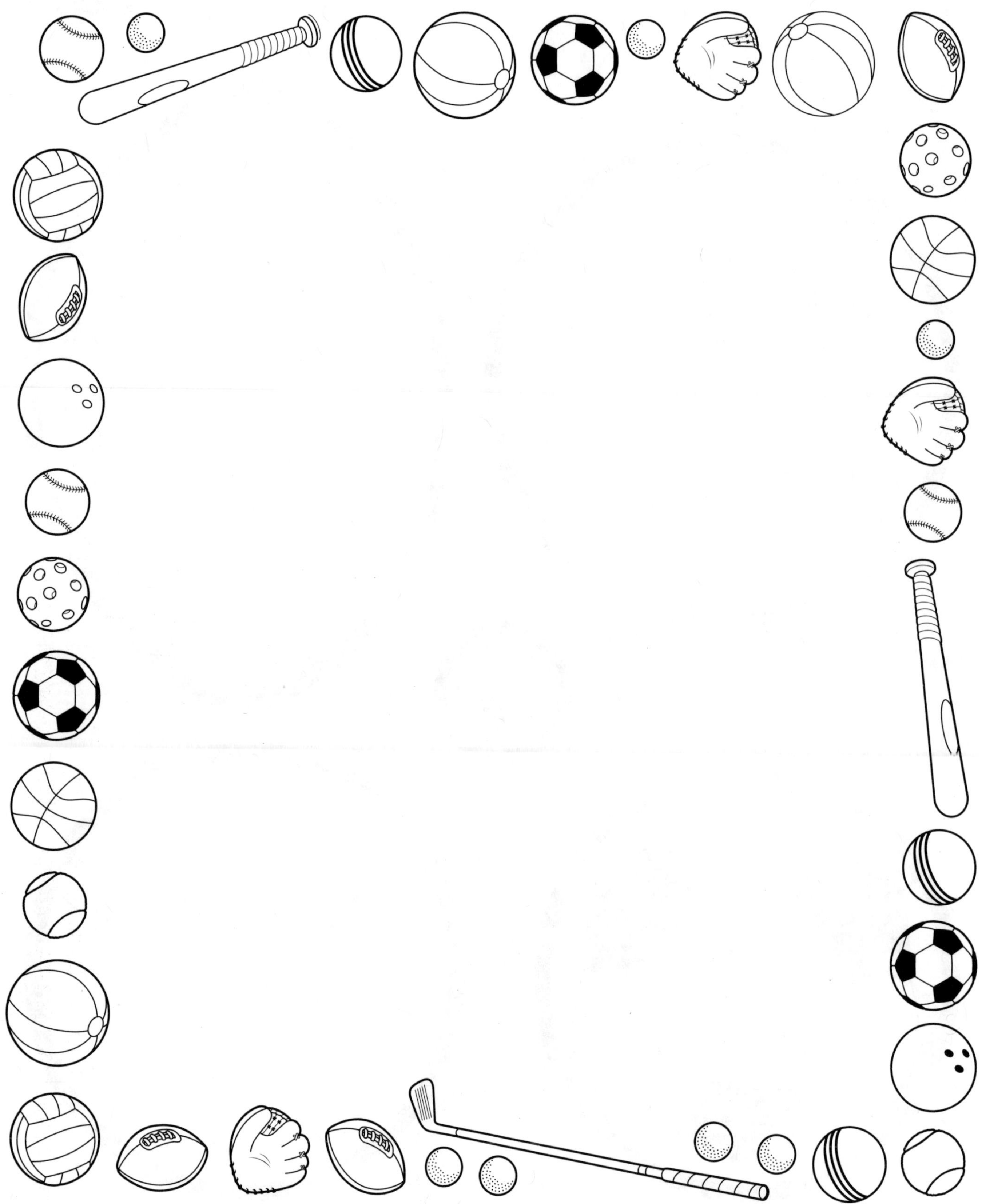

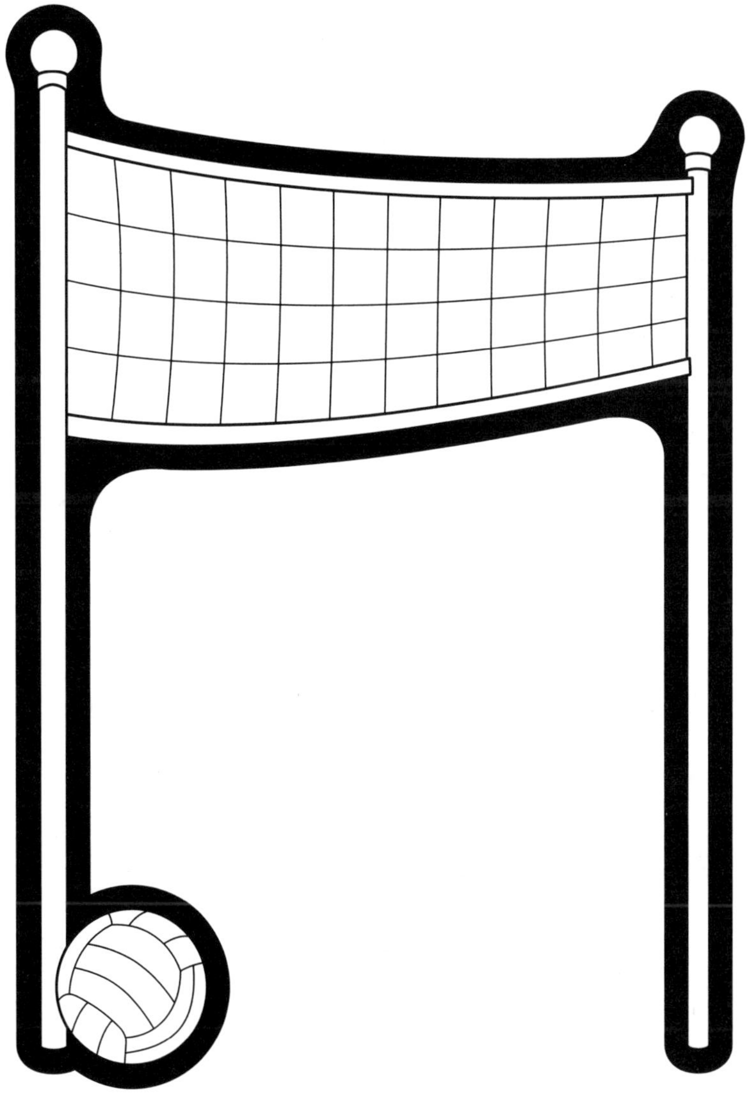

Transportation

TRANSPORTATION LITERATURE SELECTIONS

Big Book of Things That Go edited by Caroline Bingham (DK Publishing, 1994)

Cars and Trucks and Things That Go by Richard Scarry (Golden Books, 1997)

Freight Train by Donald Crews (HarperTrophy, 1992)

Harbor by Donald Crews (HarperTrophy, 1987)

I Love Boats by Flora McDonnell (Walker Books, 1995)

I Love Trains! by Philemon Sturges (HarperCollins, 2001)

My First Train Trip by Emily Neye (Grosset & Dunlap, 1999)

The Noisy Airplane Ride by Mike Downs (Tricycle Press, 2003)

Sheep in a Jeep by Nancy E. Shaw (Houghton Mifflin Co., 1988)

Sheep on a Ship by Nancy E. Shaw (Houghton Mifflin Co., 1992)

Truck by Donald Crews (HarperTrophy, 1991)

3,2,1 Go! A Transportation Countdown by Sarah L. Schuette (Capstone Press, 2003)

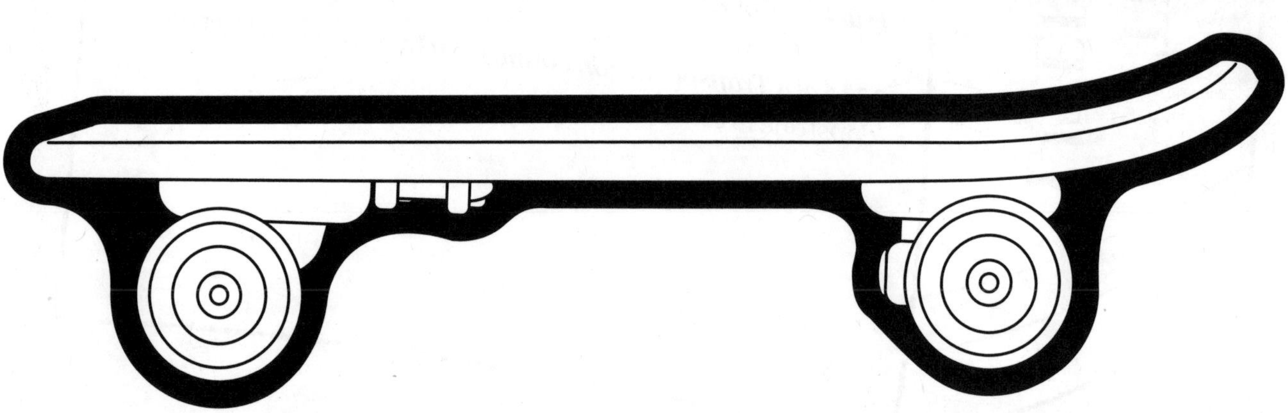

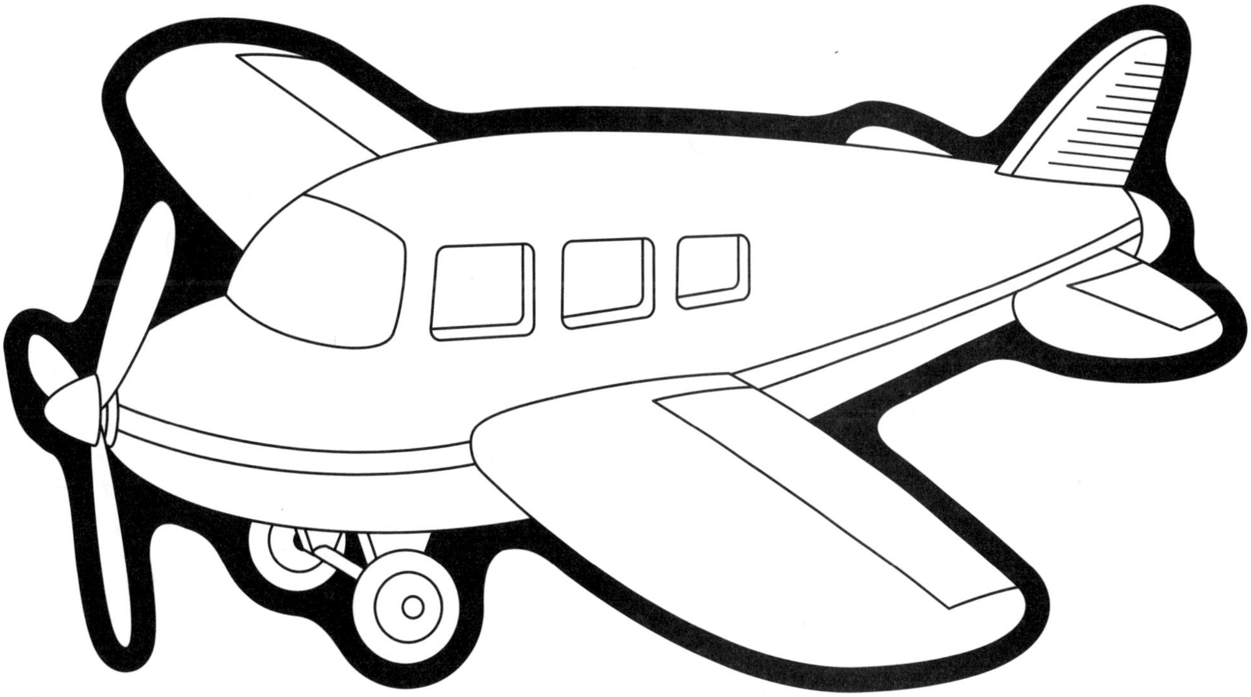

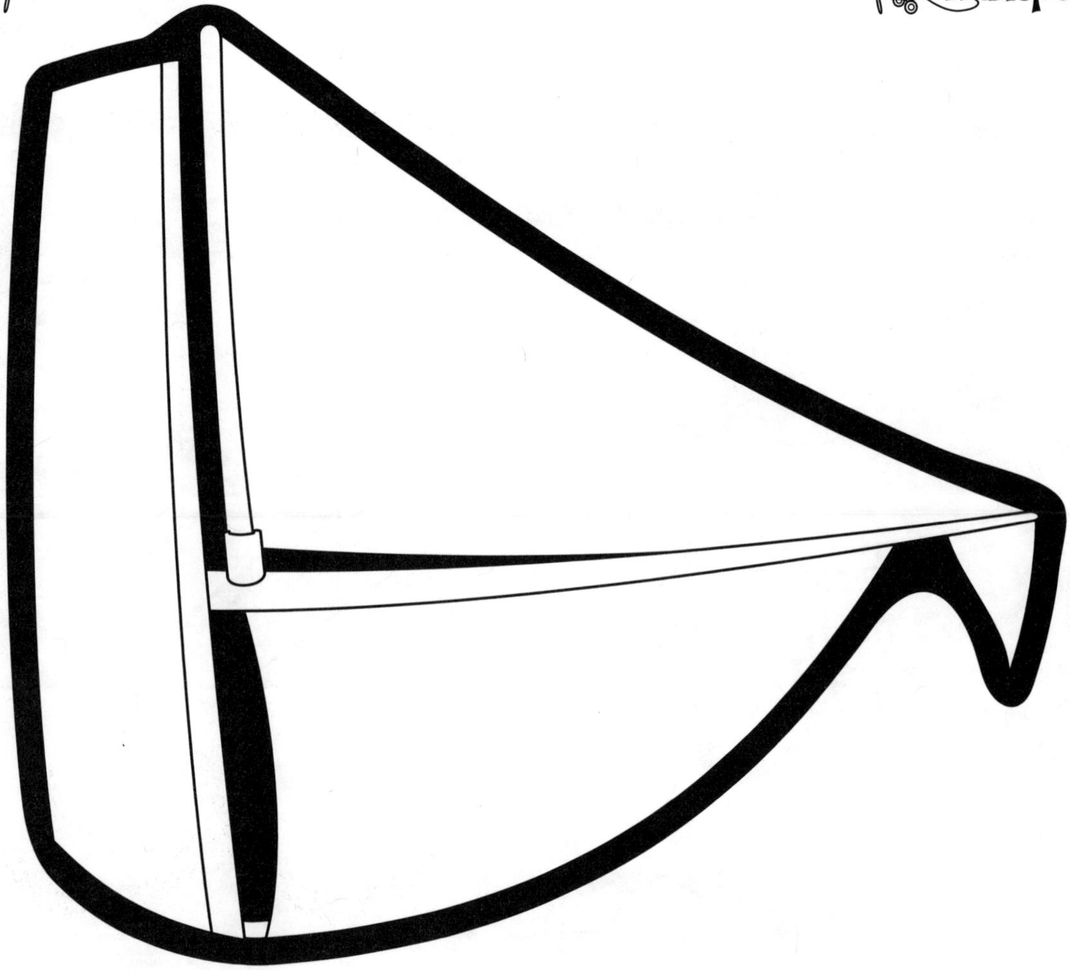

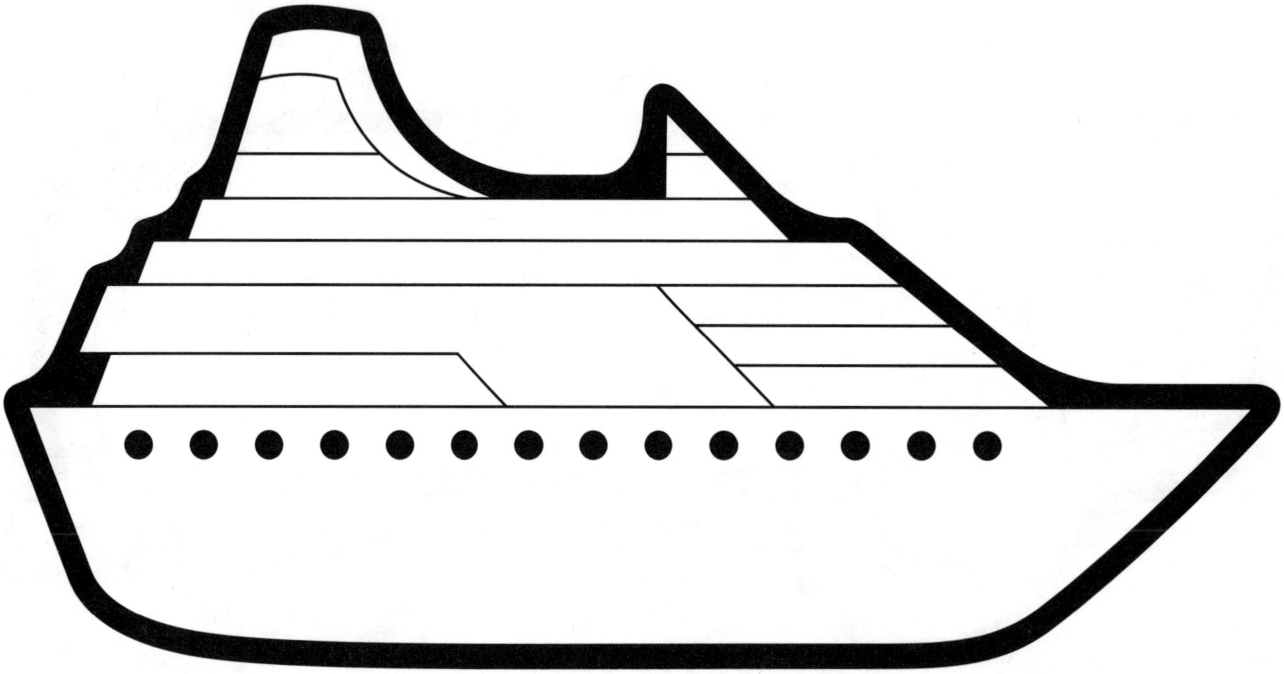

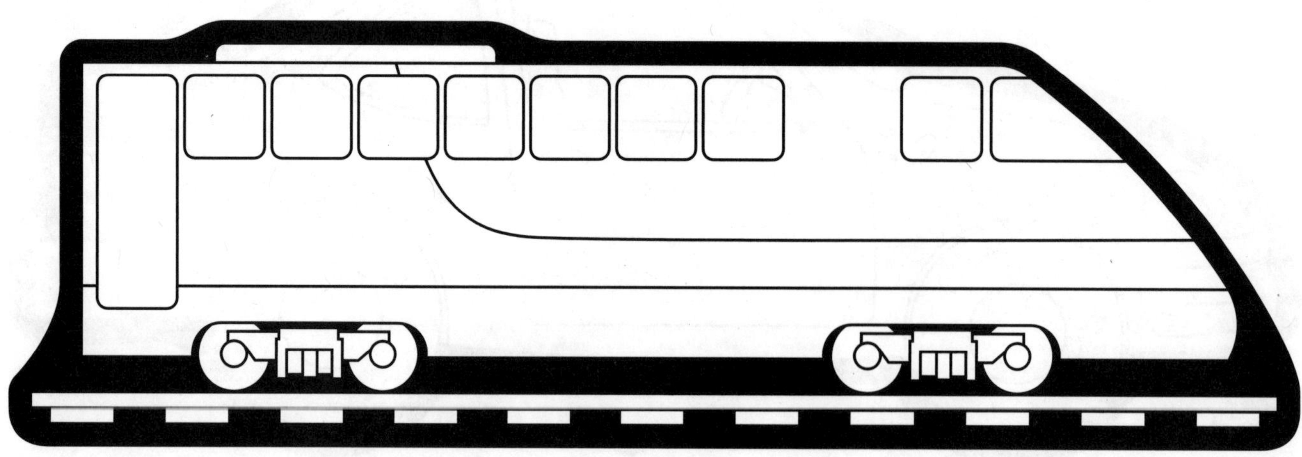

WEATHER

WEATHER LITERATURE SELECTIONS

The Cloud Book by Tomie De Paola (Scholastic, 1975)

Cloudy With a Chance of Meatballs by Judi Barrett (Aladdin Library, 1982)

Flash, Crash, Rumble, and Roll (Let's Read and Find Out) by Franklyn Mansfield Branley (HarperTrophy, 1999)

It Looked Like Spilt Milk by Charles G. Shaw (HarperTrophy, 1988)

The Jacket I Wear in the Snow by Shirley Neitzel (Scholastic, 1990)

Rain by Manya Stojic (Crown Books for Young Readers, 2000)

Red Rubber Boot Day by Mary Lyn Ray (Harcourt, 2000)

The Snowy Day by Ezra Jack Keats (Viking Books, 1962)

Snowballs by Lois Ehlert (Voyager Books, 1999)

The Storm by Marc Harshman (Dutton Books, 1995)

The Storm by Anne F. Rockwell (Hyperion Books for Children, 1994)

Weather Words and What They Mean by Gail Gibbons (Holiday House, 1992)

What Will the Weather Be? by Lynda DeWitt (HarperTrophy, 1993)

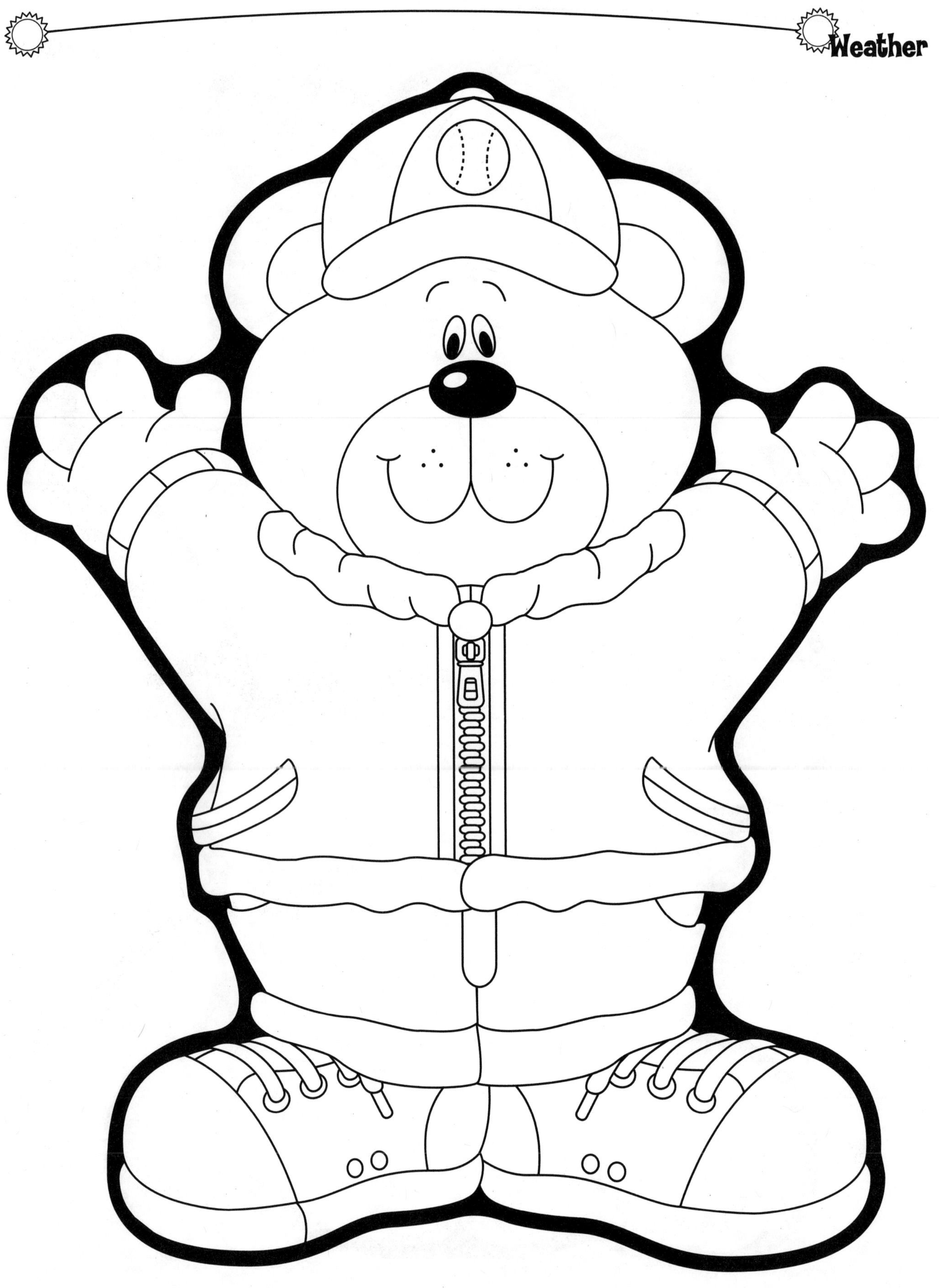

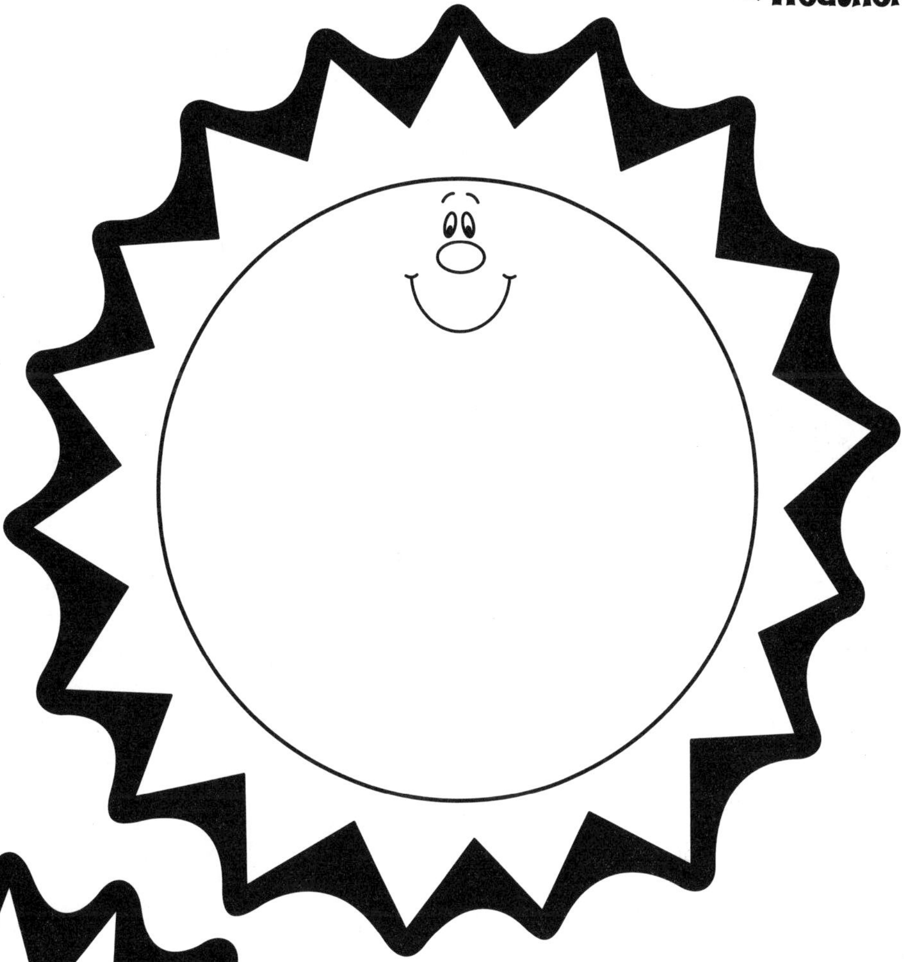

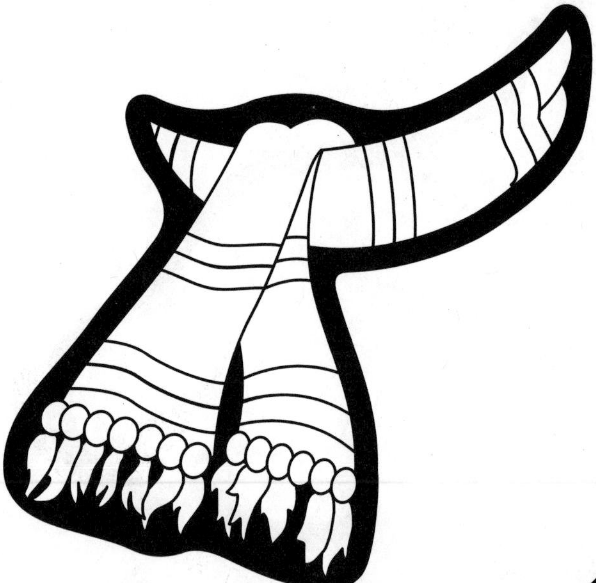

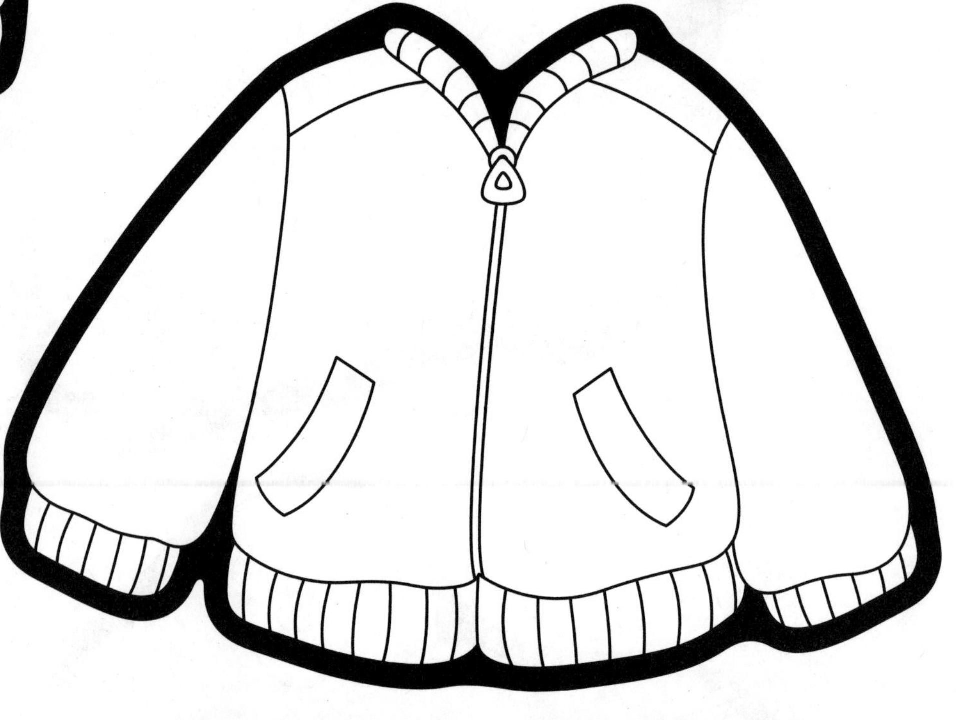

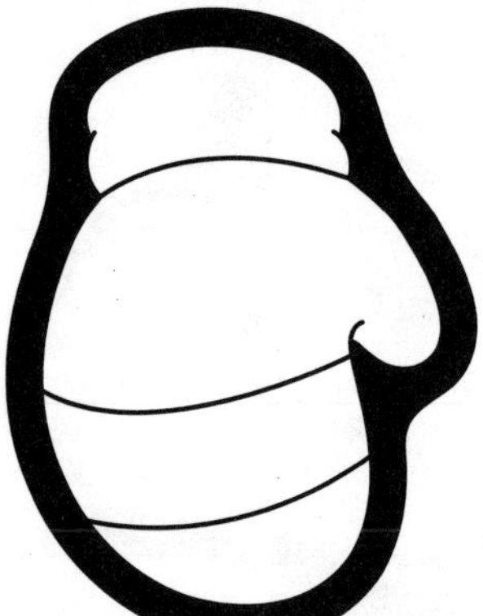

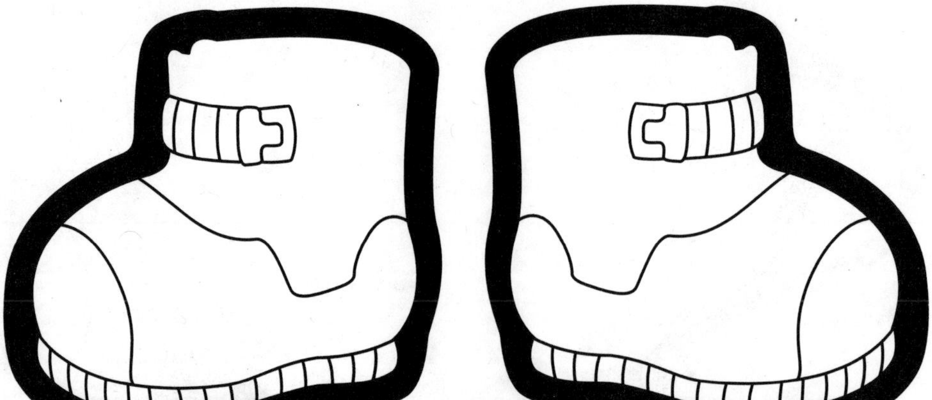

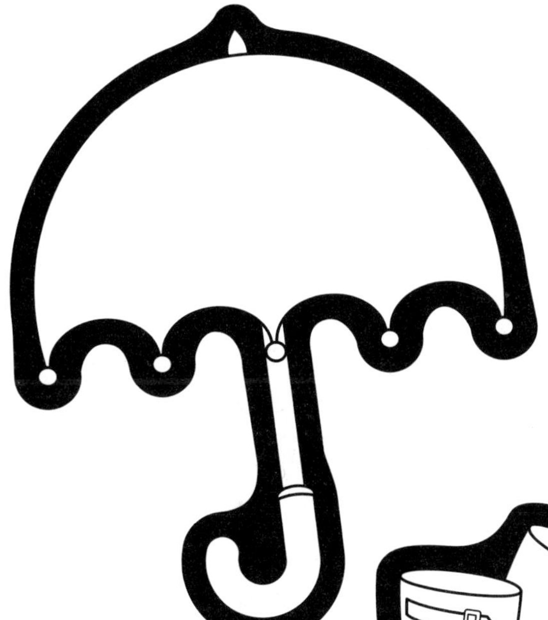

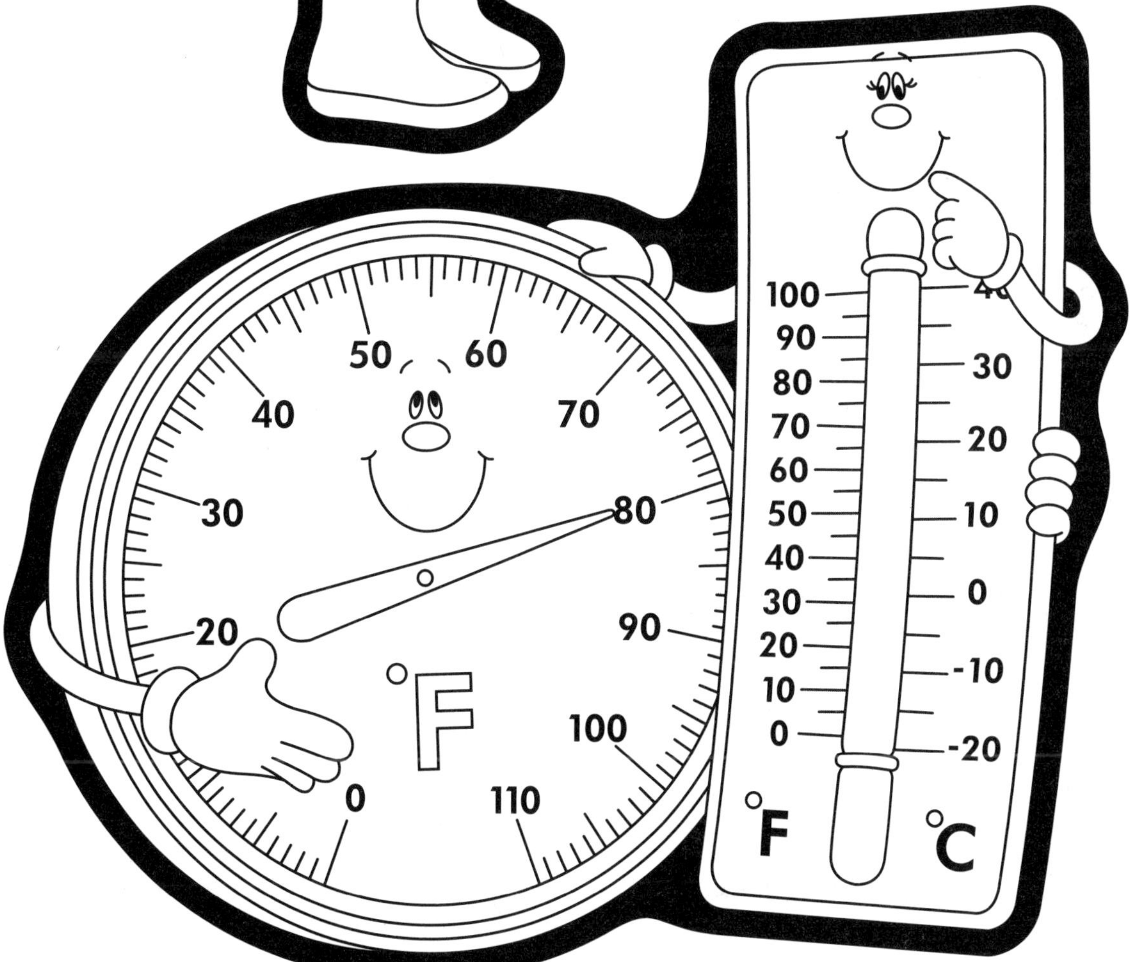

50
60
40
70
30
80
20
90
F
100
0
110
100
90
80
70
60
50
40
30
20
10
0
30
20
10
0
-10
-20
F
C

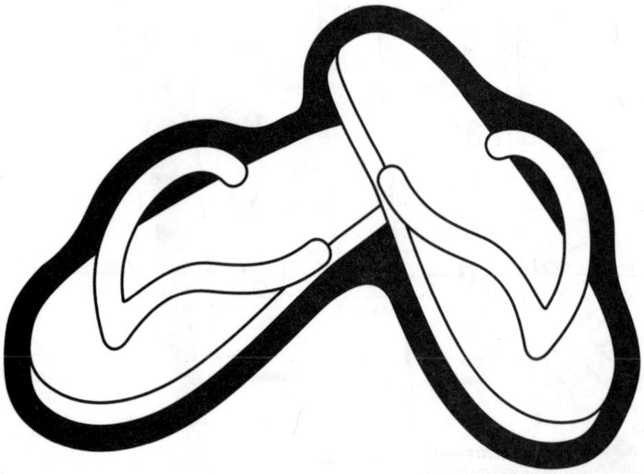

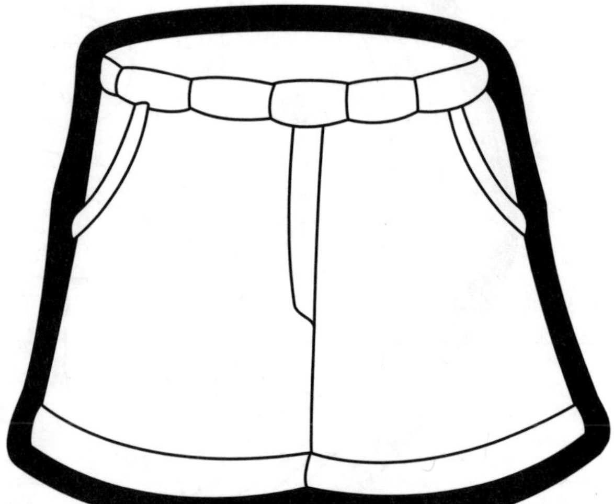